THE SURVIVAL PARADOX

This book was originally published as *De onsterfelijke onderneming*, LannooCampus, 2019.

D/2019/45/248 – ISBN 978 94 014 6138 2 – NUR 801

Final editing of the Dutch text: Sandy Panis
Translation: Ian Connerty
Cover design: Peer De Maeyer
Interior design: Gert Degrande | De Witlofcompagnie
Portrait photo: Niko Caignie

LannooCampus Publishers is a subsidiary of Lannoo Publishers,
the book and multimedia division of Lannoo Publishers nv.

LannooCampus Publishers
Vaartkom 41
3000 Leuven
Belgium
www.lannoocampus.com

P.O. box 23202
1100 DS Amsterdam
Netherlands

THE SURVIVAL PARADOX

CHANGE VS STABILITY AT APPLE AND ANY IMMORTAL COMPANY

FONS VAN DYCK

To my parents, who both left us in 2015.

CONTENTS

'You can't connect the dots looking forward; you can only connect them looking backwards. So you have to trust that the dots will somehow connect in your future.'

Steve Jobs | Stanford Commencement Speech, June 2005

INTRODUCTION

There is life after 'God'

In the summer of 2018, Apple became the first American company in history to achieve a stock market value of more than 1 trillion dollars. This means that Apple's stock market value was at that point at more than a third of the size of the UK economy and larger than the economies of Turkey and Switzerland. It is an achievement that speaks to the imagination, all the more so because as recently as 25 years ago Apple almost went out of business.

This news was in sharp contrast to the gloomy speculations made about the company following the death of its charismatic founder, Steve Jobs, in 2011. At that time, many observers expected – and feared – that Apple would not survive the demise of its 'founding father'. Over the years, Jobs had grown to become the face of the company to the outside world. Apple was Jobs and Jobs was Apple. He was famous for the manner in which he succeeded in binding his customers to the Apple brand with a loyalty that had seldom been seen before, often bordering on the fanatical. 'Which other technology brand do you ever see on bumper stickers?' *The Economist* once asked pointedly.[1] In the academic world, Jobs was lauded as the best performing CEO ever. The media also praised him to the skies. He appeared on the cover of *New York Magazine* as the 'iGod', while *Fortune Magazine* described him as 'the most innovative businessman of our time' and a special edition of *Time Magazine* claimed that he was 'the genius who changed our world'. The news of his death from pancreatic cancer was met with worldwide scenes of grief and mourning from his dedicated fans, comparable to the reaction to the death of Lady Di in 1997 or Michael Jackson in 2009. Even the American president, Barack Obama, felt obliged to comment on his passing, praising Jobs as one of the great American innovators:'Brave enough to think differently, bold enough to believe he could change the world, and talented enough to do it.'[2]

Few people could imagine that Apple would continue to reach the remarkable heights it had reached under Jobs' skilful guidance. Serious questions were asked about the ability of the new CEO, Tim Cook, to fill his predecessor's massive shoes and lead the company to the next level of success. A journalist of the respected *Wall Street Journal* expressed what many others were thinking but were often reluctant to say:'They're not re-inventing the world. They're circling the wagons.'[3]

But what is the real secret behind the success of an immortal company like Apple? Is this purely attributable to the merits of their charismatic leaders? Or is something more going on? How do they persuade their existing customers to keep on coming back time after time, whilst continuing to capture new hearts with the same enthusiasm and passion? What are the key factors that make this commercial conjuring trick possible? And – most importantly of all – will it last? These are the questions that I will seek to answer in this book. To do so, I will not simply be looking at stories of glittering success, but will also attempt to draw crucial lessons from cases of equally dramatic failure. In this sense, my book is different from most management literature, which often concentrates exclusively on triumph and ignores the possibility of disaster. But there are two sides to every coin: what goes up, must come down. It is my conviction that we can learn at least as much from the mistakes that some companies have made (and how they managed to get themselves out of the mess they had created) as from their tales of derring-do.

The history of Apple – on which I will focus in the first instance – is a case in point. It has not always been plain sailing for Steve Jobs' brainchild. On the contrary, there have been numerous ups and downs. In 1985, the annual results were so poor that the directors conspired to get rid of Jobs in a manner that was anything but elegant. In 1996, things were even worse and the company almost went out of business altogether. In other words, Apple has twice looked commercial death in the face and on each occasion managed to survive – and eventually thrive. So perhaps we should not be surprised that it has also survived the untimely departure of its founder and greatest leader.

Of course, I will not be confining my analysis exclusively to Apple, but will also be looking at other sectors. The histories of some of these companies go back a very long way. The doyens in this respect – and again, perhaps we should not be surprised – are in the wines and spirits sector. Moët & Chandon, which today is the largest champagne house in the world, dates back to 1743! The Irish Guinness brewery was founded in 1759. The Hennessy cognac brand first saw the light of day in 1765. In 2010, the average lifespan of the world's major companies was 87 years. The three branches with the greatest longevity were food and drink (141 years), pharmaceuticals (119 years) and the financial sector (117 years).[4]

That being said, achieving this kind of commercial 'immortality' is not something that can be taken for granted. While some brands are successful for decades (or even centuries), others – sometimes even iconic names – disappear forever. Think, for example, of the fate of Nokia. While Apple was climbing its way to the top of the tree with its revolutionary iPhone, Nokia's business results went into an irreversible nosedive – and this for a company that at the turn of the 21st century had been regarded as one of the most innovative in the world. By 2011, the writing was on the wall: Stephen Elop, who was then the CEO at Nokia, wrote in an internal memo to his senior managers that: 'Our platform is burning.' And he was right. Less than 2 years later, the company was sold to Microsoft for 'just' 7.17 billion dollars, a fraction of its former value.[5]

There are plenty of other examples from recent years. In 2011, the Swedish car manufacturer Saab went to the wall because it was unable to convince its potential Chinese investors to pump new money into the company. A year later, the legendary Eastman Kodak brand, which had been a pioneer in the field of photography for 131 years, found itself on the edge of bankruptcy, primarily because it had missed the digital train. In spite of all its frantic efforts to cut costs and restructure, the company still continues to be unprofitable. And when in 2015 technology pioneer Hewlett-Packard was forced to split into two separate companies – HP Inc. (printers and personal computers) and Hewlett-Packard Enterprise (servers, software, storage capacity and networks) – analysts spoke of 'the end of an era'.[6]

The future of many brands has never been as threatened as they are today. A study by Havas Media, a major advertising and media player, concluded that consumers worldwide would not be overly concerned if a staggering 77 % of brands would cease to exist. In other words, three out of every four brands have no lasting value in the eyes of the people who are supposed to buy them. They could all disappear overnight and no-one would shed a tear. In fact, they would hardly notice.[7] It looks as if brands have become an endangered species, threatened with extinction.

Linked to this is the ever-increasing expectation that many industries and product categories will move towards a 'winner-takes-all' model, in which one or at most two brands (in a form of duopoly) will establish market leadership, while the other remaining brands will need to focus on specific niches in order to survive. In many cases, the super-digital retailers - the Amazons and Alibabas of the world - will be able to secure an almost total monopoly.

The history of Apple and other iconic companies can help us to discover what more modest companies can also do to achieve their own 'immortal' status. A survey by Credit Suisse has shown that family-run companies worldwide perform 4 percentage points better than the stock market average. More recent research specifically relating to Belgian family businesses suggests that the additional annual return over a period of 15 years can even amount to as much as 7 percentage points.[8] In other words, many family companies not only have a proud past, but also a promising future. What is the secret behind their success? How will they maintain this success in the challenging environment of the coming decades? What changes will they need to make? The answers to these questions will be revealed in the pages that follow.

But the most burning question that will keep on returning in this book is the following: how can <u>your</u> company survive in these disruptive times? More important still, which factors strengthen the likelihood of future success or failure for your company and for your competitors? It is certainly not a good idea to hide from reality, or to play fast and loose with the future prospects of your company. And short-term 'quick wins' won't guarantee your survival chances in the long run, either. Along the way, you will also learn why Apple is now achieving much better results under Tim Cook than was ever the case under the leadership of Steve Jobs and how Cook's approach has confounded the expectations of so many of the armchair strategists.

It goes without saying that I will not be plucking my analyses out of thin air. Amongst other things, I will be basing my conclusions on the scientific AGIL paradigm, which was developed in the 1950s by the renowned Harvard sociologist Talcott Parsons. Using his model, supported by the results of other scientific empirical research, I will examine the reasons why some companies can survive for 100 years or more, while others sink into oblivion in less than a decade. The management lessons that this exercise will yield can form the inspiration for a strategy that will allow your company to keep its head above water, not only tomorrow but also the day after tomorrow.

What I am most certainly not going to do is allow myself to be misled by the many scare stories that are currently doing the rounds in marketing circles about the survival chances for companies in the future. I will consciously puncture a number of the most popular and persistent myths that have been drummed into the collective memory of managers and company leaders for decades, often with disastrous consequences for the companies concerned.

In contrast, the story of the rise, fall and resurrection of Apple will speak to the imagination of the business community in many different industries and offer a viable way forward for the years ahead. In that sense, this book can be seen as a scientifically based survival kit for companies in uncertain times, founded on the lessons I have drawn from the successes and failures of others. As such, it will help to set you on your way to continued future viability and to your own version of immortality. Because if you can learn from your own mistakes and those of your rivals, if you can claw your way back to your feet when fate has knocked you down, if you can re-invent yourself when all around you are clinging to the life raft of the familiar, you will be able to stand firm and secure in the chaotic and turbulent years that lie ahead.

A BRIEF HISTORY OF APPLE

In April 1976, bosom buddies Steve Jobs and Steve Wozniak started up a computer company in a garage. And the rest, as they say, is history...

But because not everyone is as familiar with that history as they might think and because I will refer repeatedly throughout the book to the often dramatic events that have coloured the Apple story over the years, it may be useful to start with a brief recapitulation of what actually happened. Although many books have already been dedicated to Apple, this is the first one that charts every phase of its progress, from the mid-1970s to the present day. At first glance, this might seem like a strange approach, but whoever consults the existing literature will soon come to the conclusion that most previous authors have either concentrated on relatively short (and often the most successful) periods of the past four decades or else have focused on the company from the perspective of the life story of its founder, as was the case, for example, with the most well-known biography by Walter Isaacson, published in 2011. As a result, most Apple books ignore the period from the mid-1980s to the mid-1990s, when the company was not under Jobs' control and had to navigate its way through some very stormy waters.[9]

In this book, I will make a distinction between two phases. The first phase, which I describe as the 'wilderness years', is characterised by the forced departure of Jobs, the desperate attempts of senior management to prevent the company from being sold off, and the very real threat of bankruptcy in 1996. The second phase, which I refer to as the 'golden years', cover the return of Jobs as the 'prodigal son', the spectacular success of the iPhone and the highly successful continuation of Apple's market dominance by Tim Cook after Jobs' death in 2011.

In the course of the book I will often refer to these two phases, not in the least because it is interesting to see whether the AGIL principles can explain both the successes and the failures of Apple – and, by extension, those of other companies.

The wilderness years (1976-1996): from hero to zero

The two Steves set up Apple Computer in Los Altos, California, on 1 April 1976. The first computer 'circuit board' that they put together was christened Apple I and the initial 200 models were sold to other computer nerds of their acquaintance. Contrary to what many people think, this does not mean that they invented the personal computer. This honour goes to Ed Roberts and his company MITS (Micro Instrumentation and Telemetry Systems). Roberts had developed his own Altair model a year earlier and this is now generally regarded as the first PC, with *Business Week* describing MITS at the time as 'the IBM of the home computers'.

Not that Jobs and Wozniak were bothered: they just got on with their work. In 1977, they launched the Apple II, a highly distinctive model that allowed them to differentiate their company clearly in the home computing market. It was an attractive unit, which stood out from the crowd thanks to its large screen (much bigger than their competitors), its provision of a keyboard and power cable as standard, and the possibility to work with coloured imaging. The real computer freaks – the so-called early adopters – fell in love with Apple II, to such as extent that when the company was floated on the stock market in December 1980 it was immediately valued at a staggering 1.79 billion dollars. Not bad for a bunch of beginners! At the time, it was regarded as the most successful initial public offering since the stock market launch of Ford Motors in 1956.

But the euphoria was short-lived. At the end of 1981, IBM decided to move into the personal computers market and soon proved itself to be a potentially dangerous rival to Apple. The IBM PC made use of Intel microprocessors and Microsoft's DOS operating system, which (in contrast to Apple) was a relatively open system that other players could easily copy. Although Apple's turnover continued to rise, its market share shrank to a paltry 6.2 % by 1982. To make matters worse, IBM had not only captured the home computing market, but their computers were increasingly seen as the standard for office environments. The consequences for Apple soon made themselves felt. The launch of the new Apple III and Lisa models failed to take off, in part because of technical shortcomings and in part because of lack of commercial acumen. As a result, the company increasingly found itself outgunned financially by IBM. Between 1981 and 1984 Apple profits nosedived by an alarming 62 %, plunging it into the deepest crisis it had so far had to face.

Apple tried to halt this downwards spiral by introducing yet another new model: the Macintosh, which was launched with great bravura in 1984. Jobs was heavily involved in this launch and staked his personal reputation on the new model, arguing that it represented a major breakthrough in terms of design, ease of use and technical ingenuity. In some ways, perhaps it did, but it was also slow and there was a lack of compatible software. What's more, the Macintosh was so expensive that there was hardly any interest among ordinary consumers. As a result, the initial launch was a failure – and as the person responsible for making the decisions, Jobs had to carry the can. In April 1985, the Apple board made clear to him in friendly but unmistakeable terms that they expected him to stand down. He duly obliged but immediately set up his own rival company, with the appropriate name of NeXT...

CEO John Sculley (who had been hired by Jobs in 1983 and moved across from Pepsi-Cola) was soon able to get the Apple train back on the rails, thanks largely to new and improved versions of the Macintosh, which provided good solutions for the rapidly emerging markets in desktop publishing and graphic design. The new versions also proved their worth in the educational field, where increasing use was being made of PCs in the classroom, to such an extent that by 1990 Apple had secured half of the market. In each of these ventures, the Apple approach was always the same: it offered users a single solution for a clearly identified purpose, so that all the customers needed to do was 'plug and play'.

This concept brought a level of success that had never previously been seen. The sales figures skyrocketed: in 1990 the company achieved a turnover of 5.6 billion dollars and captured a worldwide market share of 8 %. Apple now had cash reserves that were also in excess of 1 billion dollars, making it the most profitable computer manufacturing company on the planet.

Once again, however, this success was not destined to last. In part as a result of the difficult economic conjuncture (the world crisis of the early 1990s badly hit the computer industry) and in part as a result of increasingly fierce competition (particularly from Mircosoft and their new Windows software), the company was obliged to undertake yet another radical change of course. This involved the launch of a cheaper version of the Macintosh, which achieved little other than to increase pressure on the already tight margins. Later, Sculley decided that the time had come to play the innovation card with the marketing of the so-called Newton, a revolutionary new PDA (personal digital assistant). Unfortunately, this was an idea ahead of its time and failed to capture the public's imagination, with catastrophic financial consequences. In June 1993, it was Sculley's turn to fall on his sword and the board appointed Michael Spindler, a German engineer with a long record of service at Apple, as his replacement.

Spindler's attempts to turn the company around resulted in an even bigger fiasco. His ideas were essentially sound – for example, he made internationalisation, particularly in China, his number one priority and gave permission to a limited number of companies to clone and market Apple computers at a reasonable price – but his timing was all wrong. Most of his competitors were ahead of him, so that the company effectively missed the boat (again). An effort to develop a new operating system in collaboration with IBM also failed. Faced with these expensive setbacks, Spindler felt he had no alternative but to try and cut costs. He slashed staff numbers by a massive 16 % and reduced R&D spending to just 6 % of the total sales costs. But it was too little too late. The fundamental problems remained and by now it was clear that Spindler was not the man to solve them. Two weeks after Apple reported losses of 69 million dollars for the first quarter of 1996, Gil Amelio, one of the company's directors, was appointed as the new CEO.

Amelio attempted to increase levels of efficiency by a better streamlining of the production systems and he continued to make further cuts to the payroll in an effort to build up Apple's badly depleted cash reserves. But he was fighting an uphill battle. Notwithstanding his strict regime, Apple continued to leak money, losing a further 1.6 billion dollars during his tenure in office. To make matters worse, the price of Apple shares (not unsurprisingly) fell to their lowest level for 12 years, while the company's worldwide market share fell from 6 % to a new all-time low of just 3 %. Various attempts to sell off Apple to other important players in the sector (including IBM and Sun Microsystems) proved fruitless. Nobody was interested. Indeed, the situation seemed so hopeless that Michael Dell (founder and CEO of Dell Computers) was prompted to say: 'What would I do if I was the head of Apple? I'd shut it down and give the money back to the shareholders.' It was in these parlous circumstances that Amelio was shown the door in early 1997, allowing Jobs to reappear on the scene as interim CEO of the company he still regarded as his brainchild.

The golden years (1997-2018): the sky is the limit

When Jobs took over the helm, he immediately cancelled the licensing programme that allowed other companies to clone Apple computers, since he regarded this as one of the most important reasons for the company's recent troubles. He also reduced the number of production lines from fifteen to four: the desktop and laptop Macintosh, with versions for both professional and private use. His vision was crystal clear: he proposed to use the Macintosh, which he now renamed the iMac, as a digital hub. He was firmly convinced that the iMac offered major advantages to consumers whose lifestyle was becoming increasingly digitalised through the use of digital cameras, portable music players and (of course) cell phones. According to Jobs, the iMac was the ideal hub into which all these digital applications could be integrated and controlled. Moreover, the Apple hardware and software ensured that these applications would have an ever increasing number of possibilities. Jobs believed that this multifunctionality was one of Apple's strongest commercial trump cards: the company was one of the few remaining players in the computer market that still made both hardware and software.

This vision of the iMac as a digital hub found its fullest expression in the launching of the iPod in 2001. In many respects, this new product was unique. Not only because of its simplicity, which was always one of Jobs' signature trademarks, but also because of the almost limitless possibilities of its software. This bullseye was followed up in 2003 with the 'opening' of the iTunes Music Store, the first ever site (supported by the music industry) where music could be downloaded legally, with the users paying a fixed sum per song. The iTunes Store sent the sales figure of the iPod soaring to new heights. And this was just the start of a whole series of blockbuster successes. 2007 saw the introduction of the iPhone, which signalled Apple's intention to gatecrash a market that had previously been dominated by a limited number of major players, such as Nokia, Motorola and Samsung. At the time, few people realised just what a game-changer the iPhone would be, but its impact was immediate. More and more consumers began automatically opting for the iPhone, particularly after the unveiling of the Apple App Store in 2008, which offered Apple users an almost endless range of solutions for a thousand and one different things. But it wasn't only the consumer who benefitted: Apple retained the right to give its prior approval for all the apps sold in the store and demanded that the developers pay them a hefty 30 % of the agreed purchase price. In 2010,it was the turn of the iPad to see the first light of day and once again the public's reaction was wildly enthusiastic. This was the high-water mark of Jobs' career, the last public launch that he was able to make personally before he died.

In the years following Jobs' death, Apple continued its seemingly unstoppable progress. The iPad and the iPhone sent turnover and profits soaring. In September 2014, the new CEO, Tim Cook, added a further weapon to the company's already impressive arsenal with the introduction of the Apple Watch, which marked Apple's first move into the field of wearable technology. Apple Pay, a new mobile payment system, was also an instant success, being quickly supported by the majority of the major banks and credit card companies, as well as being accepted by a significant number of retailers. The autumn of 2017, on the occasion of the tenth anniversary of its most iconic product, saw the launch of the start-of-the-art iPhone X. Some eyebrows were raised at the high price of 999 dollars, but the strategy proved to be the right one, at least for a time. In the fourth quarter of 2018, the turnover of the iPhone division increased by a spectacular 29 %, which was largely attributable to the high profit margin on the iPhone X, since the total number of devices sold was starting to stagnate. This explains why the company's senior management decided to stop releasing figures for the total number of products sold, although by the beginning of 2019 it was no longer possible to deny or conceal the falling level of iPhone sales, particularly in the important Chinese market.

Notwithstanding the company's many successes (the gross profit margin continues to hover around 38 %), over the years a number of critical voices have been raised that question the sustainability of the Apple model. Some observers ask openly whether or not Apple is too dependent on the iPhone (good for 60 % of total sales) and how long the current level of growth can last without the further introduction of newer and more genuinely innovative products. Or is a shift in emphasis already taking place? At the moment, the biggest growth unquestionably comes from the company's new services (including Apple Music), which in the fourth quarter of 2018 yielded a turnover of 10 billion dollars, representing an increase of 27 % on an annual basis. Apple continued on this path in early 2019, with the launch of Apple TV (its alternative for Netflix), Arcade (its gaming platform), Apple News (a collection of newspapers and magazines) and its own credit card.

It seems clear that Apple – unnoticed by some – is already in the process of a major transformation, which will allow the company to re-invent itself.

The metamorphosis that Apple has undergone in the 21st century under the leadership of Jobs and Cook is nothing short of remarkable. It is still unclear exactly what the future will bring, but the underlying thinking and values remain unaltered. When he was introducing the iPhone X in the brand-new Steve Jobs Theatre in 2017, CEO Tim Cook not only praised his illustrious predecessor, but also set out the path for the company to follow in the years ahead: 'Steve's spirit and timeless philosophy on life will always be in the DNA of Apple.'[10]

How to read this book

From this point onwards, *The Survival Paradox* will be developed in the following manner:

- There will be a section for each of the four functions of the AGIL paradigm, with two chapters in each section.

- Each letter of the AGIL acronym will be linked to the story of Apple, both in good times and bad. What did Apple do well? What did they do wrong (sometimes disastrously)? What does this mean for your company?

Do you want to get started immediately with changing things for the better in your own company? You do? Then the following text elements are especially designed to help you:

Debunking the myths

- In each chapter I will debunk a persistent myth in the management literature that is still far too often blindly followed by unsuspecting company leaders.

THE DO'S-AND-DON'TS

- Learn what concrete steps you can take in any organisation.

Apple in trouble

- Discover how the mega-successful Apple company also got things seriously wrong in the past, nearly resulting in its permanent downfall.

AGIL

ADAPTATION

INTEGRATION

GOAL
ATTAINMENT

LATENT
PATTERN
MAINTENANCE

THE AGIL PARADIGM

'Apple has some tremendous assets, but I believe without some attention, the company could, could, could – I'm searching for the right word – could, could die.' With these words, a hesitant Steve Jobs admitted his doubts about the continued existence of Apple in an interview with Cathy Booth, a reporter at *Time Magazine*.[11] The conversation took place shortly after Jobs' return to the company in August 1997, when Apple was close to the edge of bankruptcy. Although his demeanour during the interview was typical – dressed in a T-shirt, shorts and a worn-out pair of sneakers, with his feet on the table and a big grin on his face – it was unusual (to say the least) for him to have second thoughts about the ability of the company he had founded to survive.

Life is getting shorter

In the meantime, we know, of course, that Apple did survive and has come a long way since then. During the past 43 years, its technology has changed the world. This actually makes it quite 'old' for a high-tech company. True, market leaders and their brands in other sectors often have a history that dates back for more than a century, but this does nothing to alter the fact that eternal success can never be taken for granted in any sector. Many famous companies have already gone under and others are still fighting to keep their head above water. So wherein lies the difference? Why do some companies fail, while others continue to prosper and even seem to remain 'young'? Is there a common characteristic that makes the winners 'immortal'?

The average age of stock-listed companies in the US in 2010 was just 31 years.[12] It is an open secret that companies are disappearing more rapidly than ever before. Research has shown that companies that were floated on the stock market before 1970 have a 92 % chance of surviving the next 5 years, whereas companies floated between 2000 and 2009 have only a 63 % chance.[13]

Sad though it is, this means that we can expect a significant number of other famous names to leave the stage in the years ahead. Because if we look at the average

age of just the largest companies, the figures paint an even more dramatic picture. Consultant Innosight researched the life cycle of the largest companies listed on the S&P 500, an American share index for the 500 companies with the highest levels of market capitalisation. In 1965, companies that made it onto the index could expect to stay there for an average of 33 years. By 1990, this average had fallen to 20 years. The prediction for 2026 is that it will fall still further, to just 14 years. In other words, during the next 10 years, half of the current S&P500 companies will be replaced.[14]

There are no sacred cows when it comes to corporate survival. At an internal meeting in Seattle, in the autumn of 2018, an employee asked founder and CEO Jeff Bezos about Amazon's future. Specifically, the questioner wanted to know what lessons Bezos has learned from the recent bankruptcies of Sears and other big retailers. 'Amazon is not too big to fail,' Bezos said, in a recording of the meeting that CNBC has heard. 'In fact, I predict that one day Amazon will fail. Amazon will go bankrupt. If you look at large companies, their life spans tend to be 30-plus years, not 100-plus years.'

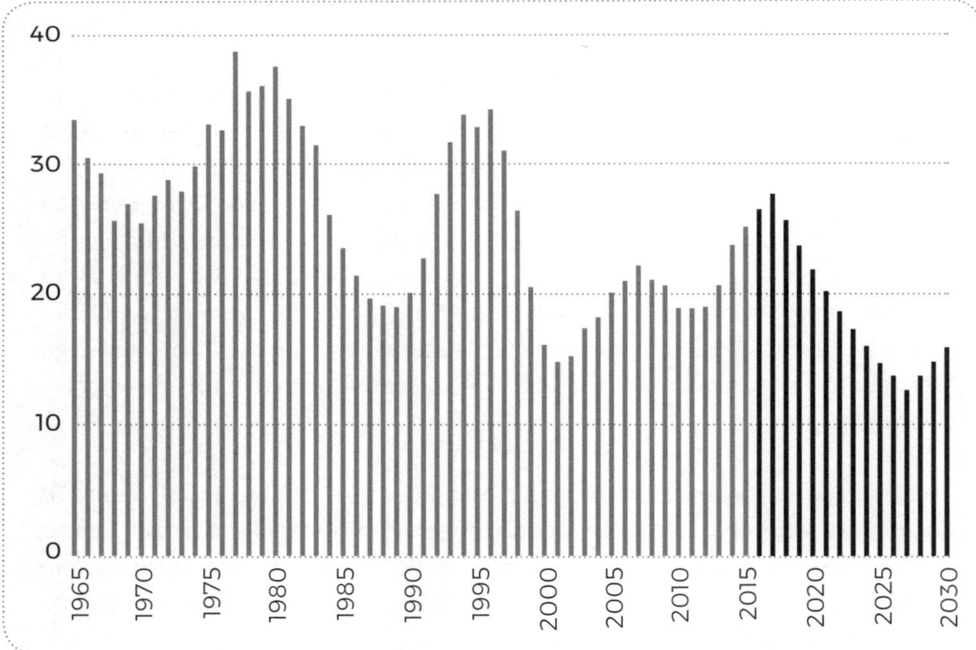

Average longevity of a company in the S&P 500 index expressed in years
(source: Innosight, *Corporate longevity: turbulence ahead for large organisations. Executive briefing*, Spring 2016)

The key to prolonging that demise, Bezos continued, is for the company to 'obsess over customers' and to avoid looking inward, worrying about itself. 'If we start to focus on ourselves, instead of focusing on our customers, that will be the beginning of the end,' he said. 'We have to try and delay that day for as long as possible.'[15]

Bezos' comments came at a time of unprecedented success at Amazon, with its core retail business continuing to grow, while the company was also winning in the massive cloud-computing market and gaining rapid adoption of its Alexa voice assistant in the home. His confessions demonstrate the point that any company, old or new, large or small, even if highly successful today, can be threatened with extinction in the next decade.

Of course, the average life expectancy of a company varies from sector to sector. A report by McKinsey has confirmed that some industries generally do better than others, especially where the relationship of trust with the consumer is a key factor.[16] Examples include professional service providers, private banking, insurance and luxury watches. By contrast, in other sectors (such as high-tech or fashion) things move much more quickly and the thresholds for starting are much lower. Viewed from this perspective, it is fair to say that a technology company that manages to survive for 15 years has done as well as a consumption goods company that survives for 30 years.

The explanation is a logical one: a company that does not need to manage factories, logistical chains or large tangible products is much easier to copy. This is certainly true for young digital companies that are often developed around 'big ideas' (for which there is not always a physical product), which make them vulnerable to imitation (or destruction) by the larger players in the market. For this reason, the life cycle of technology companies is on average much shorter than for companies in the physical world. In this respect, Apple is an exception. It is the last survivor of the pioneer companies that first brought PCs to market in the late 1970s. With over four decades of unbroken activity already on the clock, it has far exceeded the average age for the sector. So the question now is: will Apple make it to its century?

Darwin in business

One of the main reasons why companies are finding it harder and harder to survive is that they are no longer able to adapt to the increasing complexity of their environment. Since the pace of change is likely to increase still further in the years ahead, the ability of companies to re-invent themselves will become correspondingly more important. It is with this in mind that consultants (like McKinsey) now constantly stress to managers the urgent necessity of clearly mapping the challenges that they can expect to face in the future.[17]

Complexity is frequently caused by an intricate combination of rapidly evolving technology on the one hand and economic shocks (sometimes referred to as 'creative destruction') on the other hand. Companies often fail to interpret this new environment correctly or else choose faulty strategies to deal with the resultant changes. As a consequence, they miss the opportunity to adjust in ways that will allow them to profit from these changes. The most common errors include clinging on to old business models in new markets, an inability to respond to disruptive competitors in the lower market segments and a failure to know in which future markets (more than 10 years) they now need to invest.

Researchers at the Boston Consulting Group have even gone so far as to compare companies in their fight for survival with biological species. Like a biological species, companies are 'complex adaptive systems' that are continually in motion in a manner that is difficult to predict. This is largely a result of the fact that companies are now more closely connected with each other than ever before. Interconnectivity of this kind can inject great vitality into an economy, but it also increases the risk of a snowball effect when things go wrong. It is for this reason, say the experts at BCG, that the companies can now learn important lessons from biology.[18]

Culture eats strategy for breakfast

Much has already been published about how companies can survive in disruptive times. It is noticeable, however, that most of these studies focus exclusively on the short term when they search for the causes that explain the problems currently being faced by the business world. The remedies they propose are equally short-term.

Moreover, the authors in question tend to concentrate primarily on economic and technological aspects, while (more importantly) failing to develop an integral strategy that will increase a company's chances of survival. It is for this reason that in this book I will make use of the work of the renowned American sociologist Talcott Parsons, who did develop such an integrated approach in his own field, which he then applied to 'social systems' in general.

Before examining Parsons' ideas more closely, I first want to look at three other studies that are both relevant and interesting. The first was made by MIT professor Edgar Schein and investigated the spectacular rise and fall the Digital Equipment (DEC) computer company. At one point during the 1980s, DEC achieved an annual turnover of 14 billion dollars, was listed in the Fortune 50 and was second only to IBM as the largest computer manufacturer in the US. The company was responsible for many groundbreaking developments, including speech recognition applications, the mini-computer and the introduction of local networks. Yet with all these things working in its favour, it was still unable to perpetuate its initial success and in 1998 was sold to the Compaq Corporation.

So what went wrong? How was it possible that a company which had performed brilliantly for over 35 years could no longer cut the mustard? Why were its dozens of intelligent, eloquent and highly respected engineers and managers unable to deal with the problems that were clear to everyone else, both inside and outside the organisation? According to Schein, this paralysis was the result of the prevailing company culture, which was frozen in the past. This prevented DEC from making the adaptation that was necessary to reflect the trend that saw mini-computers increasingly replaced by personal computers. Their culture was still highly innovation-driven, but there were insufficient commercial impulses to follow the market. As a result, DEC created its own kind of immune system, which gradually isolated it from all contact and feeling with its consumers.[19]

Schein concluded that cultural values are not by definition either good or bad. The important thing is that everyone should be aware that values are not only capable of strengthening good organisational evolutions, but can also, depending on the circumstances, hinder necessary change. In other words, culture functions as a double-edged sword. Everything is dependent on the extent to which the company and its culture are open to the idea of change. That, says Schein, is the most important new challenge facing the managers of today: they must be capable of simultaneously detecting, analysing and responding to the changing state of technology in the market, as well as being aware of the implications this has for the state of technology within the organisation and the ability of the company culture to adjust to these developments: 'We try to manage culture but, in fact, culture manages us far more that we ever manage it, and this happens largely outside our awareness.'[20]

Beyond profits

In addition to Schein's study, the book *Built to Last* by management consultants Jim Collins and Jerry Porras is also highly recommended for anyone who wishes to discover the secret of the immortal company. They examined the evolution of 18 long-standing companies dating from the period 1926 to 1990, including General Electric, Disney, Hewlett-Packard, Procter & Gamble and Johnson & Johnson, before comparing their findings with those of other comparable companies who had not been able to stay the distance. 'Making a profit' was certainly not the primary objective of the successful companies (although it was clearly one of them). Instead, the main connecting theme between these companies was the fact that they were all ideologically driven, rather than economically driven. They were focused on a 'core ideology' or 'higher goal', which was reflected in their values and culture. It was this that gave them their seemingly perpetual forward momentum. Collins and Porras concluded that the guiding principles of these visionary organisations seldom change, 'much like the guiding principles of the American Declaration of Independence'.[21]

A similar conclusion was reached by Arie de Geus, a former head of strategic planning with the Shell Oil Company.[22] Together with his team, he carried out a study in the 1980s to establish the reasons to explain why some companies were able to survive for 100 years or more. It became clear that high turnover is only an indicator for present and relatively recent performance, but says little about the future prospects for long-term survival. The excellent financial results achieved by General Motors, Philips Electronics and IBM in the mid-1970s did little to suggest the huge difficulties that all three would face just a decade later.

De Geus and his team also found a number of common characteristics that distinguished the 'centenarians' from other companies. In particular, they seemed to have priorities that differed significantly from the values traditionally found in the business literature. More specifically, there were four key points that allowed the long-lived companies to rise above the crowd:

1. Long-lived companies have special 'antennae' that allow them to sense perfectly what is happening in the world around them. This does not simply apply to technological developments, but also to wider societal developments, such as economic conjunctures, political turning points and even military conflict. They exceed their sectoral rivals in their ability to adjust harmoniously to their environment. Although social concerns are seldom explicitly made their first priority, they are nonetheless capable of responding easily and at all times to the conditions imposed on them by the society in which they operate.

2. Long-lived companies have a strong and coherent identity. No matter how diverse the workforce might be, each employee (and some suppliers as well) feel part of the same integrated whole. Unilever, for example, sees itself as a fleet of ships: each ship is independent, but together they possess a strength that is greater than the sum of the individual elements. Most of the cases in the Shell study display the same strong sense of solidarity between everyone in the organisation, which is an essential prerequisite for surviving in a world of constant change. This community spirit is further boosted by the widespread practice of recruiting new managers internally. The new appointees regard themselves as 'next generation' successors, creating a degree of continuity with a long line of successful past managers.

3. Long-lived companies are tolerant for experiments and innovation (the Shell researchers refer to this as a 'decentral' approach). This means that when attempts are made to diversify the company at different levels, the central management pillar does not impose too many restrictive conditions. In particular, initiatives at the margin are actively encouraged, providing they fit within the broad parameters of the company's overall mission and objectives. In this way, it becomes feasible to continually explore new possibilities for future development.

4. Long-lived companies are conservative when it comes to money matters. They are economical with resources and do not easily take financial risks. They ensure that their reserves are always sufficiently large. This mentality allows them to respond flexibly and without reliance on external financing to new opportunities as and when they arise, giving them a significant first-mover advantage over their competitors.

This unique study by De Geus sheds a whole new light on the chances for companies to survive in the long term. His analysis goes beyond straightforward technological and economic thinking, providing us with new and fascinating insights into the dynamics that make it possible for some companies to break the 100-year barrier, while others disappear at a relatively early age. In short, his study is an important source for both reflection and inspiration.

A first myth debunked: dinosaurs

Dinosaurs are a much-used metaphor in management circles, when the need to change in order to survive is discussed. It is often assumed that large organisations and famous brands in particular are threatened with extinction, as was the case with the dinosaurs (although these companies are sometimes also referred to as elephants). The experiences of companies like DEC and Kodak are cited as classic examples of the potentially devastating effects of inertia and an inability to innovate and evolve.

In many such cases, reference is also made to the concept of 'creative destruction', which was popularised by the Austrian economist, banker and politician Joseph Schumpeter (although it was initially formulated by the sociologist Werner Sombart). Schumpter understood 'creative destruction' (a term which is now almost a century old) to mean a process of continual innovation, whereby the successful application of new technologies systematically destroys the old ones. According to this theory, technological innovation is therefore the only true source of economic growth. Consequently, successful innovation brings with it temporary market power, which negatively impacts the market share and profits of companies whose business model is still based on outdated technologies. This initiates a self-perpetuating cycle that sees the repeated rise and fall of 'old' companies and their replacement by an endless succession of new kids on the block– and so ad infinitum. In other words, well-established companies and technologies will inevitably be eradicated in due course, with new companies and technologies offering the only prospect of progress and growth. This implies that companies with a long history in a particular technology lack the capacity to innovate and renew, so that they will eventually be eliminated and replaced by more creative newcomers. In recent times, Amazon, Uber and Airbnb have been repeatedly put forward as examples of this kind of creative destruction, which dislocates existing markets and puts established names, interests and technologies out of business. Sounds reasonable? Maybe. And popular? Certainly. At least until now.

However, more recent research has shown that the theory does not hold water. A study carried out by the London Business School and the University of Southern California set out to identify the companies that had introduced the most radical innovations over a 140-year period. Were these new and initially small companies, as Schumpeter had suggested? Or were they large and established players?[23] The research team concluded that in 42 % of cases radical innovation originated in big companies, with small and medium-sized companies accounting for 58 %. In other words, the size of the company is not a significant variable for the level of radical innovation. The researchers further concluded that while Schumpeter's theory held good for the period before the Second World War, since 1945 the balance of innovation power has switched to the big guns, with 74 % of post-war innovation attributable to large companies and just 26 % coming from their small and medium-sized counterparts. The stories of companies like IBM (which has a history stretching back more than 100 years) demonstrate that in the right conditions the so-called dinosaurs are perfectly able to re-invent themselves time after time through a process of creative transformation.

Microsoft is one of the most recent examples of a successful transformation of a large company. The company that was founded by Bill Gates had turned into a bureaucratic dinosaur by the beginning of the 21st century. However, under the new CEO, Satya Nadella, Microsoft has re-invented itself. After just 5 years at the helm, he has turned Microsoft into a 1 trillion dollar company, a landmark reached in the spring of 2019.

In a similar vein, it is often said that the major global brands are increasingly losing ground to small, local rivals. Researchers at the Ehrenberg-Bass Institute (University of South Australia) have investigated this claim and reached a nuanced conclusion. Some large brands are still gaining in market share, while others are losing out. Whether or not a brand continues to grow seems to be largely dependent on the dominant dynamic in the sector: is the sector growing, shrinking or stationary? If the sector is growing, then brands are also likely to be growing in terms of sales revenue. Although a brand might lose market share, it can still grow its revenues, because the sector as a whole is still growing. In other words: a smaller slice of a larger pie can feed you better than a large slice of a small pie. The main takeaway is that the basic consumer need that a sector or product category fulfils is the main driver of the growth or decline of a brand. The 'category need' comes before the need which a particular brand fulfils in that category.

The most serious threat for the major brands is actually posed by the increasing number of 'house' and private label products being manufactured by retailers. The 'discerning' consumer has a growing preference for these house brands, principally because they now offer better quality and value for money than in the past: better ingredients, more attractive packaging, greater environmental awareness, etc. The house brands also represent a threat for good performing newcomers, whose products they shamelessly copy and sell, but without the need to lose time and money searching for suitable distribution channels. We can consider these private labels of the retailers as a category by itself (driven mainly by lower prices).

The Ehrenberg-Bass research has also demonstrated the inaccuracy of the contention that it is primarily young people from the so-called Generations Y and Z who are turning their backs on the big brands. The study compared the reasons for choosing a brand among a group of young people under 25 years of age and a group of 25-plussers. They concluded that there were no significant differences. In fact, in 40 % of the cases examined the famous brands had a larger market share in the young group than in the older one.[24]

Did Steve Jobs ever study Talcott Parsons?

With the exception of the studies by Schein, de Geus, and by Collins and Porras, the majority of management insights about the future of companies are based on a short-term perspective. In other words, they focus on short-term performance and short-term success alone. As a result, most of them fail to look any further than the well-trodden paths and the predictable recipes of the recent past. In nearly every case, there is no effort to develop an integrated model that is scientifically based and capable of testing. At the same time, they seldom succeed in being able to explain both successes and failures. It was for this reason that I have spent 6 years deepening my understanding of the insights from what, at first glance, might seem like an unlikely field of expertise for an economist: sociology. In particular, I have concentrated on the theory developed by Talcott Parsons (1902-1979). A fervent advocate of the work of the famous German sociologist Max Weber, Parsons became a professor at Harvard in 1944 and was later head of the sociology faculty until 1956. Although not widely known among the general public, he is regarded as the most important sociological theoretician of the 20th century, whose work is fit to stand alongside that of Marx, Durkheim and Weber. In this work, he examined how social systems – for example, religions – are capable for surviving for hundreds (and sometimes thousands) of years. What is it that often makes a social system stronger than the sum of its individual parts and how does the interdependence of those parts lead to 'functional integration'?

In this context, it is worth noting that Parsons was by no means the first academic to investigate the operation of social systems. At the end of the 19th century, the British sociologist Herbert Spencer had already developed the 'survival of the fittest' concept, which was later refined and popularised by Charles Darwin. The key difference, however, is that Parsons' theory goes much further than the purely biological aspects of the need to adapt in order to survive. He added vital economic, social and cultural dimensions.

To make this possible, Parsons developed a conceptual – albeit purely theoretical – framework known as the AGIL paradigm, which can be applied in many different fields. And that is precisely what I intend to do in this book: use Parsons' findings to examine how social systems like organisations, companies and brands can survive successfully and how they can extend their chances of continued survival over a long period.

Parsons first described the AGIL paradigm in 1956 in his macro-economic study entitled *Economy and Society*.[25] In the paradigm each letter stands for an absolute requirement or function that a social system must be able to fulfil if it wishes to prosper over a long period of time. The first two letters– the 'A' and the 'G' – are more economic in nature and focus on the external environment. The 'A' stands for 'Adaptation' (the need for a system to adjust to the environment) and the 'G' stands for 'Goal attainment' (the need for a system to have clear objectives). These two conditions can also be found in a number of other related economic theories.

What makes Parsons' thinking so interesting is the way in which he then combines these economic aspects with the 'I' and 'L' functions, which have a more internal focus. The 'I' stands for 'Integration' (the need for a system to ensure that its constituent parts form a coherent whole) and the 'L' stands for 'Latent pattern maintenance' (the need for a system to stay consistent and coherent through time by developing common cultural anchors). Put simply, systems need to have objectives and must be willing to change to meet those objectives, but at the same time they must maintain the unity that is their strength and not betray their basic values and identity. According to Parsons, whoever is able to find the right balance within these conflicting fields of tension, which involve both conservative and progressive forces, will have cracked the survival 'code' and can look forward to the future with confidence.

It has to be admitted that Parsons' work is highly theoretical and far too abstract for many people. But therein lies the strength of the AGIL paradigm: it is a universal theory, which means that it can also be used as a guide for running a company – and this in the following manner:

A · ADAPTATION

If you want to survive and be successful, you need to deal effectively with external events and changes in your environment. Not only passively, but also actively. This means that it is not enough simply to adjust to the new environment; you need to be able to turn that new environment to your advantage. Or to put it more forcefully: you need to ensure that the new environment adjusts to you. In this way, 'adapting' becomes much more than just a survival reflex, but is instead a mechanism to make 'smart' use of the new elements in the environment to optimise your own functioning. You need to monitor this mechanism constantly, but it nevertheless still requires considerable expertise to sense which new developments can be important for your company and which ones you should ignore.

G · GOAL ATTAINMENT

As a company, it is vital to have clear and unambiguous objectives, since it is these objectives that will ultimately allow you to achieve the desired new relationship with your changing environment. It is important that all your energy and all your actions are devoted to the attaining of these objectives. In a marketing environment you can easily define goals in terms of growth, profit and competition. But the G function goes much further than this. Companies are also confronted by changes in society (based, for example, on political decisions, public opinion, etc.). It is also necessary to set objectives to meet changes of this kind, which will ultimately make you stronger at the end of the process.

I · INTEGRATION

It is equally crucial to treat all members or component parts of your company – all staff, all subsidiaries, all stakeholders, all customers, all suppliers, all brands, etc. – in such a manner that a long-term relationship will not only be built up with the company itself but also between those different constituent elements. In essence, this requires long-term trust, solidarity and, ultimately, mutual dependence. This can be achieved by setting common priorities and agreeing common norms, supported by a system of social control that ensures compliance and coherence. This will help to avoid the possibility that a single element can undermine the entire system.

L · LATENT PATTERN MAINTENANCE

You must ensure that the motivation of individuals and the underlying cultural usages on which that motivation is based are constantly nourished, maintained and renewed. These processes will help to create increasing solidarity with and loyalty towards the company, also in the long term. This implies that the company must have a set of shared values that sets it apart from all other companies. These values must be promoted by all the members of the organisation, since this will provide stability and enhance the ability to remain faithful to the values when they come under pressure. This pressure can be external (for example, cultural changes that represent a challenge to the company or even a threat to its existence) or internal (for example, as a result of tension between some individuals or sub-units within the company). It is vital for a company to be consistent in the preservation of its values, so that it can continue to differentiate itself from its competitors, which in turn will enhance its prospects for long-term survival.[26]

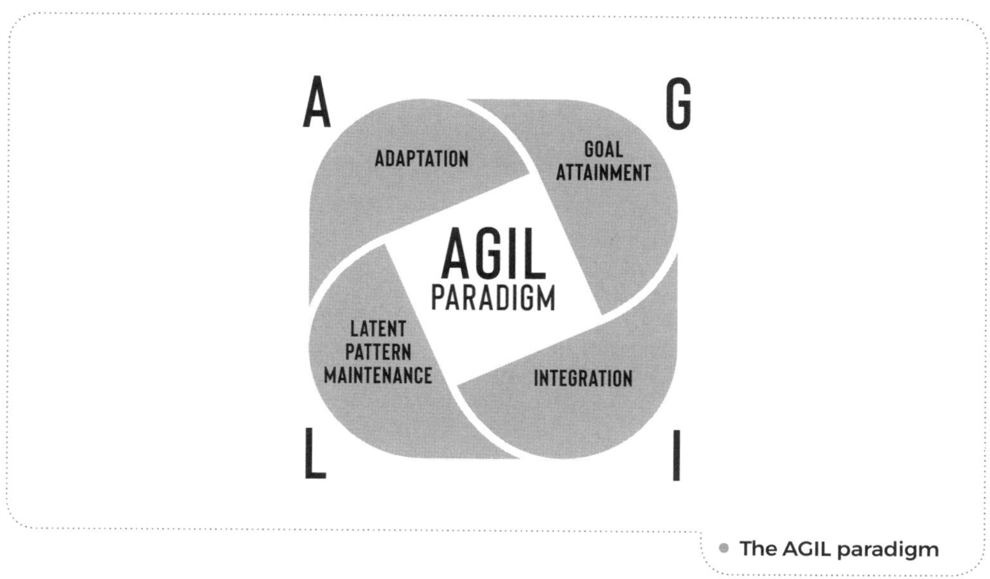

The AGIL paradigm

According to Parsons, these four functions must be met if a social system (in our case, a company) wishes to survive in the long term. In his multifunctional model, each function is necessary and each function must be attuned to the other three. Because the AGIL paradigm offers a unique 360 degree picture, it yields surprising new insights that can be directly applied within the context of the strategic management of a company. The paradigm also allows us to better understand the internal and external conflicts, the dysfunctions and the changes with which today's companies are constantly confronted.

In this sense, the AGIL paradigm is a unique model that allows the survival chances of a company to be clearly mapped out in a structured manner. The need to do this in the rapidly changing times in which we now live is great. Nowadays, nearly every company is subject to the challenges posed by change, threats and new opportunities, all of which require the company to adjust or even re-invent itself. At the same time, they must be careful not to fall into the 'chameleon trap', which persuades some organisations to attempt to follow every new trend, but at the risk of losing their own identity.

It should be noted, however, that Parsons' theory is not a 'big bang' theory. At the end of the day, it is still the managers who need to decide what steps to take, what identity they wish to establish and what opportunities they wish to pursue, both in the short term and in the long term. That being said, the AGIL paradigm can certainly help managers in every industry to make those decisions the right ones.

Long-term thinking and why it is necessary

Most companies concentrate in the first instance on short-term objectives, primarily because their agendas are dictated by quarterly reports and the need to acquire as much market share as quickly as possible. But there is now a growing realisation among managers – albeit slowly – that focusing first and foremost on longer-term objectives is the only way to ensure the future survival of their brand. Not that this is easy, because it takes both courage and patience to stand the test of time. Consider again the case of Apple: during the 1990s, it took them almost a full decade and four CEOs before they could adjust to the demands of the internet age. Even after Jobs had launched his 'digital hub' strategy, it took a further 7 years (from 1997 to 2004) before this was translated into significantly higher sales figures.

A study by McKinsey has confirmed the importance of this kind of long-term perspective. The researchers compared the financial results of companies who engage in long-term thinking with the results of companies who focus more on the short and/or medium term. Based on data from 2001 onwards, the long-term thinkers score better on nearly every parameter. The figures for turnover and income growth were higher by 47 and 36 % respectively. In terms of employment, this translated into an additional 12 000 jobs. It was also calculated that if every company in US would adopt a long-term approach, this would increase American GDP by 1 billion dollars and create some 5 million extra employment opportunities.[27]

Summary: the recipe for survival

A company will only survive if it can fulfil four key functions: adapting to its environment (A), achieving its goals (G), integrating all its stakeholders (I) and providing long-term consistency in terms of its values (L). In other words, a sustainable company needs to constantly search for a *moving equilibrium* between the need for change and the need for stability by strengthening its identity. Contrary to popular wisdom, change and stability should not be conflicting forces when it comes to managing a company, or any organisation. They are both necessary levellers of corporate survival in the long run. This is what I call 'the survival paradox'.

This main premise can be made concrete through the elaboration of two sub-premises per function, based on the AGIL paradigm.

A ADAPTATION	G GOAL ATTAINMENT
- An immortal company is a 'smart follower' of new technologies (chapter 1) - An immortal company provides relevant value for its customers (chapter 2)	- An immortal company has a clear goal and a single-minded strategy (chapter 3) - An immortal company grows by being physically and mentally omnipresent for its customers (chapter 4)
L LATENT PATTERN MAINTENANCE	I INTEGRATION
- An immortal company builds, cultivates and defends a unique identity that is consistent over time (chapter 7) - An immortal company is based on a deeply anchored culture that is difficult to change (chapter 8)	- An immortal company builds and manages a community of engaged employees, attached customers and dependent partners (chapter 5) - An immortal company is a unique system that defines its boundaries and defends them against hostile attacks (chapter 6)

The AGIL paradigm applied to the immortal company (© Fons Van Dyck)

On the other side of the coin, the AGIL paradigm implies that a company risks disappearing if it does not fulfil the four key requirements, or only fulfils them partially, or if one function is dominant at the expense of the rest, or if there are long-terms conflicts between the interests of the four different functions.

In this book I will examine how Apple Computer, from now on simply referred to as Apple, struggled in practice to satisfy these four requirements or functions during two distinct periods: a period of decline (the 'wilderness years' between 1976 and 1996, when the company passed through turbulent waters) and a period of growth (the 'golden years' between 1997 and 2018, when Apple developed into the most valuable brand and company in the world). I will further support the basic principles of my arguments with management lessons drawn from other sectors and companies, based on academic research and relevant practice. Where necessary, I will also debunk misleading myths and other sacred cows. Together, the combined conclusions will, I hope, allow any company to survive – and perhaps even become immortal.

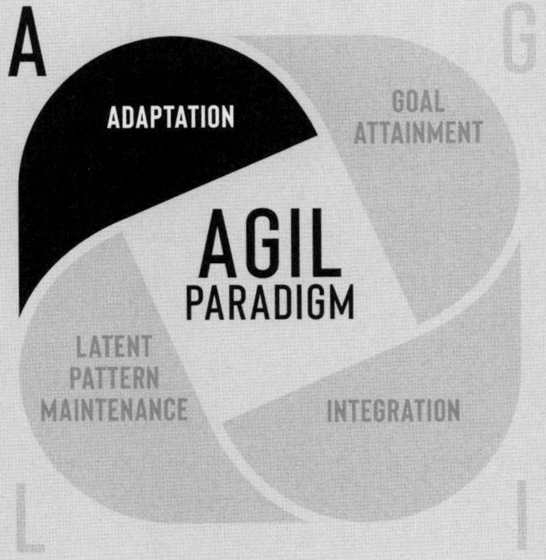

A

G

ADAPTATION

GOAL ATTAINMENT

AGIL PARADIGM

LATENT PATTERN MAINTENANCE

INTEGRATION

L

I

A ADAPTATION

AGIL

ADAPTATION

A first condition for survival is that your company adapts to a rapidly changing environment. This might seem like stating the obvious, but it is still the most common answer and one that has been touted by analysts and advisers and used by smart entrepreneurs for years. But how exactly do you adjust? How do you know what trends to follow? How can you separate the wheat from the chaff when we are talking about hypes and the whims of fashion? In our search we will discover that it is not enough for a company to adjust to its environment; it is much more important to make the environment adjust to your company. It is no good just following others; you need to be a leader, setting new trends, norms and rules that you impose on others.

I will examine the 'A' function of the AGIL paradigm from two different but parallel angles of approach. In chapter 1, I will zoom in on the technological environment, in which new technology is ultimately the motor of change and renewal. Technology ensures that history will never repeat itself and that tomorrow will always be different from today. But how should a company deal with technology? I will answer the question of whether a company needs to be a radical innovator or whether it is better to be a smart and fast follower of new technologies. We will also see the impact that this choice has on results. In chapter 2, I will focus on the importance of the market and the customer. At the end of the day, it is the customers who provide income for your company. But how far should you allow yourself to be led by the rapidly changing consumer preferences of up-and-coming generations and new trends in both the market and society? And perhaps even more importantly: how can your company create relevant and meaningful value for its customers?

A

1 THE SMART FOLLOWER

An immortal company is a 'smart follower' of new technologies.

When Steve Jobs once again took up the reins of leadership at Apple Computer in 1997, he realised better than anyone else that the company had missed too many chances and opportunities in recent years. To survive, it was essential in future to move with the fast-changing business environment and, in particular, to latch on to the new technology that was destined to change people's lives: the internet. In 2008, in an interview with *Fortune Magazine*, Jobs compared the evolution of technology with the movement of waves: 'These waves of technology, you can see them way before they happen, and you just have to choose wisely which ones you're going to surf.' He understood that Apple needed to jump on the right passing train. Jobs again: 'You also need to choose horses that you can ride for 5 to 10 years without the need to constantly change.'[28]

Here Jobs hit the nail on the head. Not only because of the prophetic nature of his comments, but also because of the wisdom they contain: a company can only survive if it adjusts to its constantly changing environment. Not by chasing after events, but by anticipating in advance what the next new world will be. This applies particularly to new technologies. Technology creates the future and ensures that the past is gone forever. It seems so obvious: if you don't adjust, you are in danger of being left behind – and going under. But the million-dollar question is this: how can you best make that adjustment? The answer to that question is the basic principle on which I will concentrate in this chapter: 'An immortal company is a "smart follower" of new technologies'. Immortal companies search their environment, looking for new evolutions and trends that they can pick up and exploit. Or as Jobs once put it: 'You can't be too far ahead, but you have to be far enough ahead, because it takes time to implement.'[29]

By the end of the previous century, this was a lesson he had learnt well – and knew how to apply. In the interview with *Fortune Magazine* shortly after his return to Apple, he stated positively – and for some people surprisingly – that 'people focus too much on entirely new ideas, as if that's what's required to grow a new business. Maybe that's not the right way to do it. Most good products are really extensions of previous products.'[30]

From the iMac to the iPad

The iMac, which Jobs launched in the market after his return from exile as a means of putting Apple back on the map, is a good example of this philosophy. The product was not faster or more powerful than other existing computers. It had no revolutionary new functions that other computers did not have. Even so, the iMac caught people's eye: in part through its neat design and in part because its start-up process was simpler than its rivals. In this sense, the iMac was more evolutionary than revolutionary. Some observers even commented that the iMac was no more than 'a cosmetic masterpiece'.[31] Perhaps – but it still paved the way for the resurrection of Apple in the 21st century.

Likewise, Apple was not the first company to bring an MP3 player to market. Jobs launched 'his' iPod in 2001, but in 1999 there were already 23 other versions of something similar in circulation. In 2000, this market was worth 80 million dollars. The following year – when the iPod arrived on the scene – the market grew by 25 % to 100 million dollars. One of Jobs' most brilliant qualities was that he always chose the right moment to enter a market. And he always added a number of 'extras' to his products, to make them stand out from the crowd. He made these products better – or perhaps re-invented them might be more accurate – by eliminating the shortcomings he saw elsewhere and which he knew caused frustration among consumers. He understood perfectly that there is no point going to market with a product that has not yet been fully developed technically. His products needed to be perfect. At the same time, he also knew that it could be fatal to wait too long, because then it becomes too difficult to establish a strong position, even if you are offering top quality. The growth of Apple in the 21st century was not generated by inventing new devices, but by perfecting existing ones and creating a new market for them (more about this in chapter 2).

Nowadays, everyone – both inside and outside the company – accepts that Apple was not the inventor of the smartphone. As early as 1992, a year before the world wide web was available to the general public and 15 years before the launch of the iPhone, a visionary engineer named Frank Canova Jr. had already developed an embryonic version of a smartphone: the Simon Personal Communicator. At the end of the 1990s, Nokia and Ericsson both launched similar devices, with a touchscreen that could be operated with a stylus and on which various apps could be installed, so that you could listen to music. For some people, these models were 'nice to have', but they clearly still had defects.

Almost everyone at Apple – from Steve Jobs and the other managers, right down to the smart engineers and designers – was fully in agreement that these early smartphones 'sucked': 'They were terrible. Just pieces of junk,'[32] or so it was said. It was in this kind of situation that Apple was at its best: fixing the problems in other company's products that irritated consumers. And with the iPhone, they did it brilliantly. As soon as it hit the market, it was an instant success. But was it 'revolutionary' in the true sense of the word? No, not really. Apple simply finished off the work that others had been sweating over for years. Were there lots of new functionalities? Again, not really. But at least the functionalities all worked – and worked properly. Should we then perhaps regard the iPhone as an incremental innovation? On this matter, Jobs himself commented: 'It was a great challenge. Let's make a great phone that we fall in love with. And we've got the technology. We've got the miniaturisation from the iPod. We've got the sophisticated operating system from Mac. Nobody had ever thought about putting operating systems as sophisticated as OS X inside a phone, so that was a real question. We had a big debate inside the company whether we could do that or not. And that was one where I had to adjudicate it and just say, "We're going to do it. Let's try."'[33]

The success of the iPhone was followed by the iPad. Once again, this was nothing new. Tablets had been circulating since the turn of the century, but had not yet taken off. People didn't really know what to make of them. They weren't a computer, but weren't a telephone either. They were something in between, but with fewer functions than a computer and with none of the communication possibilities of a phone. So what were they, exactly?

It took Apple to find the answer to this question, with yet another brilliant plan: 'The real insight was not shrinking the Mac, but growing the iPhone,' says Bob Borchers, a former director of marketing at Apple.[34] And so the company struck oil again, by simplifying and perfecting what already existed, to create the ideal mix from the best available ideas. As a result, they also took the iPad to market at exactly the right moment.

Picasso as a reference

It is no coincidence that this same pattern emerges in all the big Apple success stories. Steve Jobs knew exactly what he was doing. There is an anecdote – one that has now acquired almost legendary status – about a visit he once made to the Xerox PARC Research Center at the end of the 1970s. It was there that he was shown a user interface with icons for the very first time. He was not the only outsider to see this brand-new Xerox innovation, but he was the only one who immediately saw its potential: it made it possible to bring the computer into the home in a simple and easy-to-use version. And that is what he proceeded to do. The designers at Xerox could only look on helplessly, as Jobs beat them (and everyone else) to the market. Jobs' biographer Walter Isaacson has written that the 'Apple raid' on Xerox PARC is now regarded by many experts as 'one of the biggest heists in the chronicles of industry'.[35] Jobs was not bothered by criticism of this kind. In fact, he was proud of what he had done: 'Picasso had a saying: "good artists copy, great artists steal" – and we have been shameless about stealing great ideas.'[36]

Jobs was the best in the business when it came to turning an accusation into an advantage. Marketing guru Malcolm Gladwell once described Jobs in the authoritative *New Yorker* magazine as 'a tweaker',[37] while in similar vein a reporter for *Fast Company* magazine wrote that Apple's speciality is the remix: 'It curates the best ideas bubbling up around the tech world and makes them its own. It's also "a great fixer", improving on everything that's wrong with other similar products on the shelves.'[38]

First-mover effect?

In technology circles, but also in the wider circle of business leaders and management consultants (and not forgetting the media!), it has long been accepted that companies which are able to be the first to bring a new technology to market as pioneers will, as a result, gain a competitive advantage that will last for quite some time. In the management literature, this is known as the 'first-mover effect'. However, a number of more recent studies have shown that this is not the case. For example, researchers Tellis and Golder conducted a large-scale study that examined more than 650 products from 66 different product categories.[39] In particular, they compared the performance of the pioneers in various branches in 1923 with the performance of pioneers in 2000. Their conclusion was clear: in 64 % of cases, the company that first brought the product to market subsequently failed. And those that did not fail only managed to acquire a 6 % share of the market. In just nine of the 66 categories were the original pioneers still market leader and in recent years that score has declined still further (just 1 in 16 from 1974 onwards). On average, a pioneer holds its leadership position for 5 years. Moreover, the current market leaders arrived on that market on average 19(!) years after the pioneer had made the breakthrough.

Tellis and Golder have shown that many of the companies that are now market leader are also regarded as pioneers, but in reality that is not the case: they were simply fast followers, with the pioneers they followed having long since disappeared from the market.

In other words, we can argue with a degree of confidence that the principle of first-mover advantage needs to be taken with a fairly large pinch of salt. This does not mean that innovation is not important. Or that pioneers cannot become market leaders in due course, although this only applies to a small minority of them. Brands must continue to innovate: it gives them the necessary oxygen to keep hold of their existing customers and to attract new ones, so that they can retain their leadership position. Innovation also ensures that attention is focused on the value of the product and not on its price, while at the same time giving companies a clear purpose: it keeps them sharp and reminds them that once they have taken the step of going to the market they need to keep on re-inventing themselves, if they want to stay there.

Class	Pioneers who are now market leader (number)	Pioneers who are now market leader (%)	Number of cases
Total	6	9 %	66
Before 1940	3	8 %	36
1940-1974	2	14 %	14
After 1974	1	6 %	16
Traditional	3	7 %	42
Digital/high-tech	3	13 %	24

Market leaders or pioneers in 2000 | source: Tellis& Golder, 2002, p. 46

Of course, there are lots of different kinds of innovation. In Apple's case, it is often said that their innovative strength resided first and foremost in the way in which they approached the market. Apple was not usually first to the market, but they were always one of the smartest or fastest followers. Many of today's current market leaders – even those who supposedly have a reputation for innovation – have employed this same strategy, while the real pioneers have long since been forgotten.

The Apple story therefore illustrates the theory of the pioneer versus the smart follower in both a positive and negative sense: positively with the successes of the iPod and iPhone; negatively on the occasions when the company failed because it went too quickly to market, without taking account of the wider environmental factors.

What will never change

Peter Thiel, the founder of PayPal and one of the first investors in Facebook, Space X and LinkedIn, is someone else who does not have much time for pundits who are always singing the praises of disruptive innovation. The term, he notes critically, has almost become an obsession in Silicon Valley, whereas he regards it as a kind of self-glorifying buzzword for everything that is supposedly trendy and new. Nor is he a great believer in the so-called first-mover effect: 'It is actually better to be the last-mover.' By this he means that it makes more sense to be the last person to launch a major development in a specific market, so that you can monopolise profits for years or even decades. And how do you do this? You must first achieve dominance in a small niche within the market and then systematically upscale from there, always working with a long-term vision. It is tried-and-trusted method that will become increasingly familiar as you read this book.[40]

Thiel is not alone in questioning an obsessive focus on disruptive innovation. Amazon CEO Jeff Bezos is often asked to predict how society will change in the next ten years. His shrewd reply is well worth noting: 'One thing I rarely get asked is probably even more important and I encourage you to think about it. It is the question: What is not going to change in the next ten years?' Constantly adapting to changes around you, Bezos claims, means that you will also constantly need to change your company's strategy. He argues that it is smarter not to focus on these changes, but on particular key values that consumers will always appreciate: in Amazon's case, the certainty that their customers will always want low prices, fast delivery and a large selection of products. By focusing on these key elements in their value proposition – customer needs that are largely stable and will still be making money in ten years' time – companies can channel their resources into the fundamentals of their business: 'It changes how leaders organise their business, what they fund, what risks they take,' says Bezos. 'For us at Amazon, the focus becomes: What can we do to offer lower prices? To deliver faster? And so on.'[41]

A second myth debunked: disruption

Companies like Apple, Google and Amazon are often described as 'disruptive', because their products are capable of dislocating entire sectors almost overnight, making the existing players irrelevant. Disruptive innovation of this kind is often put forward as the success formula for growth, profit and power. But is that really the case with Apple? To answer this question, we need to go back to the original definition of 'disruption', which was first cited by Professor Clayton Christensen of the Harvard Business School in his 1996 book *The Innovator's Dilemma*,[42] a book that is believed to have had a major influence on Steve Jobs.

Christensen made a comparative study of the hard disk industry between 1970 and 1990, in which he made a distinction between what he called sustainable and disruptive companies. In his original definition, he argued that disruptive companies could easily be identified because they were simpler, cheaper and had lower standards of quality. They offered lower margins, which meant less profit for themselves, and their products were usually first commercialised in emerging or less significant markets. According to Christensen, consumers who are used to the products of market leaders are not usually interested in the products of these 'disruptive' companies – something that is often forgotten by the supporters of the disruption theory. No less a person than Jobs himself helped (in his own inimitable style) to strengthen the disruption myth. In many of his public appearances he continued to claim for years that Apple and its products had brought about a revolution in entire sectors and markets. These speeches served to lend weight to the popular belief that products and services can only be successful if they are technologically disruptive.

It is not my purpose here to evaluate whether Christensen's original theory of disruption was correct or not. But if we look at Christensen's characteristics for a disruptive company, it is clear that Apple does not fit the bill (even though many people continue to insist that it does). There is no way that Apple's products, viewed from a technological perspective, can be described as simpler, cheaper and of lesser quality. On the contrary, Apple was most successful when its products were very high-quality and sold at a premium price with a huge profit margin. Apple has never wanted to attract new customers by promising lower prices (except for a brief period in the 1990s when it changed strategies – a mistake it quickly corrected). Christensen's third criterion– the launching of products in an emerging or less significant market – equally fails to apply. For example, Apple was certainly not a pioneer in the home computer market in the mid-1970s. In the late 70s and early 80s this market grew rapidly, in large part through the arrival on the scene of IBM PCs and Microsoft software. And when Apple finally launched its iPhone, the telephone had been in existence for more than a century. In other words, Apple did not invent the phone or create the market for it; it simply took the phone to a much higher level.

In fact, Apple's 'i' series was often subjected to criticism by technology watchers, who felt that the series was not innovative enough to be disruptive. In an interview with *Business Week* in 2007,[43] Christensen himself predicted that the iPhone would fail because it was not sufficiently disruptive, arguing that it was nothing more than 'a sustaining technology relative to Nokia'. According to Christensen, all Apple had succeeded in doing was to make a better phone and this success, he was sure, would only be limited. Of course, we now know different.

Apple in trouble: on the bleeding edge

Having said all this, there were moments in its history when Apple seemed set on a highly innovative course. Unfortunately, this led to series of abject failures, which at one point even seemed to threaten the company's continued existence. This was also responsible for the forced resignation of its figureheads, Jobs and Sculley, in the 1980s and the 1990s respectively. How can we explain these disasters? To what extent was Apple not able during these periods to adjust to its environment or, alternatively, was not able to force this environment to adjust to the company and its innovations? And what can we learn from this?

A good example is the launching of the Lisa computer in the early years of the 1980s. The Lisa was described as a 'revolutionary computer', a real game-changer. It was a direct result of Jobs' visit to the Xerox innovation centre in 1979, where he saw their prototype for a personal computer. It is often said that Jobs could hardly believe what he saw that day: not only were there screen icons for the menu options, but you could operate them not by text commands but by moving a strange new contraption – which Xerox called a 'mouse' – over the work surface and clicking on a button! This was light years ahead of Apple, but Jobs immediately set his developers to work to create something similar. And with success. The Lisa had it all: a graphic user interface (with icons), a mouse, two disk drives and a detachable keyboard. What's more, Lisa took up less space than its rivals and had its own apps as standard (a spreadsheet, a drawing program, a graphics program and a word processor). And because it was intended primarily for office use, the Lisa could also be connected to a local in-house company network. In theory, the machine seemed to have everything going for it and expectations were high. In practice, its introduction turned into a nightmare for Jobs and co.

Apple launched Lisa in January 1983. By the end of 1984, the sales figures were negligible. In 2 years, just 60 000 machines had been sold. Not surprisingly, the project was terminated. So what went wrong? Although the concept was brilliant, the technology had not been fully developed before taking it to market. There were still too many teething troubles. What's more, Lisa could not be connected with IBM and MS DOS computers, which at that time were standard in the professional market. That was a huge drawback.

The Lisa story illustrates three main points of interest: (1) Technology must work. You cannot launch something onto the market if it does not satisfy the customer's basic requirements. (2) In terms of innovation, it does not pay to move forward too fast and too far; otherwise there is a risk that your customers will not be able to follow. (3) If you set your focus on a particular market segment – in Lisa's case, the professional environment – you need to go about it in the right manner. If you know that IBM machines are currently standard in that environment, you have to make sure that your product is compatible or, at the very least, try to profile yourself as a serious rival that understands the needs of the end user.

The failure of the Lisa was the start of a difficult period for Apple and led indirectly to the forced departure of Jobs (and Wozniak) just a few years later. On the other hand, the Lisa can also be seen as a kind of prototype project, which in due course would result in the Macintosh and its unique operating system. Viewed in these terms, Jobs' basic idea was brilliant, but it was one better suited to a long-term rather than a short-term perspective. In other words, he simply went too fast. He wanted to be a pioneer – and it was that ambition that cost him his job.

Once bitten, twice shy? Unfortunately not. At the start of the 1990s, Apple and Jobs' successor John Sculley made a more or less identical mistake with the Newton. Sculley wanted to bring a totally new kind of computer to the market, like Jobs and Wozniak had done with the Apple II. The result was the Newton, which Sculley said could function as a digital personal assistant. The unit was small enough to hold in your hand, but still powerful enough to perform rudimentary tasks, such as taking notes, planning appointments and communicating with people anywhere in the world. As with the Lisa, expectations were once again sky-high. Sculley, who also appointed himself as CTO, aimed at nothing less than the revolutionising of the computer market, just as the PC had done back in the 1980s.

For the second time in a decade, Apple's hopes were dashed. Ordinary consumers were not waiting for a computer like the Newton. The designers had been seduced by their own desire to create a revolutionary product. In this they succeeded, but they failed to realise that the only people interested in technology of this sophistication at that time were other people like themselves. In short, they forgot the needs of the customer. As a result, during the first 10 weeks after the launch Apple was only able to sell 50 000 Newtons, mainly to computer nerds and loyal Apple fans. After this initial period, sales slowed to around 7 500 units per month. Instead of being a game-changer, the Newton was destined to become nothing more than a footnote in the Apple story: it was not the long-awaited 'killer application'. It did, however, kill Sculley's career and he was soon shown the door. Looking back in later years, he still believed that the Newton was 'a terrific idea, but was too far ahead of its time'.[44] And he added prophetically: 'Everything Apple does fails the first time, because it is out on the bleeding edge.'

The golden formula: brand extensions

In other words, being a pioneer is not your best plan, certainly not if you are Apple. Viewed historically, smart followers have on average a much better chance of success. But what then? Let's imagine for a minute the following scenario. You have launched your product successfully onto the market and it has been well-received. So what are you going to do next? Are you going to try and develop another totally new product? Or are you going to build on your success and bring out a variant of your existing product? This latter option is the strategy that has been resolutely followed by Apple during the past 10 years. And with success. Apple has shown better than anyone else that product variants (known in the marketing world as 'brand extensions') are a sure-fire way not only to continue growing in your existing markets, but also to conquer new ones. This explains, of course, why at the end of 2017 the company brought the eighth edition of its iPhone to market and for the phone's tenth anniversary even launched a premium edition: the iPhone X. It is a golden formula.

We can talk of a brand extension when a company uses one of its existing brand products to launch a new product. Classic examples include Gillette with its different types of razor, Volkswagen with its different Golf models and Coca-Cola with its seemingly endless variants of the world's most famous soft drink. In general, marketeers distinguish between two different types of brand extension. First, there are line extensions: the producer launches the same product, but in a different colour, flavour, size or shape, or with an additional function. This is what Apple has done so successfully with its iPhone series: re-launch the same successful product time after time, but on each occasion with a significant and incremental innovation. However, you can also take this process a stage further by using your existing brand to launch a new product onto the market in a different but related product category. Here, Apple is once again a good example: the company first went to market with an MP3 player, then with a smartphone and later with an e-reader. This strategy with category extensions works best of all with strong brands – and Apple is certainly that!

The American marketing professor Kevin Lane Keller argues that 80 to 90 % of all new products that appear on the market in any given year are line extensions.[45] Why? Because there are a number of obvious benefits. Research has shown, for example, that the development of a variant takes only half the time needed to develop a new product. Similarly, the cost of taking a variant to market is significantly less and the chances of success are twice as great. On the other side of the coin, new products only have a 2 in 10 chance of being successful or, in some sectors, just 1 in 10. According to Keller, there are a number of reasons for this. In particular, consumers have more trust in products that originate from a brand they know and like. They feel that they are running less of a risk with these familiar brands. If a new product can be associated with this kind of 'trusted' brand, this significantly increases the prospect of a favourable launch. On the other hand, if there are too many variants of the same product, this can lead to consumer confusion and frustration: which one should they pick? This was one of the problems with Apple in the 1990s. Customers were overwhelmed with a seemingly endless stream of new variants and options. Psychological research has shown that when consumers are faced with choice stress of this kind, they will ultimately end up buying less. In this respect, strong brands can push things further than less well- known brands, since consumers are more inclined to give stronger brands the benefit of the doubt. That being said, even the quality brands need to be careful not to stray too far from their core business. This is a lesson that Apple has also learnt from the turn of the new century onwards (see chapter 3). In fact, Apple is the living proof of the success of the brand extension strategy, both in line extensions and in category extensions: not only with its introduction of different versions in the same product category (the iPhone), but also in other categories, with the 'i' series as the connecting factor.

Brand extensions will generally be more successful when there is a content match between the brand and the new sector or product category.[46] Such brands can count on greater consumer trust if they are seen to be making use of the expertise they built up in their original sector. In this case, it is even sometimes possible to speak of a lever effect. However, this presents managers with a difficult choice. If they ensure that there is a strong link with the characteristics of the existing products, there is more chance that the new product will enjoy more initial support, but with the possible risk that it will not be seen as innovative enough. On the other hand, if they opt for a product that is completely new, which has no real substantive link with the company's existing products, this may be viewed by consumers as less appropriate – and research has shown that for the average customer 'appropriateness' is more important than 'innovativeness'.

The advertising used by Apple in 2007 to launch the iPhone on the American market is a case in point. The film shows old and familiar scenes from films and television series in which actors and actresses simply pick up the phone and say 'hello'. Nothing more than that. Just a series of 'hellos', time after time. This was neither innovative nor ground breaking, as many people had come to expect from Steve Jobs and Apple, but it was clever of Apple to play on the common codes in the telephone category, while at the same time making clear that a new telephonic era was dawning with the arrival of the smartphone.

The recipe of using brand extensions that have small and incremental progressions (in some cases, as small as just a new kind of packaging) has also proven to be a good strategy from a financial perspective. It is certainly massively cheaper than heavy investment in R&D programs, the success of which is by no means assured. In fact, in this context it has been compared – with only some mild exaggeration and a little bit of imagination –with the so-called Lorenzian butterfly system, named after the MIT mathematician Edward Lorenz, who described how a seemingly insignificant action (like a butterfly flapping its wings in the Amazon rainforest) can result in something immeasurably more significant (like a tornado in Texas). Put simply, small steps can have big effects. And research by INSEAD has indeed shown that a less ambitious strategy based on incremental innovation can result in more sales than a strategy based on huge R&D budgets for the new development of so-called 'blockbuster' products, which more often fail in the market than succeed. For this reason, it is better for brands to focus on seemingly marginal improvements for their most important brand products, which should always seek to answer the real needs of consumers who, as a result, will be willing to pay a little bit more for the privilege (also see chapter 2).[47]

The heritage

So how are things today at Apple? Are they continuing to walk the 'smart follower' path set out for them by Steve Jobs? The answer is an unequivocal 'yes!' – and CEO Tim Cook makes no secret of the fact. On the contrary, he boasts of it as a strength. In an interview with *Bloomberg Business Week* in 2017 he said: 'We don't give a rats about being first; we want to be best in creating people's experiences.'[48] The introduction of the Apple Watch and Apple Pay are clear examples of what he means. Yet again, these were product groups in which Apple did not take the lead, but is now seen as being the best company in the respective branches. As far as the

Apple Watch is concerned, it was as long ago as 2003 at the Consumer Electronics Show in Las Vegas that Microsoft first launched the concept of a smartwatch. And as for Apple Pay, Tim Cook had this to say: 'I think we have the first mobile payment solution that can be mainstream, that people can really use. I think most of the other people that ventured into this spent all of their time on the front end thinking about how to create a business model, how to collect data, own the data, sell the data, monetise the data. They were thinking about it in those kinds of terms, not in terms of why you would want to use it.'[49]

Similarly in the field of artificial intelligence, which many experts believe will be 'the next big thing', Apple is happy to adopt a 'wait-and-see' approach. 'Because,' says Cook, 'something that you would see out in the market any time soon would not be something that any of us would be satisfied with.' As a result, they are integrating AI technology into their products little by little. Siri, the smart speaker HomePod, and the facial recognition on the iPhone X are probably the best known examples. 'We didn't feel an urgency to get something because somebody else had it. It's actually not about competing, from our point of view. It's about thinking through for the Apple user what things will improve their lives.'[50]

Apple has made a clear strategic choice to upgrade existing technologies and take them, as a smart follower, to a higher level. They search through their environment and cherrypick the things they think are most appropriate, both for the company and for their customers. And then they give these things the full Apple treatment, whilst at the same time always remaining conscious of the need not to stray too far from their core business. Adjusting to the reality around them is their golden formula for becoming – and remaining – an immortal company.

A

THE DO'S-AND-DON'TS

- ∞ Innovation is a permanent, non-stop task: it gives oxygen to your company and your brands.
- ∞ Search your environment and decide which new trends you can best latch onto, without deviating too far from your core.
- ∞ Don't focus too much on new ideas: most good products are extensions of products that already exist.
- ∞ Do not allow yourself to be blinded by disruption theory: most successes are not disruptive at all.
- ∞ Do not be concerned if your company is not a pioneer: pioneers often disappear from the scene, usually to be replaced by smart followers, who then in turn come to be regarded as pioneers.

A

- ∞ Wait for the right moment to take your product to market.
- ∞ Brand extensions with incremental innovations are the recipe for success in the long term.
- ∞ Always take account of what the customer wants, not what you want.
- ∞ Do not get too far ahead of yourself; your customers also need to follow.
- ∞ Don't forget: products should not only be 'nice to have', but must also work for your customer.
- ∞ Ask yourself what will not change in the future, and build your business on that.

A

2 THE CUSTOMER FIRST

An immortal company provides relevant value for its customers.

'You've got to start with the customer experience and work backwards to the technology.' These words from Steve Jobs created a shockwave amongst the ranks of the many hundreds of engineers and software developers who had gathered together in the spring of 1997 to hear him at the annual Apple Worldwide Developers Conference in San Jose, California. Jobs had just returned from his 10 years of enforced exile. He was 'home' again, surrounded by his last few followers, who had remained loyal to the company during his absence, often against their better judgement. During the intervening years, Jobs had become wiser and more mature, so that he now dared to confront his past failures in public ('I've made this mistake probably more than anybody else in this room'). Even so, Jobs knew that he was once again expected to take up the role of the company's Messiah, the 'chosen one' who would show his people the path to the Promised Land. And Jobs was in no doubt about the direction this path would take: it would lead to Apple's customers and to a full and proper understanding of their needs: 'What incredible benefits can we give to the customer? Where can we take the customer?' This was Apple's new mantra, which would open the door to the company's 'golden years'.

This was unquestionably a paradigm shift, both for Apple and for Jobs. In their pioneering years, Jobs and Wozniak had built computers first and foremost for themselves and for a small group of fanatical early adopters, who would later become their biggest fans. But reaching the wider public? No, that was something different. That needed something more than technological ingenuity and Jobs' legendary gut feeling. In fact, this is the fate of many pioneering start-ups, which are built on brilliant technical concepts, but lack the necessary touch to sense the needs of a large market. As a result, they fail to capitalise on the praise and success they initially enjoyed. So how can companies ensure that an initial success is not just a 'one-hit wonder'? How can they develop this hit into a lasting formula for long-term growth? The answer is simple: adapt your operations to reflect the needs of the customer, exactly like Jobs did in 1997. In this chapter, I will therefore look in more depth at the' A' (Adaptation) of the AGIL paradigm and offer evidence to support my second fundamental principle: 'An immortal company provides relevant value to its customers'.

A finger on the pulse of the world

If you want to understand your customers and their needs, you need to be constantly scanning your environment. You need to use your finely-tuned antennae to sense which developments and forces are at play. In order to survive, you must be able, right from your earliest days as a company, to detect new trends and identify changes in customer moods, as well as reflecting on what these things might mean both for you and them. To be absolutely clear: this goes much further than simply asking your customers about their wishes and desires. If you do that, you will probably find yourself chasing events rather than controlling them, certainly in matters relating to technology. Nor is it enough simply to concentrate on trends in your own sector. Things that are happening in other industries can also have an effect on your operations and might even be a source of inspiration. For example, the importance that companies like Apple, Google and Facebook attach to creating an optimum user experience has unquestionably resulted in this aspect becoming important in other sectors, such as tourism and the banking world. And you don't need to be an experienced trendwatcher to realise that the advent of artificial intelligence and virtual reality will have a major impact on many (if not all) industries and even on the way in which we relate to each other as individuals.

In addition, you also need to be alert as a company for the new sociological trends that are active in society as a whole. Society is disruptive by nature. In the late 1980s, Apple in particular was able to surf with great success on the wave created by the emergence of a new 'creative class', a phenomenon that was excellently described in *The Rise of the Creative Class* by the American sociologist Richard Florida.[51] Florida defined this new social class as people who were employed in professions such as engineer, scientist, architect, designer, artist, etc. In short, an increasingly important group of autonomous knowledge workers with new ideas, who created new products and technologies and developed creative content to match. Silicon Valley was the main playground for the exponents of this new ethos of creativity, whose rise to prominence Florida sets against the background of the counterculture that flourished on the West Coast of the United States in the 1960s, with San Francisco as its epicentre. Alternative values were cross-fertilised with a traditional Protestant work ethic to produce a fascinating cocktail that was part liberalism and part capitalism, with technology serving as the lubricant between them. Jobs liked to see himself as the child of this counterculture and so it was no coincidence that in the mid-1980s Apple introduced the Macintosh, which was specifically aimed at graphically oriented consumers: advertising agencies, publishers, graphic designers, etc. Even today, this group still form the backbone of Apple's core support, but this did not just happen by chance. It happened because Apple not only devoted care and attention to the design of its own products, but also offered the new creative class tools which facilitated their work and their ability to express themselves, specifically with products and applications for the DTP market. This makes clear that if a brand wants to survive, it not only needs to adapt to its environment, but also needs to help shape that environment and stimulate its further development.

Even so, Apple was faced with a serious problem as the new century began. The company could still rely on the support of its 'old faithfuls', but it was struggling to capture the imagination of a younger audience: the millennials of Generation Y. Young people no longer found Apple 'cool' in the same way as their parents. Moreover, Apple's products were simply too expensive for them to buy. It was not until the introduction of the iPod and iTunes in 2003 and, even more decisively, the iPhone in 2007 that Apple could finally count on the appreciation of the young. The iPod gave Apple back its 'trendy' image and thereby opened the door to a broad new spectrum of customers. 'In time,' noted the commentators, 'it would prove to be the Walkman of the early 21st century.'[52]

But it was the iPhone and the iPad that paved the way for the real breakthrough. It was these products that attracted new customers in their millions. At a Goldman Sachs conference in 2013, Tim Cook said about this: 'The tablet is attracting people who've never owned a PC, and people who have owned them, but aren't greatly experienced. And Apple is at the forefront. The iPad is absolutely the poster child of the post-PC revolution.'[53] Apple had finally succeeded in bringing its products to the wider general public by responding to the needs of a much larger group of consumers, but without surrendering the uniqueness of its own identity.

The world around your finger

Companies therefore need to adapt to their new environment, so that they can continue to meet the new needs of customers. However, according to the AGIL paradigm, this 'passive' form of adaptation is not enough. Companies must also make use of changing circumstances to alter that environment to better suit their own purposes. In other words, they don't just adjust to the environment, but also adjust the environment to themselves. Whoever plays it smart can significantly increase not only their chances of survival, but also of continued success. What's more, in this way these smart companies (re-)define or create a new market, in which they are seen as 'the example to follow'. In fact, in some cases they can even make the other players in that market totally irrelevant, because these rivals are unable to meet the new and higher standards of added value.

In short, a company like Apple does much more than simply respond to trends in its environment. It also acts positively to change that environment, so that it can continue to exercise great influence and power. The iPod, iPhone and iPad transformed the entire consumer electronics sector. Some commentators even claim that these products have transformed the world. In this way, Apple followed in the footsteps of the truly great companies like GE, Disney and Lego. They not only were market leaders, but also leaders in a more literal sense: they led the world of which they were also a part.

Today, the influence of some companies on their environment is so massive that it can even pose a threat to society. Think, for example, of the accusations in recent years laid at the door of companies such as Apple, Google, Amazon and Facebook. In addition to allegations of tax avoidance, abuses of power and privacy infringements, there is an underlying fear that they are seeking to influence public life in general and manipulate it to further some hidden agenda.

Companies that want to survive in the long term must therefore also be able to offer answers to the so-called non-market related forces: the societal expectations of (often unorganised) interest groups and individuals, who all want to have their own say. These groups are usually very suspicious of big companies and brands, and this is something that they take no trouble to hide: they express their opinions in forthright terms in the press and/or send their lobbyists to badger the political decision-makers in Washington, Brussels and Beijing. These pressure groups can have a huge impact on a company or even on a whole economy. For this reason, companies would be wise to take account of what these groups have to say and not simply adopt a defensive position. In a global economy, sustained competitive advantage arises from tackling social, political and environmental issues as part of a corporate strategy. You will not prosper simply by pursuing business as usual – or so IE Business School professors David Bach and David Bruce Allen have argued.[54]

In other words, companies must find a way to become part of the solution, rather than being the root cause of the problem.

Apple in trouble: insulting customers

The recent history of Apple reads like a never-ending success story. But as we have already seen, things haven't always gone as smoothly. Sometimes Apple got things disastrously wrong and failed to offer its customers the value they wanted. It is interesting to look at some of these instances where Apple went off the rails, so that we can learn not only from Apple's successes, but also from their failures. When they succeeded (often brilliantly), it was because they not only adjusted to their new environment, but also in turn adjusted that environment to their advantage. When they failed (often catastrophically), it was because they had lost touch completely with their environment.

The most spectacular example of failure was the unsuccessful launch of the Macintosh in 1984. Why did things go so badly wrong? It wasn't for lack of resources or want to trying. The company made a glitzy TV commercial that perfectly encapsulated all the classic marketing lessons, as well it should: it cost 750 000 dollars to make. In addition, Sculley launched a 'state of the art' advertising campaign that set

Apple back a further 15 million (!) dollars. You need to sell an awful lot of PCs to win back this kind of money, but that is precisely what the company expected would happen. The original intention of the designers (including Jobs) was to create an affordable computer with a sale price of around 500 dollars, so that they could reach a wide public in the market. However, this plan soon started to take a different direction. As a result, the development and production costs for the Macintosh eventually exceeded this 500 dollar figure. Right up to the day of the launch, there were discussions in Apple HQ about where the sales price should now be set. Jobs had a new figure in mind for a standard price of 1 495 dollars. But Sculley's expensive marketing campaign meant that that the Macintosh finally went on the market for 2 495 dollars. This was a price that was still affordable for professional users, but this had not been Apple's initial target group. In short, they had lost sight of their intended customers. As a result, the Macintosh fell between two stools or, if you prefer, between two markets. It certainly met the needs of ordinary customers, but it was too expensive for them to buy. And while professional users could certainly afford to buy it, the machine failed to live up to their technical expectations. Not surprisingly, Apple failed to get anywhere near its ambitious sales targets. What's more, the discussion over the price made the rift between Jobs and Sculley both public and permanent. A year later, Jobs was shown the door and Apple was left to face one of its most serious crises without its founder and guiding star.

Another year later, there was a second failed launch when the Macintosh Office model was released, this time aimed at the business market. On this occasion, Apple managed to get the whole business community up in arms against them – precisely the target group they were trying to reach! The cause of the problem this time was a darkly satirical advertisement, lasting just 60 seconds and televised during the final of the Super Bowl game. The advert was entitled 'Lemmings' and was inspired by the tiny rodents which, according to popular wisdom (supported by not much more than a Disney nature documentary), throw themselves to their death off a cliff once the population in their group becomes too big to be sustainable. The makers of the commercial showed an endless row of grey-suited and blindfolded business men walking one by one, lemming-like, into a deep ravine. This was an obvious dig at many people in the business world who until now had bought IBM computers, almost without thinking.

Unfortunately, the business world failed to see the joke. As a result, the commercial turned out to be a commercial disaster for Apple. Things were so bad that the marketing director at the time even suggested making a public apology in *The*

Wall Street Journal. The idea was rejected, but it would have made no difference: the damage was already done. Sculley later wrote in his biography that this 1 million dollar advert 'would later emerge as a symbol that Apple Computer was out of control'.[55]

It is indeed possible to ask serious questions about the position that marketing was given – or rather was not given – during the company's wilderness years, and this notwithstanding the fact that Sculley had earned his spurs as a top marketeer at Pepsi. The problem started with Apple I and II, which Jobs and Wozniak had developed for themselves and their friends. The early but very limited success of these models gave Jobs an almost religious belief in his own instincts. He saw himself as the prototype of an Apple user. It was a miscalculation that would cost him and his company dearly.

Even after Jobs' return, it was not the case that everything he touched turned to gold. A good example is Power Mac G4 Cube, designed by Jony Ivy and launched in 2000. Although the device was praised for its innovative industrial design (it was later given a place in Museum of Modern Art in New York), it failed to appeal to the creative professionals, because it was too expensive, not powerful enough and difficult to upgrade.

And the disappointments didn't stop there. The launch in 2005 of the Rokr, a mobile telephone developed in collaboration with Motorola, was also a flop. This was a premature attempt to bring a kind of iTunes phone to market. The aim was to get a foot in the door of the fast-growing cell phone sector, but technically the Rokr was not fit for purpose. As a result, Apple suffered another very public setback. However, it at last taught Apple some important lessons: they needed to do things better and they needed to do them alone. The seeds had been sown for the iPhone.

ISP: the holy grail

This narrative naturally leads on to the more fundamental question of how you can succeed in binding large groups of consumers to your brand, create new markets and even force the world to adapt to your company and its activities. It was long assumed that a brand had to offer customers either a unique benefit or a strong emotional experience. I am now convinced that strong and sustainable brands focus on four different but also complementary dimensions. Together, they form an

ISP: Integrated Selling Proposition. With its ISP, a company must offer its customers relevant value in four key areas: (1) functional added value, (2) emotional added value, (3) a unique user experience and (4) a noble purpose with which they can identify.

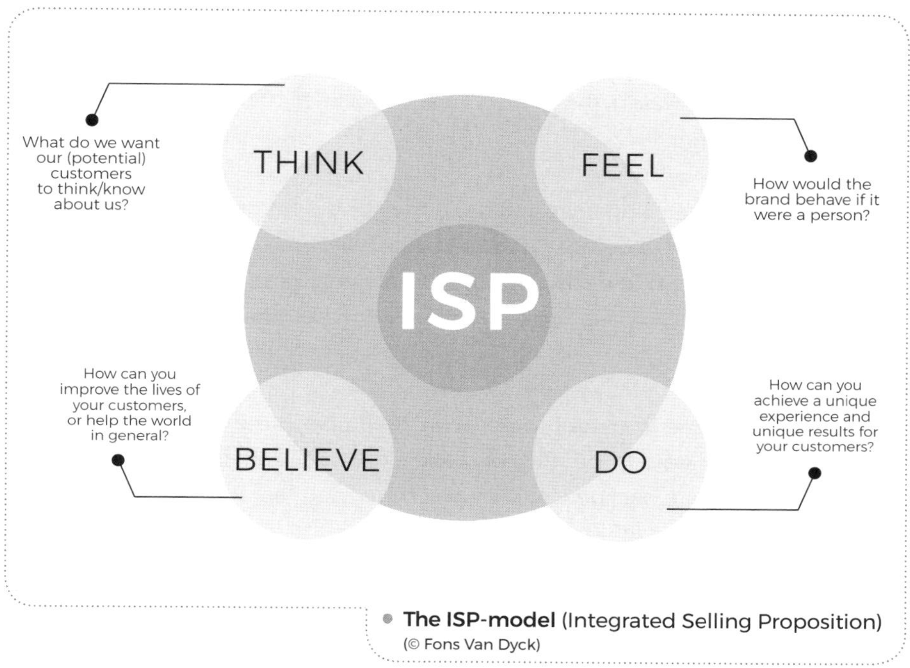
What do we want our (potential) customers to think/know about us?
THINK
FEEL
How would the brand behave if it were a person?
ISP
How can you improve the lives of your customers, or help the world in general?
BELIEVE
DO
How can you achieve a unique experience and unique results for your customers?

The ISP-model (Integrated Selling Proposition)
(© Fons Van Dyck)

I will now look more closely at each of these areas of relevant value. To do so, I will use Apple, which scores heavily in each of the four dimensions, as an illustration. More specifically, I will examine a number of Apple marketing campaigns that perfectly illustrate how during its 'golden years' the company was able to attract new customers to the brand and keep them loyal over many years. This will serve as an example to any company that wishes to do the same.

Functional added value (THINK)

The functional value of a product is the most obvious and most tangible value proposition. This relates to the visible and functional characteristics of a product, which ensure that it is experienced as 'better' than other comparable products. These attributes usually have a direct connection with the purpose for which the product or service is used: cooking for a cooking pot, printing for a printer, listening to music for an iPod.

Whoever wishes to seduce consumers with a functional value proposition will need to place the product itself in the central position. This means that external characteristics, like style and design, are important: the way the products looks, feels, sounds or even smells. All these characteristics are used in conjunction to show to potential customers that this product is better than all the others. They are also the tangible characteristics that give information about the product, so that the cognitive part of the consumer's brain is also addressed. They make him 'think' about the product. In short, the functional added value is what the product has to offer for the customer.

Unfortunately for the companies that build their brand strategy around functional added value, there are a number of disadvantages to this approach. For example, it makes it very difficult to decisively differentiate your product from the rest. And even if you do, there is a huge risk that it will soon be copied and perhaps even improved by others.

The campaign for the launch of the iMac in 1998 placed the product central and showed colourful iMacs in bright red, orange, green, purple or turquoise against a light-emitting white background. The accompanying text highlighted the product's speed, simplicity and ease of connection with the internet. In all the advertisements, there was a reference to its unique design (for example, 'Chic, not geek' or 'iCandy'). Subtle reference was also made to the 'boringness' of the competition (one advert has the words 'Sorry, no beige' above a picture of a turquoise iMac).

Apple wanted to use this campaign to try and reassure consumers that there was nothing complicated about using the iMac. The only difficult thing was picking the colour: 'The thrill of surfing. The agony of choosing', as another of their ads put it. In contrast, the rival Windows PCs were depicted as being over-complex and very difficult to use first time. The iMac was in every respect faster and more user-friendly, and this for the same price as comparable computers. Who could possibly doubt which was the best buy?

It is clear that in this instance Apple focused heavily on the functional added value of its product and this has become a part of their tried-and-tested success formula ever since. It was this campaign that formed the basis for all the later – and now legendary – product launches by Steve Jobs and Tim Cook. Rule number one: the product is the star. New features and functionalities are brilliantly depicted as 'revolutionary', even though in many cases they are only incremental improvements of existing technology. At the same time, the functional characteristics of the product are made tangible and measurable, since these characteristics form the basis for comparison with Apple's competitors. In this way, analysts and journalists from around the world have been persuaded for decades to write favourable reviews about Apple products. Perhaps the best example of this functional approach was the 'If it's not an iPhone, it's not an iPhone' campaign from 2015, in which the uniqueness of the iPhone was underpinned by what was effectively a lesson about the technology behind the product. This was a clear effort by Apple, in this instance at least, to appeal more to its customers' heads than their hearts.

Emotional added value (FEEL)

In an emotional value proposition personality characteristics are ascribed to the product. This makes it possible for the consumer to identify with that product and to feel a degree of emotional commitment towards it. In this way, the product becomes a real brand. This emotional experience of the brand or product is just as important – sometimes even more important – as the functional characteristics.[56] If a consumer opts for a particular brand because he associates it with an emotional value of some kind, this means that the brand in question offers him an emotional benefit. For example, 'I buy Volvo, because it makes me feel safe', or 'I drink Red Bull, because it gives me wings' (energy), or 'I use L'Oréal, because it gives me a certain status' ('Because I'm worth it').

Adverts and commercials can be a highly effective way to build up a personality around a product, because the product can be brought directly and visibly into connection with certain situations or users. The actors, music and drive contained in the advertising all help to give an identity to the product.

At Apple, Steve Jobs was for many years the personification of the brand. He was able to work on people's perception so well that they eventually came to see themselves – simply by virtue of using an Apple computer – as anti-establishment, creative, innovative and rebellious. 'Steve created the only lifestyle brand in the tech industry,' said Larry Ellison, the founder of Oracle. 'There are cars people are proud to have – Porsche, Ferrari, Prius – because what I drive says something about me. People feel the same way about an Apple product.'[57] Over the years, Apple has succeeded in building up its own emotional added value, to such as extent that it even survived the death of its creator. Today, Apple is still regarded as being intelligent, innovative, trendsetting and just a little bit 'quirky'.

User experience (DO)

A strong brand will not only appeal to the heads and hearts of its consumers, but will also ensure that these consumers 'do' things in association with its products that they experience as enjoyable or memorable.[58] Such brands make the user experience central, since it creates value for both the consumer and the brand holder. The pioneer of this experience culture was undoubtedly Disney. For many years, this has no longer been a brand that simply brings to life fun animated figures, but a brand that makes children all over the world dream of one day visiting Disneyland. They wear T-shirts with their favourite Disney characters, go to sleep clutching their favourite Disney soft toy and drink their breakfast milk out of mug decorated with an image of Mickey or Minnie. (A small detail: in 1986, Steve Jobs took command of Pixar Animation Studios, which was later taken over by Disney).

Companies that are able to add an experience to their brand or product are in a strong position to differentiate themselves from the rest. Linking a positive experience to a product always creates a strong added value for the consumer. One company that understood this quicker than most was Nike. The famous Nike Towns, where customers could have personalised sports shoes made, were set up as far back as the 1990s and are often seen as the inspiration that later led Steve Jobs to open the Apple Stores. Thanks to their helpful and always friendly expert staff, these stores brought Apple into direct contact with its customers. In the meantime, almost every self-respecting strong brand has opened its own concept or experience store and empirical research has shown that this kind of direct contact, providing a direct consumer experience, has a much more positive effect than printed advertising and media commercials.[59]

The arrival and explosion of digital media in recent times has added a whole new dimension to the customer experience concept. The user experience is now more than ever before a digital experience. After years of teething troubles, virtual reality (VR) is now becoming an important marketing tool for many of the major worldwide brands. As a result, companies like Facebook, Google and Samsung now invest heavily in VR platforms and headsets, which can only serve to further increase their use in the future. Although VR is currently most commonly used to test products, expectations for its inclusion in consumer products in the years ahead are high. If these expectations are met, the possibilities in terms of customer experience are almost limitless.

Noble purpose (BELIEVE)

From the start of the 21st century and in response to the anti-globalisation movement (for which the book *No Logo* by Naomi Klein was one of the catalysts), more and more companies are seeking to link their identity to a core ideal or, if you prefer, to a 'noble purpose'. Elon Musk's Space X wants to take everyone to Mars; Google wants to provide free internet worldwide (even in the deserts); Dove wants to offer all women 'real beauty' and greater self-esteem. These well-publicised raisons d'être are carefully kept separate from the more trivial matter of making a profit. Higher goals reveal a company's soul and should not be confused with short-term objectives and business strategies. Such goals are not so much a question of altruism or corporate social responsibility, but focus more on the ultimate reason for the company's existence. In short, its noble purpose.

Companies have noticed that the younger generations in particular are starting to attach growing importance to meaning, sustainability and authenticity. In the eyes of the young, companies have a responsibility towards society and are expected to exercise that responsibility wisely. As a result, the ethical dimension of a brand's identity is becoming an increasingly important yardstick for the general attractiveness of the brand worldwide. One of the interesting things about this evolution is the way in which brands who succeed in giving an 'authentic' impression in all aspects of their operations – the attitude of the employees, the methods of production, the relationships with stakeholders, etc. – are able to create a bond with their customers that is almost unbreakable. Some commentators have even compared this phenomenon with a religious movement, based on loyalty and belief. In these active 'communities' customers are no longer just customers, but become ambassadors for the company.

Apple is a past master at this fourth dimension. Few companies are able to invoke a noble purpose as a means to bind customers in quite the same way as Apple. In Apple's case, this noble purpose is their unshakeable belief that Apple technology will change the world and help to set people free. The legendary '1984' advertising film which was used for the launch of the Macintosh in that same year is a classic example of this kind of messianic message. The commercial shows an athletic young woman being chased by a group of armed soldiers. In her hands she carries a sledgehammer. She suddenly races into a darkened auditorium, where rows of workers in grey overalls are staring apathetically at a large screen, from which a Big Brother-like figure is haranguing them with an ideological speech. The Apple heroine, still pursued by the soldiers, throws the hammer through the screen, which shatters into a thousand pieces. The hall is filled with fresh air and the sluggish workers, at last, are able to see the light, both literally and figuratively. In the closing moments of the film, a voice announces solemnly: 'On January 24th, Apple Computer will introduce Macintosh. And you'll see why 1984 won't be like 1984.' The computer was never even shown, because it wasn't necessary. The most important thing was the idea that the Apple brand and its Macintosh would fundamental change not only the lives of its users, but also the world around them.

Equally impressive is the 'Think Different' campaign from 1998. This commercial consisted of a series of images of iconic 'protesters' and 'revolutionaries', who each in their own way had changed the world. This cleverly enabled the company to link Apple in the public mind with figures like Martin Luther King Jr., John Lennon, Muhammad Ali, Bob Dylan and Albert Einstein. By putting the company in the same category as these famous activists and thinkers, Apple not only showed that it was innovative, but signalled that the company, together with its users, could also change the world. Jobs later declared that the film was aimed in part at Apple's own employees: 'We at Apple had forgotten who we were. One way to remember who you are is to remember who your heroes are.' The 'Think Different' campaign once again put the company firmly in the spotlights, which at that moment in its history was more than welcome, since it was still licking its wounds from its near bankruptcy. This made it more important than ever to win back the confidence of both its own workforce and the loyal Apple support base of designers, students and publishers.

'1984' and 'Think Different' are perfect instances of the impact that ideological campaigns can have on the perception of a brand. Both films received numerous awards from the marketing world, and rightly so. They both made crystal-clear the values for which the company stands and showed how Apple is different from other companies through its desire to change the world. And both films undoubtedly also contributed to the fact that Apple continued to be seen as an innovative, disruptive and out-of-the-box brand. Together with the live performances by Jobs, these advertising films helped to elevate the Apple brand to cult status with opinion leaders, analysts and the media. Even so, the case of Apple also shows that a noble purpose, no matter how creatively presented and even with the noblest of intentions, is not sufficient on its own to bring commercial success.

That being said, some commentators argue that this higher ideological goal (the company's 'why') continues to be an essential dimension, not only for the creation of brand value, both within the organisation and beyond, but also for brand profitability.[60] Yet although it is true that strong brands do have a clear 'why', there are equally clear indications that in this context people find NGOs and citizens' movements to be more trustworthy than commercial companies, for whom the maximisation of profit will always remain a key objective, even if they try to balance this objective with societal interests. And the further the higher goal is distanced from the company's core activities, the less legitimate it becomes for that company to depict itself as socially engaged. This is something for which the millennium generation in particular now has high expectations, whilst at the same time remaining sceptical, even critical, of the credibility of most companies, based on their past record of performance. The danger of being accused of 'purpose washing' is lurking around the corner of any company and its brands.

As the ISP model shows, all four dimensions are necessary to bring about success. Consequently, all four need to be cultivated – although some dimensions will generate a greater positive effect than others, depending on the product category or the medium. In addition, it is also important to note that many (young) consumers strongly disapprove of companies which only 'pretend' that they want to change the world. Such consumers now critically monitor the actual deeds of the companies in practice, rather than being taken in by their well-packaged marketing 'zeal'.

All-in-one

For a long time, it was believed in marketing circles that it was necessary to make a choice between a functional and an emotional message. Today, however, the conviction is growing that strong bands need to integrate both dimensions into their strategy, whilst at the same time adding, if possible, a memorable customer experience. As a result, these dimensions are increasingly seen as complementary.

A Bain & Company survey has strengthened the idea that successful companies deliver on multiple elements of value. One of the researchers' key findings is that these companies obtain higher Net Promoter Scores and higher revenue growth.[61] Apple has through the years, it seems, shifted towards delivering on these multiple elements. If we look at the iMac campaign at the end of the 1990s, it is evident that Apple focused heavily on the functional benefits of its products and, by extension, the user experience. However, as the company attempted to move into new markets, its campaigns increasingly began to combine the four ISP propositions (functional added value, emotional added value, experience and higher goal), now encapsulated in a new buzzword:'storytelling'.

Let's consider, for example, the 2003 'Silhouette' campaign for the iPod. This showed a number of black silhouettes of young people dancing to different kinds of 'cool' music (hip-hop, dance, rock), being played on their iPod. The challenge for this campaign was by no means an easy one: to let the world know that there was an iPod for every different kind of computer user. But also for every age category and every taste in music, while at the same time emphasising that all that messing about with clumsy compact disc players and transistor radios was a thing of the past. The campaign rose to this tough challenge brilliantly. The message was as clear as it was simple: the iPod is small, easy to use and can be taken everywhere. In short, it gave people freedom: freedom to move, freedom to dance, freedom to express themselves. What's more, this simple message was translated into the universal language of music. Where texts were needed, they were explicit, concise and gave consumers the necessary information:'iPod. Welcome to the digital music revolution. 10,000 songs in your pocket. Mac or PC.' In this way, the campaign ingeniously combined information (Mac or PC, 10,000 songs), emotion (femininity and sensuality), experience (dancing and movement) and a noble purpose (freedom and independence).

In subsequent years, Apple built further on this success formula, culminating in the campaign for the 2018 launch of the Home Pod. In this four-minute long advertising film, directed by Spike Jonze, you can see how singer and actress FKA Twigs arrives home in her grey apartment after a tiring day and asks Siri, the virtual AI assistant in the Home Pod: 'Play me something I like.' In a matter of seconds, you see her change into a sensuous dancer, while her room is transformed into a new world, full of colour and light. The film shows the healing power of music and how easily this can be made available by a digital assistant. At the same time, it also underlines Apple's excellent knowledge of the behaviour of its customers. Research has revealed that 74.8 % of consumers use their AI assistants to stream music.

But the list of examples doesn't end there. In the widely praised 'Mac vs. PC campaign' (2006-2010) functionality, personality and user experience were all seamlessly interwoven. The aim was to demonstrate the advantages of the Mac in comparison with the average PC. In this way, the company hoped to dispel the myths that were circulating at that time among PC users, which prevented them from making the switch to Apple. The advertising team achieved this by personalising the two different types of computer and introducing them as friends. It soon became clear how fine it would be to have the Mac as a friend and how frustrating the other PC![62]

In another excellent Apple campaign, 'The Archives' from 2017, the ISP model was applied via storytelling, both literally and figuratively. The commercial shows an elderly man walking through a darkened archive vault, searching for images of his finest memories. He chooses the ones he likes best, painstakingly mounts them into a film and sets them to music. Next, we see a woman sitting at home, who clicks on the memory tab of her iPhone and watches with tears of joy the resulting film that shows a compilation of the first year of her son's life. Apple's aim in this case was to make publicity for the memory-tab on the iOS 10, which does indeed, like the old man, select the best images, arrange them into a format and adds appropriate music. It almost sounds like magic, and the fairy-tale like figure of the archivist and the gloomy setting of the vault serves to underline this impression.

What do all these advertising campaigns have in common? They are 'all-in-one' campaigns. They bring together the four dimensions of emotion, a (personal) noble purpose, user experience and functional value in a manner that allows the combined effect of the whole to be greater than the sum of the individual parts. In short, this is the ISP model at its best.

A third myth debunked: the ignorant consumer

At the end of a team presentation in 1982, Steve Jobs was asked whether or not it might be a good idea for Apple Computer to do some market research, so that they could learn exactly what the customer wants. The answer from Jobs was adamant, even combative: 'No, because customers don't know what they want until we've shown them.'[63] It was not one of his better assessments. Many experts in technology circles still cling to the myth that consumers are ignorant and can't make up their own minds, and that the companies know what is best for them. This kind of thinking has been around for a long time. Although the saying is not verifiable, tradition credits Henry Ford with the claim that if he had listened to consumers the world would have ended up with an electric horse, rather than the motor car. Instead of basing new innovations on market research, this myth still argues that the best inventions are created by the brilliant minds, instincts and gut feelings of visionary entrepreneurs. In their early days, Steve Wozniak and above all Steve Jobs liked to see themselves as belonging to this gallery of far-sighted entrepreneurial pioneers. In the case of the Apple II, this attitude led to a huge success. In other cases (the Lisa, for example), it did not. Quite the opposite. Fifteen years later, Jobs admitted: 'Apple in those early years was mainly going on common sense. We didn't think in terms of customer feedback. We never even used the word customer.'[64]

Even today, Apple continues to believe that it is not the task of the consumer to come up with new ideas for products. Asking customers for their opinions in advance is not part of the Apple development process for new products. This, they feel, is the work of the R&D people and the designers. But even though they often suggest the opposite, Apple does nevertheless carry out a form of customer research, to ensure that it can provide those customers with the best possible experience. In fact, Apple was a pioneer in the field of user-behaviour and design. The term 'user-friendly' was actually first coined by an Apple executive: Don Norman, who was one of the first exponents of user-based design. The earliest experiment dates from 1982, when the Lisa was launched on the market after months of user tests that resulted in an interface design with icons and windows. Internal sources confirm that this user-friendly reflex is still embedded in the Apple culture. In this way, for example, the super-sophisticated keyboard of the iPhone was tested externally to confirm its ease of use.[65]

As if to prove the point, in 2014 Mark Kawano, who between 2010 and 2012 was User Experience Evangelist at Apple, commented in an interview with the *Fast Company Magazine*: 'It's actually part of the engineering culture, and the way the organisation is structured to appreciate and support design.

Everybody there is thinking about User Experience (UX) and design, not just the designers.'[66]

In addition, Apple also asks the opinions of its customers about the brand and their products. It is simply that the company does not like communicating on these subjects with the outside world. This was very clear during the 2012 law suit against Samsung, when Greg Joswiak, the marketing manager at Apple, was asked to explain why Apple refused to release the results of its market research. Joswiak claimed that this would reveal too much valuable information to its competitors about the reasons why customers preferred Apple devices to the Android devices marketed by Samsung. In particular, it would show which applications customers most used and how satisfied they were with them.[67]

Conclusion: the story that Apple is not interested in the opinions of its customers is simply not true. Which only goes to show that some myths are more stubbornly defended than others, so that in the end they survive longer than the reality– or even replace it.

Finally...

Much has been written about the way in which Apple approaches its customers and succeeds in creating a binding relationship. Viewed from a distance and through the mists of time, some academics now even argue that the various Apple campaigns I have described above are symbolic for a culture that embraces technology as a religion.[68] In this respect, the cult of the individual is central. The Apple campaigns of the past 40 years have all shown how Apple followers can live 'the good life', thanks to the company's technology. Their advertising films are built up as medieval morality pieces, in which the forces of good (the Mac) are pitted against the forces of evil (other PCs). At the same time, the campaigns implicitly underline the belief that technology is the basis for human progress. This belief is presented as an absolute truth. Technology is the greatest good. Full stop. End of story. True, this technology can be challenged, but only by other technology. Apple can challenge Microsoft or Samsung can challenge Apple. But the divine status of technology per se remains inviolable. It is a world of its own with its own internal logic. Apple's success is that it has managed to engage its 'believers', its broad customer base, in this tech-world. I can think of no other company that has been able to do this in quite the same superlative manner. At the same time, there is also something slightly disquieting about it: it demonstrates the powerful hold that some companies can exercise over their customers – which is not always necessarily an influence for good.

A

THE DO'S-AND-DON'TS

- ∞ Always take the customer and his user-experience as your starting-point.
- ∞ Be curious enough to learn about the world in which your consumers live.
- ∞ Constantly scan your environment, so that you can detect new trends quickly.
- ∞ Do not limit this scanning to your own sector. Be prepared to learn from other sectors and other worlds, as well as from the trends, streams and forces at play in wider society.
- ∞ Adapt to your environment, but do so in a way that is smarter than your rivals. Show that you understand the world of your consumers and are able to offer them relevant added value.

- ∞ Learn from customer feedback and do something with it.
- ∞ Even if there are tendencies that result in your sector coming under attack, never react defensively but try to think actively about positive answers. In this way, the outside world will see you as part of the solution rather than as part of the problem.
- ∞ Try to develop an Integrated Selling Proposition that offers your customers relevant added value in each of the following four dimensions: (1) functional benefits, (2) emotional benefits, (3) a memorable user experience linked to your product and, increasingly, (4) a story about a noble purpose with which the customer can identify.

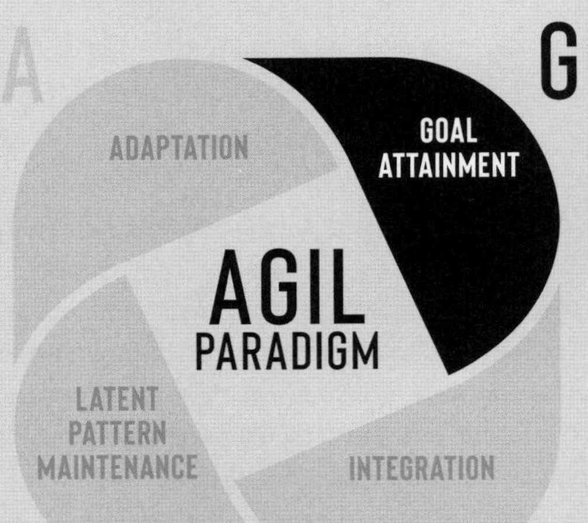
A
G
ADAPTATION
GOAL
ATTAINMENT
AGIL
PARADIGM
LATENT
PATTERN
MAINTENANCE
INTEGRATION
L
I

GOAL ATTAIN-MENT

G

GOAL ATTAINMENT

Even though it is very important, it is not enough for a company simply to adapt to a rapidly changing environment and to provide relevant value to its customers, as I have shown in chapters 1 and 2. Ultimately, a company will only be able to survive if it sets a clear goal and develops a single-minded strategy to achieve that goal. The economic success of a company is determined, in part at least, by its ability to reach its goals, both in quantitative terms (numerical targets) and qualitative terms (the fact of survival itself).

In chapter 3, I will discuss the importance of having a clear and uniform strategy for goal attainment. We shall see, for example, how Apple was most successful as a company during periods when it developed a single strategy with a very strong focus, from which it did not deviate. Conversely, when it adopted a 'flip-flop' approach to strategy, constantly changing course in the short term to achieve a series of artificial injections, the company eventually found itself in the longer term slipping into a negative spiral from which it was difficult to escape.

In chapter 4, I will show how a company can implement its strategy in practice. This involves creating a mental and physical presence in the hearts and minds of customers and stakeholders. What is the importance of paid advertising in this process? Does paid advertising actually still work in our modern world? Or should we instead place our faith (and money) in word-of-mouth advertising and influencers on social media? How effective is their impact? And what is the value of the physical store in an age of e-commerce? Why did Apple invest so heavily in its own network of Apple Stores, in addition to the App Store on the internet?

G

3 FOLLOW THE MONEY

An immortal company has a clear goal and a single-minded strategy.

In the autumn of 2017, Apple celebrated the tenth anniversary of the iPhone with the launching of the iPhone X, with its heavy price tag of 999 dollars. At the time, many observers regarded this as a commercial gamble. Even so, Apple persuaded its customers to open their wallets and purses. From Sydney to Beijing and from Dubai to New York, people stood in queues outside Apple stores to make sure that they could be among the first to get their latest Apple 'toy'. Contrary to the predictions of the analysts, the company did not burn its fingers with the iPhone X. Quite the reverse. Thanks to sales of the iPhone X, turnover increased by 14 % in the second quarter of 2018 (even though overall unit sales 'only' increased by 3 %).More impressive still, during a full six month period after the launch the X model was still selling better than the 'cheaper' iPhone 8 and 8 Plus. CEO Tim Cook was quick to emphasise the fact that for the very first time the top model was also the most popular. 'We are very bullish on Apple's future,' he announced with pride.[69] It was the success of the iPhone X that fed the expectation in the spring of 2018 that Apple was set to become the first company in history to be valued at more than 1 trillion dollars.[70]

The success of the iPhone X brings us seamlessly to the second function of the AGIL paradigm: the 'G' of 'Goal attainment'. Companies need to do more than adapt, if they want to survive. They must also set a clear goal and develop a clear and single-minded strategy to achieve that goal. In marketing circles, you often hear discussions about which strategy is the best. Trying to win market share as quickly as possible? Or setting a higher margin, so that you can remain profitable with a lower sales volume?

In this chapter, I will use the Apple case to show how a company can increase its chances of survival not simply by aiming at market share, but also by focusing on profitability and a non-stop search to find new and 'good' customers.

It's the product, stupid

When Jobs returned to Apple in 1997, he quickly re-established some semblance of order. He cancelled the licenses for the cloning of the Macintosh and set a clear focus on a select number of high-quality products. He had long argued that it was best for Apple to concentrate on premium computers for the top segment of the market. He did not want the company to compete on price, which was the strategy of the market leader at that time, Dell Computer. Apple's goal must be to make first-class products that were sufficiently profitable to allow new products to be developed. Trying to compete on volume would simply lead to prices being forced down.[71] At a 2007 conference, Jobs made this point about Apple's product leadership strategy very clear, when he said: 'We don't ship junk.'

This was a clear and simple choice, and it remains Apple's mantra today. In an interview with *Fortune Magazine*, Cook later explained: 'There's a lot of companies that have much higher margins. We price for the value of our products. And we try to make the very best products. And that means we don't make commodity kinds of products. And we don't disparage people that do; it's a fine business model. But it's not the business that we're in.'[72] This was a more diplomatically expressed version of a comment he had made previously in *Business Week* in 2013, in which he echoed Jobs' 2007 sentiments: 'We're not in the junk business. (...) There's a segment of the market that really wants a product that does a lot for them, and I want to compete like crazy for those customers.'[73]

The iPhone X is a textbook example of how Apple's strategy is focused on product leadership. For example, the device has a function that is completely new for a smartphone: facial recognition or Face ID. This technology scans the face of the owner, who can therefore unlock his phone simply by looking at it. This is made possible by a True Depth camera, which can recognise the salient characteristics of individual faces, a technique that is similar to that of Touch ID, Apple's fingerprint scanner.

Choosing your battles – and your strategy

Any company that wants to assume a position of 'product leadership' needs to push beyond the current known boundaries of performance, as stated by Treacy and Wiersema in their 1995 book *The discipline of market leaders*. It needs to explore the unknown, the untried and the untested. Such companies, the authors suggest, have a culture that relies heavily on individual imagination, out-of-the-box thinking and a thoroughly future-minded approach.[74] However, this is not the only way. There are two other alternatives.

The first of these alternatives is 'operational excellence'. An operational excellence strategy allows companies to 'provide their customers with a combination of quality, price and ease of purchase and use that no-one else in the market can match'. By focusing on end-to-end product supply and the streamlining of the basic service, which maximises cost and efficiency; by centrally planning and tightly controlling internal operations; and by developing management systems that result in 'integrated, reliable, high-speed transactions and compliance with norms', companies like Dell Computer have managed to satisfy their customers' desire for easily obtainable and easily affordable products that still offer the advantages of high technological standards and quality.[75]

Amazon is another successful example of a company with an operational excellence strategy. This strategy is also reflected in the company's culture and values, which reward efficiency and value frugality, right down to the smallest detail. As a result, Amazon employees are expected to pay for their own parking places and for their cups of coffee in the office. Founder and CEO Jeff Bezos is famed for his determination to drive his people ever harder. For example, he often calls meetings over the weekends and even started an executive book club that only met on Saturday mornings. His oft-repeated quote about working 'smart, hard and long' has become legendary. Of course, all of this does have a potential downside. As Brad Stone mentions in his seminal book on Amazon, *The everything store*, the company is not noted for being family-friendly and some executives left when they wanted to have children. Not that Bezos was unduly worried. 'Jeff didn't believe in work-life balance,' a former employee is quoted as saying. 'He believed in work-life harmony. I guess the idea is that you might be able to do everything all at once.' When a female employee pointedly asked Bezos when Amazon was going to establish a better work-life balance, he replied bluntly: 'The reason we are here is to get stuff done. That is the top priority. That is the DNA of Amazon. If you can't excel and put everything into it, this might not be the place for you.'[76]

The second alternative strategy, according to Treacy and Wiersema, is 'customer intimacy'. It was this strategy and culture that allowed IBM in the 1960s and 1970s to offer its customers 'the best solution', not by delivering what the market wants, but by delivering what it knew its specific customers would want. A company focusing on customer intimacy therefore needs to build up a close relationship with its customer base, rather like that of a 'good neighbour'. In this way, the company develops a detailed knowledge of the people it sells to and the products they need.[77]

Whichever of these strategies a company chooses, the message is simple: failure to stick to a single-minded strategy over time can endanger your very existence. If you do not choose a clear strategy, you will end up implementing a series of hybrid models that cause nothing but confusion, tension and loss of energy, resulting in a rudderless ship that has no clearly defined way to resolve conflicts or set priorities. Not choosing means allowing circumstances to control your destiny, rather than taking matters into your own hands. The Apple case, and more particularly the events in the early 1990s, underlines this point all too painfully.[78]

Sticking to one particular strategy should also not make any CEO feel guilty about missing out, about losing potential customers because of this choice. As Fred Crawford and Ryan Mathews have argued in *The Myth of Excellence,* it is impossible for one company to be great at everything. Even assuming that any organisation could excel in every area, it would without a doubt have difficulty communicating a clear value proposition to consumers. Companies should focus on what their customers value most. An organisation should never serve too many masters at a time.[79]

Luxury brand

With the iPhone X, Apple has moved almost seamlessly into the luxury products segment, which is an exclusive league apart. Luxury goods, such as certain fashion and car brands, can permit themselves to ask the highest possible price for their products, more even than the premium brands. Jean-Noël Kapferer, who is an expert in this field, says that the luxury brands are far more than just the product alone; they represent a dream that allows the buyers or users to acquire an 'elite' status that sets them apart from the 'plebs'.[80] In this respect, fashion is a very strong case in point: you are not just buying a few bits of fabric; you are buying an image. This is something that Steve Jobs understood perfectly, so that it came as no surprise when he insisted on recruiting the very best fashion designers from Yves Saint Laurent and Burberry's to help give shape and form to the Apple concept stores.

There is good news for luxury brands and brands like Apple who focus heavily on the selling of a dream or a story. Research has shown that the millennium generation (born in the 1990s) and Generation Z (today's teenagers) attach more importance than their parents to self-expression. And one way that they can express themselves is through the brands and products they buy. These brands and products help to define who they are as a person, a process in which quality is very important to them. By 2025, these younger generations will be good for 45 % of the global market in luxury goods.

The premium price

Whichever way you look at it, the price of a product is the only factor in the marketing mix that generates real income. For this reason, it is important that we should look here at how brands set their prices. Consumers often automatically classify and assess products on the basis of price categories. Apple is more expensive than Samsung, Samsung is more expensive than Huawei, etc. Strong brands can allow themselves the luxury of asking a higher premium price for their products. This is possible, providing the customers know that they are getting sufficient value and quality in return for their willingness to pay the extra amount. Studies have shown that strong brands can ask up to 25 % more than their weaker rivals and up to 200 % more than private label brands. In addition, the margins of strong brands are much bigger, because they can get away with organising fewer promotion actions and advertising campaigns.[81]

Whoever (justifiably) sets a premium price also sets in motion a kind of self-fulfilling prophecy. Strong brands are in a position to ask such a premium price. Consequently (or so the consumer often reasons), this must mean that they also offer higher quality – and quality is what most consumers are looking for, and so they buy more. In this sense, setting your product in the market with a price that is too low is not a good idea. Instead of attracting more customers, you might just as easily have the opposite effect, if they think that there must be some reason – such as poor quality – for the price difference with other products. To tip the scales even more heavily in their favour, strong brands are less sensitive to the possible negative impact of a price increase. And so the circle is complete.

It is also necessary to make a clear distinction between the real value of a product (the cost of making it) and its perceived value (comprising all the different ISP value propositions we discussed in chapter 2). The 'value' that the customer attaches to the iPhone X is a good example. TechInsights, a company specialised in calculating the true cost price of technology, estimates that an iPhone X can be made for 357.50 dollars. In other words, the product has an intangbile margin of a massive 64(!) %. This is therefore the perceived value of the product, which immediately underlines the strength of the Apple brand.

The iPad is another instance of Apple's premium price strategy. Initially, Jobs and his team wanted to develop the device for use in education. But as the development phase progressed, it became clear that the iPad offered so many possibilities that it would also be able to reach a wider and more public market. The marketing team was so sure of this fact that they increased the price they originally had in mind by 100 dollars to 499 dollars.[82]

In short, the art of price setting is to find the right balance between: (1) the quality of the product, (2) the lowest possible production cost compatible with delivering quality, and (3) a correct estimation of the perceived value of the product for consumers and, on this basis, how much more these consumers will be willing to pay over and above the production cost.[83] At times, Apple was brilliant at making this delicate balancing act!

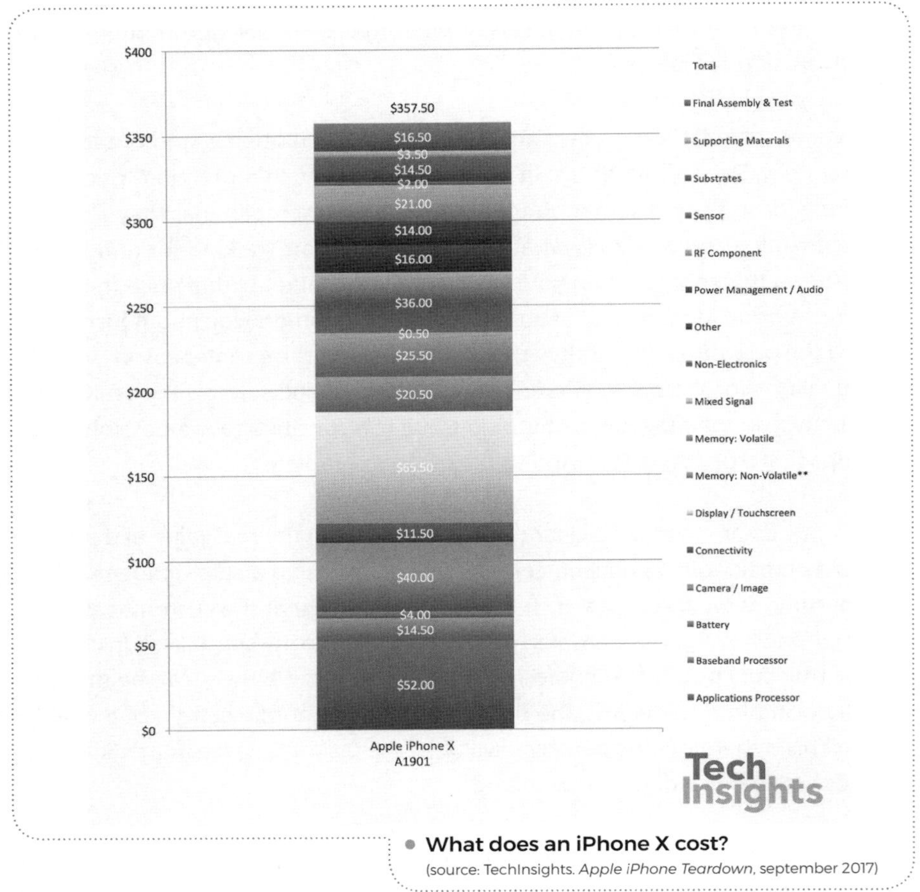

What does an iPhone X cost?
(source: TechInsights. *Apple iPhone Teardown*, september 2017)

It is an approach that many other companies are increasingly trying to copy. They are turning away from attempts to grow volume (in terms of market share) and are investing instead in so-called 'premiumisation'. This means making more money from each item you sell. In this way, volume growth is replaced as the main objective by value growth. Value growth can be achieved by upgrading an existing product or service in such a way that it justifies asking a higher price. In many cases, this is done through brand extensions: new versions of a core product that add extra value for consumers, so that the product can be sold at a premium price. As long as the percentage of profit for the core extension is the same as for the original version, this will result in additional profit for each unit sold. Might this not lead to the 'cannibalisation' of volume from the existing products by the new variant? Perhaps. But even so, overall profit will generally increase.[84]

These arguments have certainly convinced AB InBev, the world's largest brewer. CEO Carlos Britto believes that the days of a single power brand serving all consumer needs are gone forever. He sees fragmentation of markets and the resulting growth of more specific customer needs as an opportunity, with 'premiumisation' as the answer. 'In the past, everyone sold his beer at the same price', as he states it. 'But by positioning your brand as the premium in the market, you can ask more. There is also a market for a super-premium and for traditional, craft-made beers. Consumers are prepared to pay extra for these products. (...) If you focus on this aspect, you can exploit the complexity of the consumer market to your advantage.' Regarding the question of volume cannibalisation, Britto does not seem all that concerned, stating that providing the public with a wide portfolio will even benefit AB InBev rather than damage the company, adding that 'you attract a greater share of the profits from the beer market, but this also has knock-on effect on volume growth.'[85]

In other words, value share instead of market share is now the new mantra at AB InBev – as it has always been at Apple, at least during the past 20 years. In this respect, there is one aspect of marketing that should never be forgotten: it is not a popularity contest. Former AB InBev CMO Chris Burggraeve argues that 'marketing is finance'[86]. As a result, the absolute number-one priority remains the creation of pricing power. Any branded business model must focus on maximising the value that the company is able to secure. To a large extent, this is a psychological process, as companies like Netflix and Amazon Prime have successfully demonstrated in recent times. Both have found subtle ways to increase their brand equity without scaring off their customers, so that their brand health remains as good as it ever was.

Most luxury brands apply this theory: higher prices create the perception of higher quality, status, taste and wealth, which in turn boosts demand among a clear segment of people interested in 'the (perceived) best'. Or as Burggraeve puts it: 'The stronger the brand, the lower its price elasticity. To maximise value for the firm, the best marketers will then continuously test how high they can go before consumers turn elastic again.'[87]

Growth through new customers

Having a quality product is not enough by itself to allow a brand to grow. You need customers as well. It is often said that the success of Apple is based on its hard core of almost fanatical followers, who continue to follow the company through hell and high water, to such an extent that some people even talk about a cult movement. It is certainly the case that Apple right from its earliest days has had a very loyal fan base, starting with the Apple II and continuing through to today's 'i' series. That the company was able to survive during the debacle years of the 1990s was due in no small measure to the customers who remained faithful to the brand, notwithstanding all the negative publicity at the time. Even so, the history of Apple shows equally that the brand is at its best when it succeeds in attracting new customers, as was the case, for example, with the 'creative spirits' and the Macintosh in the late 1980s and the young people of Generations Y and M with 'i' series during the past decade.

This brings us to a question that is frequently and fiercely debated among marketing and brand specialists: what is the best way to grow a brand? Is it by selling a greater volume of products and service to loyal customers (which is therefore generally known as a loyalty strategy)? Or is it by selling a similar volume of products to a greater number of new customers (known as a penetration strategy)?

Empirical research has revealed that sustainable growth does not occur solely by selling products to existing loyal customers, but also by attracting new customers. It was long assumed that Pareto's Law also applied to sales; namely, that 80 % of income was generated by the most loyal 20 % of customers. However, research by the Australian professor Byron Sharp has now shown that this is not the case. He investigated a dozen or so brands from different product categories and demonstrated that for the sale of consumer goods over a period of three months the Pareto percentage was as low as 35 %. In other words, the loyal 20 % of customers were only good for 35 % of turnover. Viewed over a period of a year, the 35 % eventually rose to around 50 %, but failed to come close to the Pareto level of 80 %, which is almost never achieved. Sharp therefore concluded that half of all sales are made to incidental customers – he calls them 'light buyers'– who only occasionally buy a particular product.[88] Not surprisingly, he further concluded that it is well worth the effort to try and attract this group and, if possible, increase their size.

An analysis of marketing campaigns in the UK that received an IPA award for effectiveness showed that the winners focused much more heavily than others on attracting new customers and less on creating growth through selling more products to existing customers. Even when a winning campaign was focused on loyal customers, the high level of effectiveness still resulted primarily from sales to new customers, who nonetheless still felt attracted by the campaign. This does not mean, of course, that companies should turn their back on loyal customers. On the contrary, a truly happy customer can be converted into a brand ambassador, who will attract even more new customers. The IPA databank demonstrates clearly that the most effective campaigns target both new and existing customers.[89]

The Apple case also illustrates that a brand can benefit more from a two-pronged strategy, which attempts both to stimulate existing customers to buy new products and invests in increasing the group of light buyers who are not attached for life to a different brand. This latter group can be attracted by developing the right value proposition (ISP). The phenomenal success of the iPod, iPhone and iPad was due primarily to Apple's ability to persuade large groups of new customers – in part from the West's Generation Y of digital natives, in part via expansion into the huge Chinese market – to buy their products. It was not the result of their ability to hold on to their 20th century PC customers from Generation X. This certainly helped, but it was the new customers that really made the difference for Apple – as they do for every brand.

Apple in trouble: in the middle of nowhere

Apple's survival chances were greatest during the periods when the company succeeded in achieving its commercial and financial goals. It did this by developing a clear and single-minded strategy on which it was not prepared to compromise and which was implemented with almost military discipline. This was not the case in the early years. Jobs and Wozniak had no big plan and no idea of where they really wanted their company to go. Jobs would later explain that Wozniak was primarily interested in the technology, so that it was left to him to try and work out how to run a company.[90] He had no idea how to draw up a business plan; in fact, he had never even heard of one, according to Michael Scott, Apple's first CEO.[91] In spite of the fortune he acquired at the start of the 1980s, Jobs still regarded himself as a child of the counter-revolution. Walter Isaacson, his biographer, reports him as once saying: 'I never did it for money (...) I made a promise to myself: I said I'm not going to let this money ruin my life.'[92] Sculley also noted that Jobs had a remarkable attitude towards fame and fortune: 'Apple grew from a desire to change the world, not to make money.'[93] The result of this altruistic approach was that by the mid-1980s Apple was in deep trouble and Jobs had been dismissed from his own company.

Apple's brief revival in the late 1980s can be attributed to Sculley's premium price strategy. Although some of his managers put him under pressure to change, he opted resolutely for a strategy based on products of high technological quality that were sold in the market at a correspondingly high price. In a price-quality diagram, Apple products at this time nearly always featured in the top-right segment: high quality, highest price. However, this model eventually fell out of balance, because the price was set too high. During the 1989 financial year, Apple had a gross profit margin of 49 %, but its market share had fallen back from 9.1 % in 1987 to just 7.6 %. Cynics commented that Apple was only 'for the elite among us'.[94 95 96]

It was for this reason that Apple, still under Sculley, made a sharp U-turn at the beginning of the 1990s. From then on, the company intended to back two horses in its attempt to achieve its ambitious commercial and financial goals. Its new target was a market share of 10 %. As a result, in October 1990 Apple launched the Mac Classic, a computer costing 999 dollars that, it was hoped, would attract new customers at the bottom end of the market, where it was competing directly against cheap IBM copies. At the same time, however, Sculley still also wanted to target the top end, with products like the portable (but pricey) Powerbook. Yet notwithstanding the new strategy and the serious efforts made to support it, the company still failed to reach its targets. In 1994, Apple was even overtaken by Compaq as the number two player in the market, after IBM. The first sign of cracks in the Apple bastion were starting to appear. For a time, things still seemed to be going well: in 1995, the company generated a record turnover of 11 billion dollars with 37 % profits, but this hid the fact that during the fourth quarter turnover had plummeted by 48 %, leaving a profit margin of a paltry 21 %.Not even the board of directors had seen this coming.[97] One of those directors, Gil Amelio (who later took over as CEO) commented that: 'We suddenly heard that although there had been record sales, the company would lose money. Apple was selling more and making less... To say we were stunned would be putting it mildly.'[98]

Even so, Apple persisted with its double strategy. During the Christmas period in 1995, Apple prices were lowered still further, so that the difference between the Mac and other comparable PCs fell from 1 000 to 320 dollars. This made the Mac more attractive for the customer, but less attractive for the company, whose margins decreased still further. Even then, the action did not have the desired effect. Instead of winning new clients with cheaper starter models, these new customers and the Apple veterans opted to take advantage of the lower prices for the more advanced models. As a result, Apple continued to grow in overall terms but had effectively signed its own death warrant: its market share continued to fall, because the rest of the market was growing faster. The company's cash reserves began to melt like snow in the sun, to such an extent that people soon began to notice. A week before Christmas 1995, Standard & Poor's and Moody's both published negative credit ratings for Apple. As a result, the price of Apple shares went into free fall: from 50 dollars in the middle of the year to just 30 dollars at its end. The company was trapped in a negative spiral, which translated into losses of 816 million dollars in 1996 and 1 045 million dollars in 1997. By then, worldwide market share had slumped to a miserable 3.3 %, light years removed from Sculley's ambitious 10 % target. The company was up for sale, but nobody was interested in buying it. How much lower could Apple's fortunes possibly sink?

A fourth myth debunked: market share

The fight for a bigger market share is still regarded as an absolute must in many business and marketing plans. Until the late 1980s, growth in market share and achieving market leadership were the main goals for any company and were seen as the conditions for profitability and success. This belief was strengthened still further by articles from trendsetting academics in respected publications like *Harvard Business Review*. These articles confirmed the popular idea that doing business is similar to waging war, with the only objective being the elimination of your opponents. This idea was perhaps most neatly expressed in 1989 by Bruce Henderson, founder of the Boston Consulting Group, when he commented in the *HBR*: 'Darwin is probably a better guide to business competition than economists are.'[99]

Since then, however, research has demonstrated that profitability is not a direct consequence of market share. Researchers attached to the Wharton School (University of Pennsylvania, USA) investigated to what extent companies took measures to try and win market share from their competitors. The results of this survey were then compared with the ROI (return-on-investment) (after tax) of those companies during five periods of 9 years between 1938 and 1982. The correlation for companies focused on market dominance proved to be negative. In contrast, companies that made profit maximisation their primary goal achieved a much better ROI. Put differently, companies that are only concerned with their rivals and attempt to become the biggest player in the market threaten to jeopardise their profitability. Other more recent research has also confirmed these findings.[100]

Even so, this myth continues to persist with remarkable stubbornness in the minds of many entrepreneurs, since it reflects what many of them regard as their gut feeling. Researcher J. Scott Armstrong has predicted that as long as management books and strategic advisers continue to perpetuate this myth companies will continue to suffer serious economic loss. This does not mean that companies should not pay attention to what their competitors are doing, but they should not make being bigger than these competitors their main objective. The main objective must always be maximum profitability. This is a lesson that Apple has learnt well in the 21st century and they are now reaping the rewards of this wisdom in abundance.

A study conducted in 2015 illustrates the nature and the importance of Apple's strategy in this respect. The study concluded that the iPhone accounts for no less than 92 %of the profits made by all the smartphone companies combined, even though the iPhone's global market share is on average only 20 %.[101] In the second quarter of 2018, the market share of the iPhone amounted to just 15.1 % worldwide (in comparison with 22.6 % for market leader Samsung).[102] Even so, just a month later Apple was declared to be the 'richest' company on the planet. This is further evidence that, in contrast to what is often believed, a large market share or, by extension, market leadership is certainly not enough on its own to guarantee good profitability, never mind make a company immortal. Apple's history also demonstrates the more negative side of this argument. On occasions when the company has focused exclusively on the winning of market share, as was the case in the turbulent 1990s (by offering low prices for less qualitative products, with shrinking margins as a result), it soon found itself in difficulties. Fortunately, Jobs after his return and, later, Cook both understood this. Since the debacle of the mid-1990s, the company has steered well clear of the battle for market share and has concentrated instead on the sale of premium products with high profit margins. Viewed over the long term, this has proven to be a highly successful strategy.

Moreover, companies with a dominant market position also need to deal with an additional handicap. Precisely because they are so dominant, they are carefully watched not only by their competitors, but also by consumer organisations and regulatory authorities. This was something that was noted as long ago as 1975 in an article by marketing professors Philip Kotler and Paul Bloom in *Harvard Business Review*.[103] The companies that were dominant in their sector at that time included IBM, Gillette, Eastman Kodak, Procter & Gamble, Xerox, General Motors, Campbell's, Coca-Cola, Kellogg and Caterpillar. In each case, their market share had already become so large that any attempt to acquire still more would have aroused suspicion and opened the floodgates of criticism. According to Kotler and Bloom, in some cases it is even better to let your market share fall, basing this contention on the legal actions brought against IBM, Xerox and eight dominant oil companies in the 1970s. In each of these actions the relevant regulatory authority claimed that the market share of the offending company was so huge that it was no longer possible to meaningfully speak of competition in their market. In reality, they were being punished for their success, as a result of which they were forced to split up their organisation or, at the very least, to operate in an entirely different way.

Half a century later, the conclusions of Kotler and Bloom are still relevant. Consider, for example, the position of the new giants, like Apple, Amazon, Facebook and Google, who are viewed with deep mistrust by the European Commission and the US regulators for their supposed abuses of power. There are even some voices who argue that these perceived monopoly positions should be broken, with greater regulation and enforced sub-division again being proposed as the weapons to achieve it.

Asked about the possibility of the American government cracking down on 'big tech' and the position of companies that are perceived of as 'too big', in a 2019 interview Tim Cook explicitly stressed the point that 'nobody reasonable is going to come to the conclusion that Apple is a monopoly. Our share is much more modest. We don't have a dominant position in any market... We are not a monopoly.'[104] But in this case, Apple should also acknowledge that very often perceptions are stronger than mere facts.

Finally ...

Finally, I would just like to look briefly at the point (or lack of it) of temporary price discounts and promotions. Earlier in this chapter, we saw that good price setting is extremely important, but that it also needs to be supported by a constant search for new customers. Many brands try to attract these new customers through various special offers and promotional actions. In the short term, this tactic can perhaps result in higher sales figures, but in the long term there are a number of pitfalls of which you need to be aware.

For example, research has shown that incidental customers may well buy a product if the price is reduced, but will go back to their previous purchasing habits once the price returns to normal. Worse still, temporary price cutting has the effect that the promotion price becomes the reference price in the mind of the consumer, so that he/she is no longer prepared to pay the normal, higher price. Sometimes retailers ask brands to reduce their prices, so that they can pass on these reductions to their customers. But this, too, is not a good idea, since its gives the retailer a degree of power over the brand. If the brand refuses to give a discount, there is a risk that the retailer will replace it with another brand.

Even so, price promotions remain popular with marketeers, precisely because it is the short term that is most clearly visible in their sales figures. They entice customers by giving them the feeling that they are getting 'more value' for their money. But here again research has demonstrated that, in general, price promotions are more expensive than marketing campaigns to increase the perceived value of a product (based on the Integrated Selling Proposition). During price promotions, profit margins are automatically lower, which means that as a brand you need to sell bigger volumes. In other words, the greater the price discount, the greater the volume and the smaller the margin. The cost of those lost margins is always greater than the cost of the value increasing actions. What's more, promotional actions always run the risk of tipping you into a negative spiral, because your sales figures usually shrink the moment the price reduction comes to an end. In short, the effect of price promotions is dubious, to say the least. At best, they are a way for brands to 'subsidise'(primarily) their most loyal customers (and the retailers), who would buy the product anyway.[105]

The idea of attempting to win market share by promotions and price discounts can be fatal to the survival chances of a company in the long term. This is one of the most painful lessons from the wilderness years of Apple.

G

THE DO'S-AND-DON'TS

∞ Companies must set clear objectives and achieve them.

∞ Focusing exclusively on market share is not a good idea.

∞ The bigger your market share, the more careful you need to be when making every decision, because you will be more closely monitored by your competitors, society and the authorities.

∞ Margin per product and per customer is crucial for the income of your company.

∞ The stronger your brand, the higher the price you can ask.

∞ A price that is too low creates a negative perception about the quality of your product.

∞ Find the right balance between: (1) the quality of the product, (2) the lowest possible production cost compatible with delivering quality and (3) a correct estimation of the perceived value of the product for consumers and, on this basis, how much more these consumers will be willing to pay.

G

- ∞ Your loyal customers are obviously important, but also invest sufficient time and money to grow the large group of incidental customers.

- ∞ Attract new and incidental customers by adding value to your product that corresponds with the four dimensions of the Integrated Selling Proposition.

- ∞ Do not expect too much from price promotions. Avoid at all costs the traps usually associated with such promotions.

- ∞ Expand your customer segment by appealing to new 'groups' of consumers; for example, young people and minority communities. Also remember to explore new geographical markets; for example, neighbouring countries, but also more distant locations.

- ∞ No matter what you do and who you approach, remain authentic at all times!

4 OMNIPRESENT

An immortal company grows by being omnipresent, both physically and mentally, for its customers.

San Francisco, January 2007. Steve Jobs is standing in front of a packed auditorium. The public is sitting in the dark, but a bright spotlight is focused on Jobs. In his back pocket sits the brand-new iPhone, but at the moment his spectators have no idea what it is or what Jobs is planning to do. He begins. 'Today, Apple is going to re-invent the phone.' The public – many of whom had been queuing all night to get in – is visibly excited. The up-beat music increases the tension still further. A picture of the iPod appears on a huge screen, together with two symbols that represent a telephone and an internet connection. When combined, the three images form a single whole: the iPhone. 'iPhone is a revolutionary and magical product that is literally 5 years ahead of any other mobile phone.' Jobs talks and talks and talks. His narrative is regularly interrupted by applause or cheering from the hall. Everyone is hanging on his every word. The next day, the price of Apple shares rose to what was then a new record level: 97.80 dollars.

Jobs knew like few others how to get an audience in the palm of his hand, time after time. He was without doubt the best orator in the business world of his day, perhaps ever. His public performances were compared with rock concerts, including cheering fans and frantic journalists, like groupies anxious not to miss a single second of their hero's act. It is often thought that these performances were the reason why Apple was able to perform so well and break all commercial records. And it is certainly true that they made a significant contribution to familiarising and popularising Apple products and services with the general public. But to claim that this was the only reason for Apple's huge success is taking things a step too far. The truth of the matter is that Apple understood (far better than any other company at that time) that you need much more if you always want to be ever-present in the hearts and minds of your customers. This is only possible by focusing on the golden triangle of marketing: word-of-mouth advertising (also known as buzz marketing), advertising campaigns in the media, and distribution (both physical and online, the so-called 'bricks' and 'clicks'). Within this triangle, Jobs' public performances served simultaneously as both catalyst and flywheel, a kind of motor that kick-started the entire process into action. But the real secret to success was a perfectly orchestrated synergy of all the component parts.

This brings me neatly to the theme for this chapter (remember, we are still in the 'G' for 'Goal Attainment'). We have already seen that companies can only survive if they set clear goals and achieve them. To make this possible, a clear strategy is essential. If you want to grow as a company, you need to generate income and make profit. We saw in chapter 3 that you can do this by attracting new and profitable customers. But before you can attract them, you first need to reach them and stimulate them. And to do that, you need to go to all the places where your customers are or make sure that you are present in all the places where they can meet you. The principle that I will investigate further in this chapter is therefore: 'An immortal company grows by always being omnipresent, both physically and mentally, for its customers.' Using the Apple case, I will show how you can realise this in three key areas: via word-of-mouth advertising, paid advertising campaigns in the media, and physical and online distribution, close to the customer.

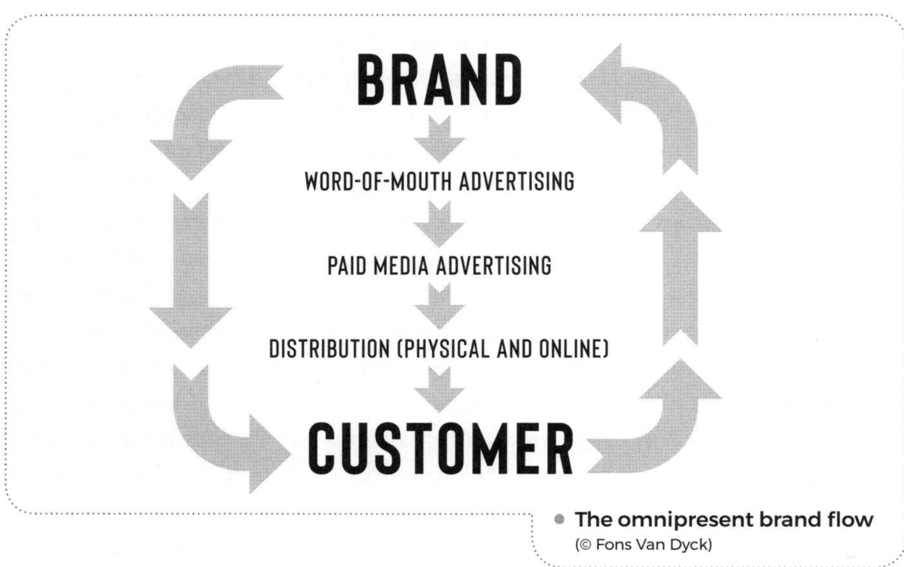

The omnipresent brand flow
(© Fons Van Dyck)

The 90/10 rule

Apple is truly expert at word-of-mouth advertising or buzz marketing, in part because they understand better than most the classic principles on which it is based. It was back in the 1950s that the American sociologists Paul Lazarsfeld and Elihu Katz first launched the theory that when people are forming an opinion they are primarily influenced by the so-called opinion-makers, who in turn are influenced by the mass media. In the past, this meant media like newspapers, radio and television. Today, their role has been supplemented (or perhaps even supplanted) by social media. According to Lazarsfeld and Katz, each social group of people consists of 90 % opinion-followers and 10 % opinion-makers. Nowadays, these 'ten' are known as influencers. It is very important for a company or brand to be able to reach and convince these influencers in a positive manner. They will then reach and convince the 'ninety'.

This was a field where Apple was an absolute pioneer and trendsetter. Buzz marketing was part of the Apple DNA before the term was even invented and dates back to the launch of the Apple II, now more than 40 years ago. The man regarded as the architect of this tradition is the American PR consultant, Regis McKenna. During the 1970s, McKenna had built up an impressive reputation in Silicon Valley, based in part on his successful campaigns for Intel processors. Jobs was keen to work with him, but that was by no means straightforward. McKenna's outlook and life style were very different from those of Jobs and Wozniak. In fact, to begin with, McKenna and his team were very sceptical about Jobs, who came across as a kind of modern-day John the Baptist: an eccentric loner who wore sandals and had unkempt hair and a wispy beard. It seems that the first meeting between the three men was 'uncomfortable'. In particular, it was Wozniak who initially had a problem with McKenna. When McKenna commented critically on the excessive technical content of an article that Wozniak had written, the Apple man is reputed to have replied heatedly: 'I don't want any PR man touching my copy.'[106] Jobs served as a diplomatic mediator between the two men, but he had to use all his powers of persuasion before he was able to convince McKenna to work for them. He even offered him 20 % of the shares in Apple, which at that time was still little more than a start-up. McKenna declined, later commenting that it was the biggest mistake he ever made in his entire life.[107] Jobs in typical fashion just wouldn't take 'no' for an answer and kept on badgering McKenna until he finally agreed to a collaboration.[108] This, too, would bring him fame and lots of money – but not as much as 20 % of Apple shares. And it also proved – once again – that Jobs' gut feeling was usually spot on.[109]

Although McKenna launched a successful advertising campaign for the Apple II, he still felt that he was more of an expert in public relations than a marketing guru. He was convinced that it was much more important to build up long-term relationships with journalists instead of simply sending out press release after press release, in the hope that someone would pick them up. According to him, this 'scatter-gun' approach was even inherently risky, since there was a danger that it would confuse or even scare off the majority of people who knew very little about technology. 'Winning a quick endorsement from the market is crucial to success,' he wrote. 'Once a product wins rave reviews, it picks up momentum in the marketplace. Success builds on itself. The product develops a positive image, and customers flock to it. On the other hand, once the market sticks a product with a "loser" label, the product has a tough time recovering.' McKenna believed that it was not possible to gain control over these processes simply with press releases and advertising. Instead, he believed, like Lazarsfeld and Katz, that people are much more inclined to take certain decisions when they are directly encouraged to do so by others – friends, experts or even salesmen.[110] 'If one person has a good experience with the product, he'll tell others about it, and they in turn will tell still others. Credibility builds and builds. But the process works in reverse as well. A role of thumb: if a customer has a good experience, he'll tell three other people. If he has a bad experience, he'll tell ten other people.'[111]

In other words, McKenna was a powerful advocate of the 90/10 rule: 90 % of the world is influenced by the other 10 %. In his view, the most important opinion-makers were the financial community (with its risk capitalists and investors), the business consultants, analysts and futurists, the press, the distribution partners, the community of customers and the company's own personnel.[112] With this in mind, McKenna prepared each new campaign in great detail, but always focused to reach as many of the 10 % of opinion-makers as possible. He also invested a lot of time in building up good relations with journalists and other decision-makers. For example, he began the preparations for the media campaign for the Macintosh a full 2 years before the launch was scheduled, organising special viewing days for the opinion-makers and sneak previews for the press, all at different moments. In this way, he tried to keep the buzz going. At the same time, he also carefully selected the magazines in which information about Apple would appear, with the aim of reaching the broadest possible public. This not only meant specialised computer magazines and trade magazines, but also more low-brow publications: he once even gave a scoop to the popular *Rolling Stone Magazine*.[113] It was with these building blocks that Apple developed the strategy it would continue to follow during its most successful periods.

Later on, Sculley was also a big fan of the 90/10 rule. He reasoned that in one way or another the opinion-makers of different groups of people are always in contact with each other. When a journalist wants to write a story about a particular subject, he will listen to the different representatives of those different groups – and if those representatives have already heard about the product in advance, they will be more inclined to talk about it positively. Based on this philosophy, Sculley arranged, for example, for 'celebrities' and important decision-makers to receive a free 'trial model' of the Macintosh, including CNN founder Ted Turner, the mayor of San Francisco, writers and artists (Andy Warhol) and captains of industry (Lee Iacocca and David Rockefeller). In this way, a groundswell of support was created before the product was even launched.[114]

Word-of-mouth advertising continues to be a very successful formula for influencing large groups of consumers. Recent research has shown that customers who are influenced by word-of-mouth advertising generate twice as much long-term value for a brand than customers who are influenced by advertising campaigns in the media. It is fair to say with no exaggeration that word-of-mouth advertising makes the biggest contribution to the overall profitability of a brand.[115] It will therefore come as no surprise to learn that Tim Cook has continued to use this same formula with great success. The launch of iPhone X in the autumn of 2017 and the launch of Apple TV in the spring of 2019 were both reported worldwide on the front page of quality newspapers, in television news bulletins and in fora on social media. In this way, Apple brilliantly set the agenda for the opinion-makers, who in turn did their bit to make large groups of consumers enthusiastic for the latest Apple hit.

Nowadays, there is a strong word-of-mouth dynamic active in social media and we increasingly hear about the growing trend of influencers on the internet. According to the World Advertising Research Center, 'influencer marketing', as it is now called, is 'the partnering of brands with influential and popular individuals on social media who share the same target audiences, to deliver a branded marketing message and content. It can help brands communicate with their audience in an authentic way and win distracted customers' attention.' In 2018, influencer content generated 72 % of all activity in the US on Facebook, Twitter and Instagram. By 2020, the market is expected to be worth over 10 billion dollars.

Even so, not everyone is convinced. Some marketeers question both the ROI of influencer marketing and its prospects for long-term survival. Is the bubble about to burst? The plethora of transactional sponsorships and the frequent absence of a real connection between brands and their influencers is being viewed with increasing suspicion, enhanced still further by the lack of transparency surrounding the entire process and the growing rumours of dubious practices, such as the buying of fake followers.[116]

What's more, although the importance of influencers for brands on social media continues to increase (for the time being, at least), this should not blind us to one of the most crucial marketing facts of life: studies have revealed that 90 % of all influential conversations still take place in the real world. In other words, nine out of every ten conversations about brands, companies and their products happen in bars, on the train, at home or in shops – and not on Facebook or Twitter![117]

Advertising works – but not as it used to do

Its spectacular product launches make it possible for Apple to harvest immediate brand awareness and admiration in the media, so that it can profile itself as an innovative and 'revolutionary' company (a phrase repeatedly used by Jobs). But when the initial storm of interest has passed and the journalists and photographers have left to find the next 'breaking news' story, this is when the real work begins for Apple. They already have people's attention; now they have to make good use of it. This is the moment when Apple's gigantic marketing and advertising machinery moves into action. Its aim: to win new customers all over the world. From the launch of the 'i' series onwards, this strategy has reaped huge rewards for Apple. The figures do not lie.

Three months after the launch of the iPod 'Silhouettes' advertising campaign in 2003, sales were 50 % higher than in the quarter preceding the launch. In the US, total Apple revenue increased by 25 % in comparison with the previous year and income also rose significantly in other parts of the world: in Europe by 48 %, in Japan by 13 % and in the Far East by 55 %.[118] In the first quarter of 2003, Apple recorded a loss of 8 million dollars; a year later, they had turned that into a net profit of 68 million dollars, a success largely attributable to sales of the iPod.[119]

Another extremely successful advertising campaign was the 'Mac versus PC' commercial (2006-2010), in which the two rival computers were depicted as 'real' people: the smart and innovative Mac against the slow and conservative PC. The market share of the Mac doubled in no time at all, while all the rest of the market could do was to lick its wounds. The sales of the Mac catapulted Apple from a company with a market capitalisation of 76 billion dollars in 2006 to more than 300 billion dollars in 2010.[120]

Of course, the key question for marketeers is always how much to spend on (often very expensive) advertising campaigns in the media. Is the investment proportional to the return it yields? Does offline advertising still work in our new online age? The answer to all these questions is an unequivocal 'yes'! Yes, it is still necessary to invest in paid advertising. And yes, this paid advertising does bring in more – much more – than it costs. Dozens of reliable studies have been carried out to prove this point. On average, we can say that a 1 % increase in the advertising budget translates into increased sales of 12 percentage points in the short term and 22 percentage points in the long term – although it needs to be added that these figures (sometimes referred to as advertising elasticity) are now showing a downwards trend. In 1984, the comparable figures were 24 percentage points for the short term and 41 percentage points for the long term.[121] It also needs to be recognised that this elasticity can vary from product category to product category: it is higher for consumer durables (like cars, domestic appliances, electronic devices, etc.) and lower for non-durables (like foodstuffs, razors, etc.). Apple's products are clearly in the durables category, which means that the effect of its advertising is significantly greater.

Since the advent of social media there has been much speculation about the difference in effect of earned (word-of-mouth), owned and paid media, and how these different types interact with each other. If marketers are considering switching from traditional advertising to other channels, they not only need to look at cost but also at effectiveness. Paid advertising can ensure that more messages get to more consumers and that these messages are then shared with even more consumers. This gives marketeers a greater influence over the conversation. If this process is carefully and cleverly orchestrated, it will generate a flywheel effect that will lead to improved sales figures.[122]

Paid advertising campaigns also lead to a subsidiary positive effect on the stock market value of the company. Research has demonstrated that the presence of a company's advertising in the streetscape or in the financial markets media creates a perception that the company is financially healthy, which translates over time into a higher stock market quotation. What's more, this positive effect casts a negative light over the image of rival companies. In other words, you win twice over! This means that even in bad times it is a good idea to continue investing in paid advertising media. Of course, it is not the case that if you invest non-stop in advertising you will also continue to grow non-stop. There is an unwritten marketing law which determines the 'optimum' amount that a company can invest in advertising. If the market gets the feeling that a company is deviating too far from this amount (either positively or negatively), it will withdraw its confidence and the company will suffer accordingly. In other words, increased investment in paid advertising can have a positive influence on the value of a company, but only within the limits of what is generally accepted as being economically reasonable.[123]

A fifth myth debunked: a brand without advertising

In the marketing literature, many experts claim that the success of Apple in general and of the iPhone in particular is first and foremost due to Jobs' spectacular public performances, amplified by positive critical reviews and word-of-mouth advertising. It is certainly true that Jobs generated a huge amount of free advertising for Apple in every possible media channel: radio, television, newspapers, social media, blogs, etc. The value of this advertising for the launch of the iPhone in January 2007 has been estimated at 400 million dollars. No-one had ever seen anything like it before.[124] As a result, it fed the popular myth that Apple was a company that grew into a powerful brand without the need for paid advertising. In fact, some pundits go even further and would like us to believe that products in general do not need paid advertising at all to make them sellable. Products, they argue, should be capable of selling themselves, exclusively on the basis of word-of-mouth advertising (alternatively known as earned media).

However, in reality the sky-rocketing growth of Apple after the launch of the iPhone was by no means based purely on the charismatic Jobs and his appearance in well-staged public events. During this period, Apple spent astronomical amounts on paid advertising campaigns. Between 2009 and 2012, for example, the company doubled its advertising budget to 1 billion dollars, with the bulk going to the iPhone and the iPad. In the 2014 financial year, this trend was taken to the next level, with a budget of no less than 1.8 billion dollars: an increase of more than 50 % in less than 2 years. In comparison, in 2004 the advertising budget amounted to 'just' 206 million dollars.[125]

Two important transformations underpin this spectacular rise. The first was Apple's change of focus to concentrate more on mass consumption products for a broader market. The second was the company's increasing attempts to break into foreign markets both near and far (especially China). This resulted in a much wider radius of action, which needed an increased scale of marketing campaigns to support it. And this, of course, costs money. Lots of money. In this context, it is interesting to note that from 2016 onwards Apple no longer reports on its marketing figures. The reason for this has not been made public, but analysts assume that the 2016 budget reached new record levels. Disquieting levels? That remains to be seen. Even so, the figures that are available prove beyond doubt that Apple is a major investor in paid advertising (as well as enjoying plenty of earned media) and that, consequently, the myth that the company does not need paid advertising can be consigned to the dustbin of history.

The Apple Stores

A brand needs to be mentally omnipresent in the hearts and minds of consumers. To make this possible, it is not enough just to be well-known and popular; your customers also have to be able to buy your product. The third element of the golden marketing triangle (alongside word-of-mouth advertising and paid advertising) is therefore the constant presence of the brand through its distribution channels, both online ('clicks') and, above all, physically ('bricks').

Once again, it was Steve Jobs who understood following his return to Apple that the company needed to get its products closer to its customers, so it could get a better sense of exactly what those customers wanted. In the period around the turn of the century, Apple had become increasingly dependent on the mega-retailers: companies that had neither the incentive nor the knowledge to recommend Apple's unique products to their customers. Jobs realised that this had to change. To make it happen, he hired in two external experts: Ron Johnson, head of merchandising at the American retail chain Target, and Mickey Drexler, to the top man at Gap Stores.[126]

The idea that Apple would open up a complete distribution channel of its own was initially met with scepticism. Some commentators even predicted that the stores would be a flop and would soon be closing their doors.[127]

The first Apple Store was opened on 19 May 2001 in Virginia and was an immediate hit. That same year, a further 25 stores were opened at trendy and frequently visited locations. These stores also quickly became a commercial success. Jobs once commented on the reasons for their popularity: 'The Apple Stores offer an amazing new way to buy a computer. Rather than just hear about megahertz and megabytes, customers can now learn and experience the things they can actually do with a computer, like make movies, burn custom music CDs, and publish their digital photos on a personal website.'[128] Jobs insisted that the stores should be located in the main shopping streets, where there were lots of pedestrians. Money was no object, because, as he said: 'The store will become the most powerful physical expression of the brand.'[129] And indeed, the layout of the stores reflected the Apple image: frivolous, simple, creative, hip and overwhelming, all at the same time. The days of the PC freaks and early followers were now a thing of the past – these were stores for everyone.[130]

In 2004, Apple stores had an average of 5,400 visitors per week and booked a turnover of 1.2 billion dollars, a record figure for the retail sector.[131] The Apple Store on Fifth Avenue in New York, which opened in 2006, attracted no fewer than 50 000 visitors per week during that first year, significantly more than other famous flagship stores like Saks, Bloomingdale's and Tiffany. The New York store was head and shoulders above the rest, but the other 174 outlets still received an average of 13 800 visitors per week, which is a good score in retail. What's more, there seemed to be no end to their success. Talking at a Goldman Sachs conference in 2013, Tim Cook said: 'We're going to continue to invest like crazy in them, and our team members are the best in the world. And the financial results are great: the average store last year (2012) was over 50 million dollars in revenue. Who would have thought a store could do that?'[132]

In addition to these outstanding sales figures, the Apple stores also have another, even more important purpose for the company: they serve to cement the relationship between Apple and its customers. In reality, only 1 in every 100 customers actually buys something in an Apple store. The remaining 99 chill out in the Genius Bar, try new products, check their e-mails, meet their friends, take part in a training session or watch live music.[133] This was precisely what Apple had in mind: they wanted to create something that was nothing like a computer store. Quite the reverse. They took as their inspiration the lobby of the Four Seasons luxury hotel chain, where there is always a friendly member of staff waiting to welcome you. However, in the Apple stores this welcoming element was transferred to the Genius Bar, where an Apple assistant was available for customers, who were free to examine Apple products without any expectation that they would buy them.[134] In this way, the Apple stores became so much more than just another shop. To use Tim Cook's words, they were 'community centres'. As he explained: 'The store acts as a gathering place, as a community–it's a place that has an important role in the community. And so if you look at an agenda on an Apple store for any given day, you might find that there's a youth programme going on, where the kids from a local elementary school are coming into the store as a part of their field trip. You might find that there's a local musician who is entertaining people in that store, on that night. It's incredibly exciting what these stores do.' With some justification, he concluded: 'I'm not even sure that "store" is the right word anymore. They've taken on a role much broader than that. They are the face of Apple for almost all of our customers.'[135]

In 2016, Cook took things a stage further. He upgraded all the Apple stores and gave them a new look. To create this look, he turned to Angela Ahrendts, a former CEO of the Burberry luxury fashion chain. As she had done with chic handbags and jewellery for Burberry, at Apple Ahrendts was given the task of giving the brand a more luxurious image. The basic idea was to apply the philosophy of top fashion to the world of computers. In the fashion world, people are prepared to pay far more for an exclusive item than its intrinsic value is worth. Cook wanted people to feel the same way about Apple products. Ahrendts created this effect by, amongst other things, displaying the Apple Watch and design speakers in glass showcases. But she also did much more than that. She was convinced that it was the personnel in the Apple stores who were the key to a unique shopping experience, resulting in enthusiastic customers and higher sales figures. For this reason, she invested heavily in training and incentives to motivate the staff (some 100 000 employees, 60 % of whom are in the retail branch) to even greater efforts. 'If you're going to employ people anyway,' said Ahrendts, 'why not make them the differentiator? They're not a commodity.'

As Cook had done, she regarded the stores as community centres where much more was going on than the straightforward serving of existing and potential customers. Explaining their significance, Ahrendts said: 'In my mind, store leaders are the mayors of their community.' And we all know that nowadays it is the mayors who are the real world leaders.[136]

Ahrendts' program has since been rolled out worldwide under the title 'Today at Apple'. At the launch, she outlined the thinking behind the concept: 'We are creating a modern-day town square, where everyone is welcome in a space where the best of Apple comes together to connect with one another, discover a new passion, or take their skill to the next level. We think it will be a fun and enlightening experience for everyone who joins.'[137]

In addition to the physical stores, Ahrendts has also devoted her attention to Apple's online channels. In particular, she has ensured that both channels are better attuned to each other. Historically, the online stores tended to do their own thing, divorced from their physical equivalents, a situation that initially arose because Jobs wanted Apple's e-commerce in a separate department. The physical retail department reported to Jobs. The online department reported to Cook, when he was COO. In a world in which customers are constantly switching between online and offline sales, this silo approach was no longer viable. Ahrendts took the necessary steps to correct this outdated configuration before she left the company at the start of 2019. It is worth noting that she was the best paid of all Apple employees. Her salary was even higher than CEO Tim Cook's, which says much about the importance the company attaches to its stores and to the tasks that Ahrendts was given.

Apple in trouble: 'channel stuffing'

Apple is a classic example of a company that succeeds in being ever-present both mentally and physically for its customers. But it hasn't always been that way. During the 1990s, Apple tried to achieve its ambitious commercial and financial targets through an aggressive price promotion strategy (see chapter 3) and via 'agreements' with distributers (about the buying of products) that were on the border of legality or sometimes even over it. In effect, this was panic management at its worst, generating dubious short-term effects that threatened the entire brand in the long run.

At the end of 1995, Apple had a surplus of products with an estimated value of 1 billion euros. These products were outdated and needed to be written off.[138] Various distributers have claimed that Apple offered huge discounts, simply to have these excess products taken off their hands.[139] It soon became clear that Apple's strategy to generate additional market share, almost at any cost, was also leading to a perverse side effect: 'channel stuffing' or the parking of as much stock as possible in the distribution network. Gil Amelio admitted as much in his autobiography: 'The step beyond price cutting is to stuff the channel.'[140] This was standard practice at Apple for many years and involved obliging distributors to buy in stock valued at X million dollars in a given quarter. In this way, it was possible for the quarterly targets to be met. If the distributor refused to co-operate, Apple threatened to terminate his contract. Amelio described the process: 'So the chains buy product they don't need that's going to sit on the shelf for weeks, and Apple starts the next quarter with essentially zero orders coming in because of all that unsold product already in the stores. And when the company gets to the middle of that quarter, the same panic sets in, and the cycle repeats itself.'[141]

To make matters worse, channel stuffing also gave rise to other temptations. Amelio again: 'With these huge amounts of money involved, there were just too many opportunities for people to be tempted. Suppose Apple drops prices by $100 per computer. The channel partners might pass only a portion of this reduction through to the customers, knowing that with this particular type of product, a price drop doesn't result in much of a sales boost. Most of the $100 would then go into their own company's pockets. When Apple was selling about 1 million machines a quarter, a $100 price drop would mean some $100 million in discounts – a lot of money. Nobody would be very surprised if the partners were interested in showing their appreciation to the tune of a few hundred thousand dollars or so in gifts, paid vacation trips, or cash to the salespeople, who had helped make their improved profits happen.'[142]

These confessions by Apple's former CEO illustrate that not only did Apple fail to meet its commercial and financial objectives, but also that the questionable channel stuffing policy became institutionalised, whereby each quarter over many years the company effectively subsidised its own sales in an artificial manner, so that it could meet its short-term targets. The result, however, was that the company sank deeper and deeper into the mire. Market share fell to a paltry 3.3 % and Apple was soon on the verge of bankruptcy. All of which again proves that the only way for a company to grow sustainably is by setting ambitious goals – and then being able to achieve them.

Push and pull

The Apple marketing approach during times when things were going well is a textbook case of the push and pull strategy. On the one hand, brands need to directly attract new customers via paid advertising and word-of-mouth advertising (social media, articles in newspapers, etc.): this is 'pull'. On the other hand, the brands need to make sure that they can put their products under the noses of their prospective customers via a dense network of online and physical stores: this is 'push'. Many brands grow sustainable through the opening of new shops, since the constant strengthening of their physical proximity to existing and future customers is a condition for healthy growth. In this sense, paid advertising is not only necessary to provide a supply of new customers in the short term, but also as a preparatory step towards greater turnover in the long term.[143] The public appearances of Jobs and Cook certainly gave a push in this direction, but, as is usually the case with such performances, the effect of the resulting buzz is temporary and therefore insufficient. The fact that most of Apple's current crop of Generation Y customers have never even heard of Jobs legendary performances (unless they work in advertising) confirms this.

One final note: although e-commerce has been on the rise in many countries over the last decade, to this day most purchases – about 90 % of global retail sailes – occur in brick-and-mortar stores. At least in the foreseeable future, consumers will continue to shop 'offline', where brands will remain influential. In that perspective, Jobs' and Apple's decision to invest in physical stores instead of exclusively focusing on online stores as well as in brand equity, has proven to be a move of visionary proportions. It also explains why a platform like Amazon, which is an online platform by nature, has introduced physical Amazon Go stores in many cities, and has acquired the Whole Foods chain. Smart companies reap the advantages of both retail models to survive.[144]

G

THE DO'S-AND-DON'TS

- ∞ Make sure your company is always omnipresent by making use of the golden triangle of marketing: word-of-mouth advertising, paid advertising campaigns and effective distribution (both physical and online:'bricks' and 'clicks').

- ∞ Each social group of people consists of 90 % opinion followers and 10 % opinion-makers or influencers. Companies and brands must therefore make it a priority to approach the opinion-makers in a positive manner.

- ∞ Build up long-term relationships with your stakeholders and opinion-makers. Invest both time and money in these relationships.

- ∞ 20 % of all positive word-of-mouth advertising arises as a result of information sourced from paid advertising campaigns. For this reason, it is well worth continuing to invest in paid advertising.

- ∞ The most brilliant advertising campaigns focus on two important fields of attention. (1) They attempt to prompt action amongst the opinion-leaders, so that they spontaneously share films, images or messages via social media and, more specifically, YouTube. (2) At the same time, they use paid advertising to target consumers directly. These two elements mutually strengthen each other.

G

- ∞ Never underestimate the value of your distribution channel! It is only in a store of some kind – physical or online – that the customer actually pays for your product. Distribution is probably the most important marketing function.

- ∞ A physical store can be much more than just a sales point. It is the public 'face' of your company and can grow into a community centre, not only for customers but also as a meeting place for other members of the local neighbourhood.

- ∞ Word-of-mouth advertising has a much greater effect in a face-to-face conversation than in short and fleeting conversations online. 'Human to human' communication remains the most impactful form of communication.

- ∞ Bearing in mind the increasing importance of social media, today's marketing experts need to find a healthy and balanced mix between owned media, paid media (advertising) and earned media (word-of-mouth).

- ∞ Never allow yourself to be tempted to channel stuffing, simply to achieve your short-term targets. This is a form of self-deception that always does more harm than good in the long run.

A G

ADAPTATION

GOAL ATTAINMENT

AGIL PARADIGM

LATENT PATTERN MAINTENANCE

INTEGRATION

L I

A

INTEGRATION

I

INTEGRATION

The 'A' and 'G' functions of the AGIL paradigm have shown us the importance for a company not only to adapt in a smart manner to its ever-changing environment, but also to try in turn to reshape that environment to the company's own advantage. This will make it possible for the company to achieve its objectives, provided it has a clear strategy that it applies consistently over a long period. We also saw that it is advisable for companies to be mentally and physically omnipresent for its customers and stakeholders. These are the most commonly proposed economic insights for success and they are focused on the external environment.

But one of the unique aspects of the AGIL paradigm is that it not only formulates economic but also cultural conditions for survival in the long term. In other words, technological and economic supremacy is not enough. The company also needs to put its own house in order. Optimal internal organisation is essential, certainly when facing the challenges of a disruptive environment. The 'I' function must ensure that the company remains a well-oiled and coherent machine in the increasingly fragmented world in which it needs to operate. The 'I' function also ensures that the whole is greater than the component parts. It creates cohesion and harmony, although it also results in a degree of pressure and control.

In chapter 5, I will deal in particular with the importance of integration at the level of personnel, the ecosystem (the entire value chain consisting of partners, suppliers, advisers and other opinion-makers) and customers. In an immortal company, the customers are also part of the social system that every successful company must be. But how loyal are today's customers to companies and their brands?

A well-integrated company therefore forms a unique social system that is capable of distinguishing itself from other companies. Such a company also knows when and where to set boundaries, if necessary, and, above all, maintains and defends them against hostile attacks. In this sense, the company is also a closed system (as I will describe in chapter 6), but on occasions briefly opens its doors to allow it to survive.

5 THE ALIGNMENT PACT

An immortal company builds and controls a community of engaged employees, committed customers and dependent partners.

'My model for business is The Beatles. They were four guys who kept each other's kind of negative tendencies in check. They balanced each other and the total was greater than the sum of the parts. That's how I see business: great things in business are never done by one person, they're done by a team of people.' This was the remarkable symbolism that Steve Jobs used during a television interview in 2003 to typify the Apple model. It not only testifies to his great love for the music of The Beatles (and Bob Dylan), but also revels him as a systems thinker.

The chance is minimal that Steve Jobs ever studied the social system theories of Talcott Parsons and, sadly, it is no longer possible to ask him. Even though he liked to cultivate an image for the outside world of being something of a free-spirited maverick, Jobs actually had a highly holistic view of the world around him. He was able like few others to see the big connections, the coherence and interrelatedness of things, the necessity of combining elements that most people felt did not belong together. In this sense, Jobs was – either consciously or unconsciously– a true systems thinker. And it was this philosophy that to a large extent led to the revival of Apple's fortunes after the turn of the century.

Immortal companies behave like social systems of the kind envisaged by Talcott Parsons. Companies strive to achieve long-term mutual dependence, loyalty and commitment with the members of their community. They attempt to develop a continuous, broad and many-facetted relationship with their employees, business partners and customers

This brings us to the third function in the AGIL paradigm: the 'I' of Integration. In this chapter I will look more closely at the principle that an immortal company builds and controls a community of engaged employees, committed customers and dependent partners.

For Parsons, integration was a key concept in his study of social systems. This was not only the case when he was developing the AGIL paradigm, but also continued to attract his attention in his later years. For example, he examined how social systems confronted with internal and external change are able to strengthen themselves by integrating more closely. He saw this as a double process. The increasing complexity of the environment prompts the systems to adapt, so that they also become more complex through their differentiation. The sub-systems that are created in this manner will become increasingly distinct and autonomous, and will have their own function. At the same time, the social system works towards greater integration, to prevent its unity as a system from falling apart. Instead of working separately or against each other, the system obliges its 'independent' sub-systems to mutually strengthen each other by exchanging experiences, helping each other and pushing each other to a higher level of attainment. In this way, the whole becomes greater than the sum of the parts. This is precisely what Jobs had in mind when he made his reference to The Beatles. According to Parsons, this symbiosis can best be achieved through 'value generalisation', which effectively means taking a helicopter view of the values and identities that bind the different sub-systems together. This can be interpreted broadly, as long as the result is coherent and can be linked to a higher and common ideological goal. On this basis, it then becomes possible to see which position each sub-system occupies within the integrated whole and to assess its added value.

The same applies to brands. Given that continuity is crucial for the creation of a strong identity, the key question for brands is how they can adjust in a credible manner to a market that is becoming increasingly fragmented, with more advanced products and changing customer needs. I discussed this in some detail when we looked at the adaptive capacity of companies under the 'A' of the AGIL paradigm, where we saw that this capacity is focused externally and is generally progressive. This leads us to the next important question: once you have adapted and differentiated yourself as a company, how can you provide the integration that will forge your organisation into a powerful whole? This is, of course, the 'I' in the AGIL paradigm and is internally focused, connective and binding.

In this respect, Apple is a particularly interesting case, because at different times in its history it has experienced both ends of the systems spectrum: from extreme integration, resulting in an almost totally closed system, to far-reaching disintegration and differentiation, so that its sub-systems were sometimes even working against each other. I will look at both extremes – the good and the less good – at three different levels: (1) the internal cohesion (within the company, between different departments, management and employees); (2) the ecosystem (the network of business partners, such as external developers, distributors, content providers, etc.); and (3) the relationship with customers (both B2C and B2B).

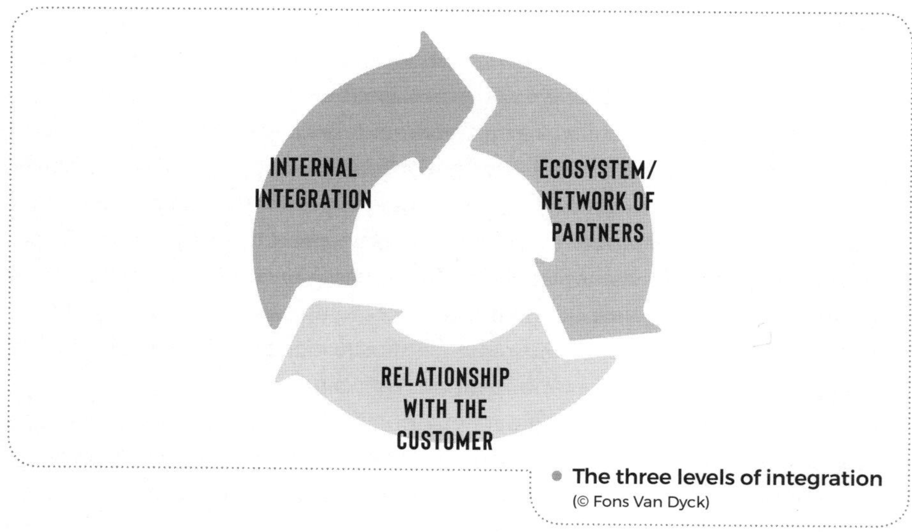

The three levels of integration
(© Fons Van Dyck)

Level 1: internal integration

Many companies, certainly when they are growing or transforming, find it difficult to maintain their internal cohesion, usually as a consequence of conflicts, internal political manoeuvring, a silo mentality or overdeveloped sub-cultures. In fact, it is probably fair to say that in most cases a homogenous culture is the exception rather than the rule. Sometimes these internal divisions are so serious that they threaten the company's future progress.

This is also what happened at Apple. In the early days, the company's success was primarily based on the Apple II, but during the 1980s the product range became increasingly diversified. There was little sign of integration. Quite the reverse! There are legendary stories about the clashes between the teams working on the Lisa and the Macintosh, which were both being developed at more or less the same time. At one point, things went so far that the Macintosh team, which was then under the leadership of Jobs, hoisted a 'skull-and-crossbones' flag above their building to differentiate themselves as pirates from the rival Lisa team. The Mac team looked down condescendingly on the Lisa, which they thought was inferior, and they compared the bureaucracy of the larger Lisa division with the hated IBM. None of this escaped the attention of the outside world. *Time Magazine* talked about 'Byzantine office politics' and said it seemed as though two different computers were being developed by two totally different companies.[145]

Worst of all, this was not just an isolated incident. There were also internal conflicts between the Macintosh and Apple II teams. Most people saw the Mac as the replacement for the Apple II. In other words, the Mac threatened to make the Apple II – and its team – obsolete. Once again, the language used was hostile. The Mac people called the Apple II team members (including Steve Wozniak) 'bozos', which effectively means a bunch of idiots. The street that separated the two divisions on the Apple campus was known as the 'DMZ', standing for 'demilitarised zone' (referring to the neutral zone between two countries in a state of war, like between North and South Korea). 'You crossed it at your own peril,' Sculley later recalled.[146] Wozniak, an Apple II fan from day one, complained that his team was getting much less money than the Mac team. 'I thought that wasn't fair,' he concluded.[147]

As a result of these rivalries, Apple was unable to integrate its technological platforms and activities internally. All its products had different names with no degree of similarity (Apple II, Lisa, Macintosh). They each had a different brand positioning, which led to confusion in the market and to the cannibalisation of each other's value propositions. But the biggest problem of all was the fact that not only were the different products incompatible with each other, but they also stole each other's customers. Before long, Apple found itself ship-wrecked as a disintegrating company with not much hope of rescue, notwithstanding the efforts of successive new CEOs (Sculley, Spindler, Amelio) to get everyone's nose pointing in the same direction.

Even though he had been one of the biggest trouble-makers in the early 1980s, it was only after the return of Jobs in 1997 that the situation began to change for the better. He now understood that things could not be allowed to carry on in this way and immediately initiated a program of vertical integration for the different products. He referred to this as 'the whole widget': from design and hardware via software to content. He then took a further crucial step by organising the different departments centrally – marketing, sales, production, finance – rather than de-centrally (per team), as had traditionally been the case at Apple. Jobs wanted all the departments to work in parallel. Instead of products being made and then passed on to the next department, all the departments were now working on the product simultaneously. Jobs commented: 'Our method was to develop integrated products, and that meant our process had to be integrated and collaborative.'[148] The results are well-known: the development of the successful 'i' series. In practice, however, it meant that Jobs was keeping a tight hold of all the strings. This was integration dictated by God.

Tim Cook took a radically different approach from Jobs, preferring to focus on collaboration and collegiality within the company. He also practiced what he preached in the way he led the company. One of the first actions he took to instigate this 'new culture' was to recruit Professor Morton Hansen (INSEAD, Harvard and Berkeley) to teach managers how they could benefit from the fruits of cross-teambuilding and internal collaboration. Hansen was not just any professor: he was the best-selling author of books like *Great at Work* and *Collaboration*, and a leading authority on social networks and co-operative processes. Today, he still teaches at Berkeley and at the Apple University.

It is interesting to pause for a moment and look a little closer at some of the ideas that Hansen preached at Apple. In his book *Collaboration* he argues forcefully for the necessity to set a common goal rather than individual objectives. You need to create a common destiny, a feeling of 'we are all in this together'. To do this, you need to generate passion and there can be no room for competition and rivalry. Hansen talks of 'disciplined collaboration' – a concept that first appeared in a Hewlett-Packard study from the 1990s – in which the advantages of a decentralised organisation are combined with intense interaction and co-operation.

When this leads to the desired results, it becomes possible for departments to work independently from each other. In this way, people get full control over their own part of the work, which enhances their sense of responsibility and gives them opportunities to be enterprising in their own right. As a result, they become capable of achieving great things. This approach needs to be supplemented with – and not replaced by – an open mind towards the idea of collaboration. Employees must be able to identify when (and when not) opportunities for collaboration arise, not only within their own team but also with other teams. And to underline the importance of teamwork and collaboration, it is vital that the senior management team also displays this same coherence.[149]

So how is all this applied in Apple under Cook? In short, the management works in accordance with Hansen's principle of 'disciplined collaboration'. In his interviews, Cook often describes Apple as a collection of functional experts, who each have their own specialty. But when it is necessary, they know how to collaborate. 'The work really happens horizontally in our company, not vertically,' says Cook. 'Products are horizontal. It takes hardware plus software plus services to make a killer product. So, all of these people, if you were to line us up and talk to everyone, you know several of them, you would see we're all different. And that's the power of it. We're not trying to put everyone through a car wash, so they look alike, talk alike, think alike at the end of the day. We argue and debate. (…) But we have great respect for one another and we trust one another and we complement one another. And that makes it all work.'[150]

Cook makes a direct connection between this manner of working and the excellent user experience that makes Apple so popular with consumers. If you want seamless integration between the iPhone, iMac and iPad, if you want customers to be able to switch without difficulty from one product to another, this is only possible if the people creating these products were able to do the same. And this, in turn, is only possible if they collaborate.[151]

The successful integration of the physical Apple Stores with the e-stores by Angela Ahrendts and her team is the metaphorical icing on the cake for this new way of working. This internal fusion was by no means easy. It required the joint training of different online and offline teams. The offline people had to learn (and accept) how customers can buy Apple products online when they want to, whereas the online people had to learn how products are sold in a physical environment. For both groups, this demanded a different way of thinking, in which the customer – and not the sales channel – is central.[152] Was this the reason, perhaps, that Ahrendts was often tipped as the favourite to one day succeed Tim Cook?

Level 2: the ecosystem

Having a sufficient degree of differentiation and integration is also crucial in your ecosystem or network of business partners and stakeholders. Initially, the Apple ecosystem functioned well and contributed significantly to the huge success of the Apple II. Marketeer Regis McKenna, who was jointly responsible for the launching of Apple II, talks in this context about the unique marketing 'infrastructure' of Apple, consisting of software developers, retailers, analysts and journalists. 'If a product can win the support of the infrastructure, it is almost certain to win in the marketplace.'[153]

By the 1990s, this had all changed and Apple was on collision course with a number of its stakeholders, primarily because the company was pursuing its own interests in an aggressive manner that took no account of anyone else. Consider, for instance, Apple's plan to target the lower segments of the market with the low-priced Macintosh Classic. This created consternation within the existing distribution network, in which the company had invested so heavily in the 1980s. 1 700 Apple dealers quite literally had to read in the newspapers that the company was planning to extend its distribution network to include hypermarket chains like CompUSA, Montgomery Ward and Walmart. Understandably, the original dealers were not impressed. To make matters worse, the strategy was a failure, resulting in a declining market share that tipped Apple into a negative spiral. Why? Because it made Apple less interesting for software developers, so that the flow of new products dried up, which in turn had a further negative effect on future growth.[154] And so the vicious circle continued.

During the second half of the 1990s, Apple found itself completely isolated from the rest of the PC industry. It urgently needed to realign itself with its 'infrastructure' and devote some serious attention to developing a real ecosystem. Steve Jobs was the man for the task. Almost at once, he took the drastic decision of cutting a deal with arch-rival Microsoft. In contrast to many others, Jobs understood that Apple could not survive in the long term without the support of Microsoft, a company that now had a dominant position in the computer world. The deal included an exchange of licenses and other technological agreements. Amongst other things, Microsoft would continue to make Mac versions of Microsoft Office and Internet Explorer. In return, Apple would install Internet Explorer as its standard browser on the Mac OS. All existing differences relating to patents were made open for discussion and settled, while Microsoft further agreed to pay 150 million dollars for 150 000 Apple shares.[155] Initially, there was huge scepticism amongst the true Apple fans, but Jobs knew that there was no choice. It was a case of ' if you can't beat them, join them'.

Jobs went on to conclude other mega-deals. For example, he extended the hand of friendship to the music business, which paved the way for the huge success of the iPod and iTunes. Apple was able to convince the five largest record companies to offer digital versions of their songs for sale in the iTunes Store for 99 cents. 70 cents went to the record companies; the rest was for Apple. This smart move transformed Apple into an important link in the value chain of the worldwide music industry and allowed iTunes to become the lever that launched the company's revival, especially now that the service was also available to Windows users.

Another Apple deal saw a partnership with American telecom giant AT&T for the launching of the iPhone in 2007. AT&T was granted exclusivity, which gave its network a serious and necessary boost. In return, AT&T paid Apple the full price per phone, instead of the standard distribution price, which was usually 200 dollars under the store price. 'It was a clean arrangement for both sides,' was the opinion of most commentators.[156]

The launching of the App Store, one of the most important drivers for the success of the iPhone, is another good example of how Apple now works consciously to build up its ecosystem. The company made it possible for external app developers, following approval from Apple, to sell their applications in the store. Most of these apps were free, but if a price was asked, 30 % of it went to Apple. Of course, Apple also retained the right to decide who was allowed into the store (and who not) and the apps needed to be built in accordance with strict Apple guidelines. This illustrates how the company, even while developing its collaborative network, still likes to have control over its partners. And in view of the huge success of the store, the partners have little option other than to agree. '[The App Store] was an absolutely magical solution that hit the sweet spot,' said Apple board member Arthur Levinson. 'It gave us the benefits of openness while retaining end-to-end control.'[157]

This, of course, is fine for Apple, but not so fine for others operating in the same field. In early 2019, for example, the online music streaming platform Spotify filed a complaint with the EU anti-trust regulators against Apple, arguing that the iPhone-maker unfairly limits rivals to its own Apple Music streaming service. Spotify (founded in 2007) claimed that in this way Apple's control of its App Store deprives consumers of choice and rival providers of audio streaming services, all to the benefit of Apple Music (founded in 2015). What particularly riles Spotify, is 'a 30 % fee that Apple charges content-based service providers to use Apple's in-app purchase system.'[158]

In other words, Spotify is accusing Apple of unfairly misusing the App Store to benefit its own music service. In effect, it is claiming that Apple is both judge and jury. And at one level it is an understandable claim. Given the huge popularity of the App Store, Apple does indeed hold the keys of the door to Spotify for many of its users. At the same time, the more recently launched Apple Music is increasingly overtaking pioneer Spotify in a number of key market segments. Put simply, Apple wins twice over: from the commission it receives on the Spotify app and from the income from its own music service. This means that at a time when revenue from the sale of smartphones is stagnating worldwide, Apple is using this streaming service to penetrate and exploit a lucrative new market, with consumers paying a fixed subscription fee each month for its use. What's more, this approach is likely not to be confined to music alone. In the near future, Apple is expected to challenge YouTube and Netflix in the field of video streaming services.

European publishers are likewise unhappy that Apple 'dictates' all the terms and conditions for every app in its store. Writing in *Financial Times*, their chairman, Christian Van Thillo, CEO of DPG Media, the largest media company in the Netherlands and Belgium, commented: 'It [Apple] also takes ownership of the customer relationship, keeps the valuable customer data, insists on using only its own payment system and imposes a commission of 30 % of the fees paid by the consumers.'[159]

This is a classic example of what a dependent relationship can mean for a company and its partners in terms of daily operational practice within an eco-system. In this particular instance, it seems clear that the partners are more dependent on Apple than vice versa. Will it stay that way? In the final analysis, it will be for the regulators and the courts to decide.

Level 3: the relationship with the customer

The third and probably the most important level on which a company or brand needs to focus if it wishes to develop an integrated social system, is the relationship it is able to build up with its customers. In marketing circles, it is generally accepted that brands seek to establish a long-term relationship with their customers, based on mutual dependence, loyalty and trust. Loyalty can be defined as the yardstick of the confidence and trust that the customer has in the brand. The greater the loyalty, the less vulnerable the brand becomes to competition from others. Moreover, loyal customers are usually prepared to pay a premium price for the brand's products, because they experience them as being part of their identity.

Marketing specialist Kevin Lane Keller argues that a brand must seek to achieve the highest possible degree of resonance with its customers. This implies the need for a harmonious relationship between the brand and the customer, in which the customer is prepared to engage actively on the brand's behalf; for example, by sharing his brand experiences with others. If this can be taken a stage further, so that the customer is prepared – irrespective of his own level of purchase and consumption – to invest energy, time, money or other resources in a brand, it then becomes possible to speak of the customer as a brand ambassador. In that case, the customer at his own initiative will take steps to ensure that the bond between the brand and other customers is further strengthened.[160]

When Steve Jobs returned to Apple in 1997, he quickly realised that one of the few riches the beleaguered company still possessed was its hardcore of loyal customers. What's more, there were a lot of them: by then, more than 25 million people had a Mac in their homes. Jobs saw that if they could be persuaded to continue buying Apple products, this might form the basis for a comeback. As soon as he was reappointed as CEO, he paid a public tribute to the Apple fans and their motives: 'I think you still have to think differently to buy an Apple Computer,' he said. 'The people who buy them do think different. They are the creative spirits in this world, and they're out to change the world. We make tools for those kinds of people.'[161]

From this moment onwards, everything the company did – from technology, design and apps to the layout in its stores – was done with the customer in mind. In contrast with the past, every effort was now made to find the right balance between excellent technology and marketing. This resulted in the unique 'Apple experience', which managed to claw back many of the customers who had previously turned their backs on the company. Jobs was convinced that every moment when a customer is in contact with the brand is important: as a buyer, a user, a visitor to an Apple store or even as someone just seeing an Apple advert on a billboard or TV. Each contact adds extra elements to the image that the customer has of the brand in his imagination.[162]

This radical 'customer first' philosophy also implied that Apple wanted total control over the customer experience. It further implied that once you were in the Apple system, it was not easy to get out again. Apple forms, as it were, a world of its own, with its own technology, own systems and own rules. In terms of Parsons, we can even speak of a closed system. This last aspect was sometimes held against Jobs. For example, he was heavily criticised for the imperious way he (and he alone) could decide which apps could be downloaded on the iPhone and the iPad, and which could not. Apps that denigrate others, or are politically sensitive, or are regarded by the Apple 'censure police' as pornographic are simply banned from the App Store, without recourse. In spite of a storm of protest, Jobs held his ground: 'You can disagree with us, but our motives are pure.' The App Store, he wrote, 'offers freedom from programs that steal your private data. Freedom from programmes that trash your battery. Freedom from porn. Yep, freedom.'[163] Even Jobs' biographer Isaacson was not wholly without criticism when he commented wryly that at times Jobs needed to be careful that he didn't turn into the Orwellian 'Big Brother' that he had so cheerfully destroyed in his '1984' Macintosh commercial...[164]

Be that as it may, with its unique focus on the customer and its radical control over its entire system, Apple set a new trend. After customers had sampled the uniform excellence of Apple's products and services, they started to demand the same standard of other companies. In this sense, it is fair to say that Apple gave a new definition to the word 'quality', so that other companies increasingly felt obliged to meet the higher expectations of their consumers.[165]

Tim Cook is still a strong advocate of organising all the company's activities in function of an integrated user-friendliness: 'It's part of our own ecosystem. And we do that because it all works together. It just works when you do it that way.'[166] Or to put it in slightly different terms: 'Our strategy is to help you in every part of your life that we can, whether you're sitting in the living room, on your desktop, on your phone, or in your car.'[167] In other words, Apple wants to be omnipresent for its customers 24/7/365. And wants its customers to be there for them.

The ever-connected customer

In the past, companies used to interact with customers only spasmodically, whenever the customers came to them. This might be once a week in a supermarket, once a month in a hairdresser's or once a year in a travel agent. Those days, however, are long gone. Today's development in technologies means that companies can and must address customer needs the moment they arise (and sometimes even earlier). 24/7 customer relationships are now a fact of life and this must be reflected in a company's business model through the development of connected strategies that make possible deeper ties with customers and improved customer experiences – or so argue Wharton professors Siggelkow and Terwiesch. This new business model can take (or combine) different forms, ranging from a simple and efficient response to basic customer demands (fast delivery, minimal friction, maximum flexibility and precise execution), to curated offerings (the provision of personalised but non-binding advice), coaching (proactively reminding customers of their needs) and even automatic execution (allowing companies to meet customer needs even before the customer is aware of those needs).[168]

Many companies see AI as the new holy grail when it comes to optimising their relationship with customers, making increasing use of chatbots as a reduced-cost way of dealing with inbound service calls. Yet while the companies seem to be sold on chatbots, the majority of customers are not. They do not trust them to resolve their service issues and remain sceptical about their ability to provide a similar level of service as humans. A report from Forrester showed that 54 % of US online consumers expect interactions with customer service chatbots to negatively affect their service experience. The main complaints are that that chatbots 'do not understand questions fully, so cannot deliver useful answers; do not provide an easy path to human assistance; and even if they do transfer to a human agent, the transition experience is far from easy or satisfying'.[169]

It therefore appears that chatbots are currently sowing the seeds of discontent with American – and non-American – consumers and the companies deploying them are likely to experience a rude and potentially costly awakening.

Apple in trouble: a loss of confidence

Apple has always been able to rely on its loyal base of fanatical fans. But when the management attempted to broaden this base in the 1990s by opting for a strategy to increase market share (see the section on the 'G' function above), it made the mistake of ignoring its own identity as a high-tech and unique premium brand. As a result, they created the opposite effect. Instead of attracting new customers, it alienated the loyal old ones. Large groups of Apple loyalists and stakeholders began to jump ship in increasing numbers – something that was soon picked up by the media. The trade press was full of articles about people who had long been Apple customers, but were now thinking of looking elsewhere. 'I can see future directions for the PC, but I can't see it for the Mac,' said one Apple fan in *Business Week*. In the same article an analyst commented: 'The Mac still has a certain magic, but consumers are increasingly in a Wintel state of mind.'[170]

Professional customers also began to lose their confidence in Apple, once they saw how the company was zig-zagging from one strategy to another. As a result, they doubted the wisdom of investing in the company and its products in the long term. Major customers like US West, Deloitte & Touche and Electronic Data Systems gradually turned to other suppliers.

This was already bad enough, but things started to go seriously downhill when media reports appeared about a revolt among Apple customers. On 5 September 1996, *The Wall Street Journal* published an article with the headline 'Companies Dump Macs as Loyalists Lose Faith'. In his autobiography, Gil Amelio wrote of this article that 'it was enough to give a strong man heartburn'. The brand had slipped into a negative spiral from which there seemed no escape. After losing its customers, it was now losing its stakeholders. The entire Apple system was falling apart.

By the beginning of 1997, even the loyalest of loyal supporters were expressing doubts about the company's chances of survival. Walter Mossberg, an influential columnist at *The Wall Street Journal* and a known Apple fan, stunned the computer world when he wrote: 'After carefully reading the plan and interviewing top Apple executives, I believe the strategy makes buying a Mac a relatively risky investment for consumers and small business owners, compared with buying a computer running Microsoft's Windows 95 or Windows NT operating systems.'[171] In its June edition of that year, *Wired Magazine* published an article about the company under the heading:'101 Ways to Save Apple'.[172] And in early July, a columnist at *The Boston Globe* neatly summarised what everyone was thinking:'Apple is nearly extinct.'[173]

The final nail in the coffin – or so it appeared at the time – was the loss of stock market confidence. Apple investors began dumping their shares, whose value sank to under 41 dollars.'The company, it seemed, was now worth as much for its buildings and capital equipment as it was for its business,' said Roger Mc Namee, chairman of the technology investment company Integral Partners.'This is like a shark at the beach: people eventually go back in the water, but you want to make sure you get rid of the shark.'[174]

A sixth myth debunked: the 'cult'

One of the most stubborn of all the Apple myths is that the company's success is due first and foremost to a small group of fanatically loyal followers. In this context, the word 'cult' is often used to describe these followers, implying that they worship the Apple brand with an almost religious fervour. And it is true that all the ingredients we usually think of in terms of a sect are present: the strong story or creed built up around the figure of Jobs, the unquestioning dedication of his 'disciples', their belief in the higher goal of the Macintosh (the democratisation of technology), the existence of a number of 'satanic' opponents (Windows, IBM, Android), etc. There were also true Mac believers who tried to 'convert' other computer lovers to the Apple gospel, believing that in this way they could free people by transcending the limits of corporate capitalism. It is also true that in the past Apple has done everything possible to try and maintain this aura of myth and mystery around the company.[175] The same 'rebel' status was even accorded to the company's own employees. Jobs once said: 'Apple is an Ellis Island company. Apple is built on refugees from other companies. These are the extremely bright individual contributors who were trouble-makers at other companies.'[176]

In the early years of the 1990s, the Mac users were seen as the new Illuminati. They drove around with Apple stickers on the bumpers of their cars, met each other at the Mac Expo to discover and discuss the latest products, and read magazines like *MacWorld* and *MacUser*. Michael Malone wrote in 1999, following the return of Jobs: 'Apple had created a vision of a new kind of enterprise, a new way of approaching the world that had resonated now with generations of computer owners. It had proved to be only a minority view, but that only cemented its case. This myth was Jobs' and Woz' greatest invention and it had now long outlived them at the company they founded. It there weren't enough of these true believers to keep Apple strong, there were enough to keep it alive.'[177]

Even so, the importance of this group of fanatical customers needs to be put in perspective, particularly in light of Apple's spectacular growth in the 21st century. Empirical research has shown that this group is 'small' in relation to the number of potential customers and that their word-of-mouth advertising only reaches as far as the (also relatively small) number of people they know. Moreover, 'pure' brand fans are quite rare. People often spread their loyalty over different brands: they are, as it were, 'polygomously loyal'. Consider, for example, Apple and Harley Davidson: two brands with a strong identity and a reputation for being able to bind customers emotionally. If, however, you look at the company figures, a different picture starts to emerge. In the early years of the new century, 55 % of Apple customers (owning one of the brand's PCs) and 33 % of Harley Davidson customers were categorised as 'loyal', in the sense that after their initial purchase they would continue to buy their favourite brand. This may sound impressive – until you know that the comparable figure for a less 'sexy' brand like Dell was 71 %.[178] Conclusion: it is certainly important to have loyal customers, but it is even more important to have a constant flow of new customers, as we saw when we discussed the 'G' function.

Even so, brands continue to invest heavily in their long-term relationship with their existing customers. The reason for this is obvious: loyal customers represent a fixed source of income, are prepared to pay a higher price, can be reached with a lower level of marketing cost and, with a bit of luck, might even become ambassadors for the brand. But this does not mean that this group is also the most profitable group of customers. In general, it is the much larger group of incidental customers who bring in the most revenue. Moreover, it often happens that at some point loyal customers expect lower prices in return for their years of loyalty. In short, companies need to avoid becoming too heavily dependent on their biggest fans. Managing loyalty and generating profits are two separate activities that ideally should work in parallel, but with sufficient attention for both components.[179]Finding the right balance is crucial.

A difficult relationship with the outside world

In the summer of 2018, Apple was the first American company to pass the landmark of a stock market value of 1 trillion dollars. With more than 1 billion Apple devices and gadgets in circulation, it is no exaggeration to say that the company has indeed changed the world and had an influence on the lives of millions of people. Tim Cook has successful continued the work started by Steve Jobs: both internally and externally, he has perpetuated and strengthened a tightly integrated social system that seems invincible.

However, there is a 'but' in this story – and it is a big one. The Apple system has an important weak spot: its corporate reputation in the outside world. This seems to get worse as the years go by. In the annual ranking published in 2018 by the authoritative Reputation Institute, Apple occupies a lowly fifty-eighth spot. By comparison, back in 2011 Apple stood proudly in second spot! Since then, it has been downhill all the way, with the company scoring particularly poorly for parameters like 'open and transparent' and 'citizenship'.

As a result, Apple has come under increasing fire from different quarters in recent years. One of the most painful issues was the appalling working conditions at the company's manufacturers and suppliers, in particular at the Foxconn plant in China – a story that received wide media coverage. In 2017, Apple was also named in the leaked Paradise Papers, which allowed journalists (from, amongst others, *The New York Times* and *The Guardian*) to uncover international tax avoidance on a massive scale. The company was accused of hiding itself in Ireland (where it has had a factory employing 6000 people since the 1980) and, more recently, in the tax-haven of Jersey. Apple strenuously denied this allegation, protesting in November 2017 that: 'We pay every dollar we owe in every country around the world.' But the damage to the company's image had already been done– and the fact that the company claims to pay a worldwide average of 24.6 % in tax has done little to alter this.

In other words, Apple still has plenty of work to do in terms of its reputation management. CEO Tim Cook is well aware of this and plans to do something about it. And so he should: social systems often fall into decline through a combination of internal inertia (complacency) and external attack. This does not simply mean attacks from business and other rivals, but also from neighbouring systems, including dissatisfied customers, government authorities (like the EU Commissioner for Competition, Margarethe Vestager) and public opinion.

You can't build up a reputation overnight. It takes more than a few classy photos and flashy advertisements. Your reputation is also based on things people associate with your brand. It is about how innovative you are, how you treat your employees, how your senior management behaves, how socially committed you are, how financially honest you are. In this sense, a reputation can be seen as the total 'gestalt' of a company. Research has shown that only 18 % of a company's reputation is determined by its products and services. The impact of the other parameters is each estimated at between 13 and 14 %.[180] In particular, the parameters 'workplace', 'vision and leadership' and 'social responsibility' have been increasing in importance in recent years. These are all areas where Apple needs to improve.

A strong reputation is important, even if only to create a buffer of goodwill that you can draw on in times of crisis. Reputable companies are always allowed more time and credit by policy-makers, stakeholders and customers to get themselves out of trouble – even if they have created the trouble themselves. Think, for example, of the Coca-Cola dioxin crisis in Belgium in 1999 or the Volkswagen emissions scandal in 2015-2016. Because both these companies could fall back on their previous good reputation, allied to their strong financial performance, they were able to ride out the storm. In fact, looking back, they emerged from the crisis stronger than before. Research has revealed that a strong reputation has no direct impact on the financial value of a company: this is determined by profitability and growth. Even so, it has been shown that a good reputation is vital to the survival of a company in the long term.[181]

To maintain a good reputation, companies like Apple (and also Google, Facebook, Amazon, etc.) need more than ever to take account of societal forces that act independently from the market: the government, interest groups, activists, the public at large, etc. Trying to keep these elements under control is very different from controlling the market. A market can be measured in figures, but you can't quantify social forces in a spreadsheet. Other rules apply. Large companies like Apple often find it difficult to deal with this. According to Harvard professor Michael Porter, these companies get stuck in their own outdated and far too narrow perception of value creation. They focus too much on financial results in the short term, so that they lose sight of what is happening in the world around them. For this reason, Porter argues in favour of 'shared value', by which he means creating economic value in such a way that major societal challenges are tackled, thereby allowing social value to be created.[182]

Fortunately for Apple, this is something at which Tim Cook excels. His appointment as CEO was not greeted with universal applause and a number of analysts predicted that the company would soon go downhill under his leadership. History has shown that they were wrong. Cook's technological record might not be as dazzling as his illustrious predecessor's, but he has shown himself to be innovative and trendsetting in other fields, particularly in terms of social engagement.

Whereas Jobs was often reluctant to take a stance on social issues, Cook has shown himself to be a thoroughbred modern CEO activist. In his biography, Leander Kahney illustrates how Cook has taken progressive and often bold steps in many societal domains; from ensuring improved working conditions at Apple's supply companies to the protection of user privacy.[183] In his 2019 commencement speech at Stanford University, Tim Cook made his point very clear on a growing number of issues directly related to Silicon Valley (which he describes as a 'chaos factory') and social media in particular (singling out privacy violation, hate speech and fake news). 'If you want credit for the good, take responsibility for the bad', Cook argued. 'If we accept as normal and unavoidable that everything in our lives can be aggregated, sold, or even leaked in the event of a hack, then we lose so much more than data. We lose the freedom to be human', he said.[184]

Cook left the attending Stanford graduates with the idea that a world without digital privacy might lead the public to start imposing some form of self-censorship, and might ultimately even endanger the possibilities of 'doing nothing wrong other than [thinking] differently' – nothing less than a brilliant nod to Apple's iconic catchphrase by Cook. To drive home his point, he decried the 'small, unimaginative world we would end up with' in an age of digital surveillance. 'Not entirely, at first. Just a little, bit by bit. Ironically, it's the kind of environment that would have stopped Silicon Valley before it had even gotten started.'

It was without a doubt one of the strongest messages a CEO has ever shared with the next generation of the technology and business elite. In other words, Cook knows – like very few before him – how to link Apple's business interests to matters of wider public interest. He may be different from Jobs in many ways, but he has the same forward-thinking and visionary approach. All that remains to be seen is whether this increased level of social commitment will ultimately have a positive influence on Apple's sometimes problematic relationship with the outside world.

THE DO'S-AND-DON'TS

- ∞ Try to achieve a permanent, broad and multi-facetted relationship with your employees, business partners and customers.

- ∞ If there are different departments within your company, make sure that they strengthen each other through the exchange of experiences, by helping each other, and by pushing each other to a higher level.

- ∞ Always search for and encourage the things that bind employees and departments together. Find a common goal and define everyone's place within the 'big picture'.

- ∞ Do not tolerate conflicts, internal political games, a silo mentality or overdeveloped sub-cultures.

- ∞ Opt for 'disciplined collaboration': combine the benefits of a de-centralised organisation (in which everyone has his own responsibilities) with the advantages of intense interaction and co-operation.

- ∞ Invest in long-term relationships with all your stakeholders.

- ∞ Seek to establish a long-term relationship with your customers, based on mutual dependence, loyalty and trust.

- ∞ At the same time, do not lose sight of the larger group of incidental and potential new customers, since this group brings in more revenue. Finding the right balance between both groups is crucial.

- ∞ Never forget or deviate from your core identity.

- ∞ Pay careful attention to all the elements that determine your reputation: your products and services, how innovative you are, how you treat your employees, how your senior management behaves, your financial performance, who sits on your board and your social engagement.

- ∞ Aim to create shared value, by creating economic value in such a way that major societal challenges are tackled, thereby allowing social value to be created.

6 US AGAINST THEM

An immortal company is a unique system that sets its boundaries and defends them against hostile attacks.

San Bernardino, California, December 2015. A married couple force their way into a care centre and shoot 14 people dead. Sixteen others are wounded. Four hours later, the killers are themselves killed in a firefight with the police. The FBI asks Apple to develop special software that will allow them to crack the pin code of the perpetrators' iPhone 5s. Apple refuses. Tim Cook later said of this incident: 'It felt bizarre to have ended up in a position where we are defending the civil liberties of the country against the government. Who would have ever thought this would happen? I never expected to be in this position. The government should always be the one defending civil liberties. There's a role reversal here.' Cook felt very uncomfortable about the situation. 'Fighting the government is not a thing we choose to do.'[185]

Even so, Apple set a clear boundary and refused to cross it. This brings us to the second principle of the integration function of the AGIL paradigm: 'An immortal company is a unique system that sets its boundaries and defends them against hostile attacks.' The FBI's request ran counter to Apple's core values. If Apple had agreed to the request, it would not only have betrayed its own values, but also itself and, more importantly, its millions of users.

So what was really going on? If Apple had agreed to the request, the FBI would not only be able to crack the code to the terrorists' phones, but also to Apple's jewel in the crown: its remarkable operating system. It is probable that many people were surprised by Cook refusal. If so, these people underestimated the strength of Apple's conviction, right from its very earliest days, that this operating system is superior to all others. It is this, the company believes, that makes it unique and sets it apart from its rivals. The system must be protected at all costs from external threats, no matter where these threats come from. For Apple, this incident was a matter of principle: it would create a precedent that might lead to a flood of similar requests from the government. This might ultimately compromise the privacy of every Apple user. The company was therefore faced with a dilemma: security versus privacy. Tim Cook was in no doubt where his priority should lie: 'Privacy, in my point of view, is a civil liberty that our Founding Fathers thought of a long time ago and concluded it was an essential part of what it was to be an American. Sort of on the level, if you will, with freedom of speech and freedom of the press.'[186]

For Apple, protecting people's privacy has always been an important guide to its actions. To go against this now would have been a direct and self-inflicted attack against its own core identity.

Defining and marking your territory

If it wants to survive, the fact that a company needs to grow into a strongly integrated social system implies that it must have powerful internal drivers that allow it to distinguish itself from and defend itself against (hostile) external forces. There is a clear dividing line. Parsons compared it with a 'watershed' that is kept in place by mechanisms that mark the system's boundaries and protect it against outside threats.[187] At the same time, this idea of 'the enemy without' has a motivating effect on both employees and loyal customers.

Immortal companies define and mark their territory carefully. Their boundaries help to determine their identity and what makes them unique. They represent everything by which a brand wants to distinguish itself from the competition. Companies and brands can demarcate their territory at three different levels: (1) by a strong brand positioning; (2) by setting up market barriers; (3) by taking legal measures (this is the most drastic approach).

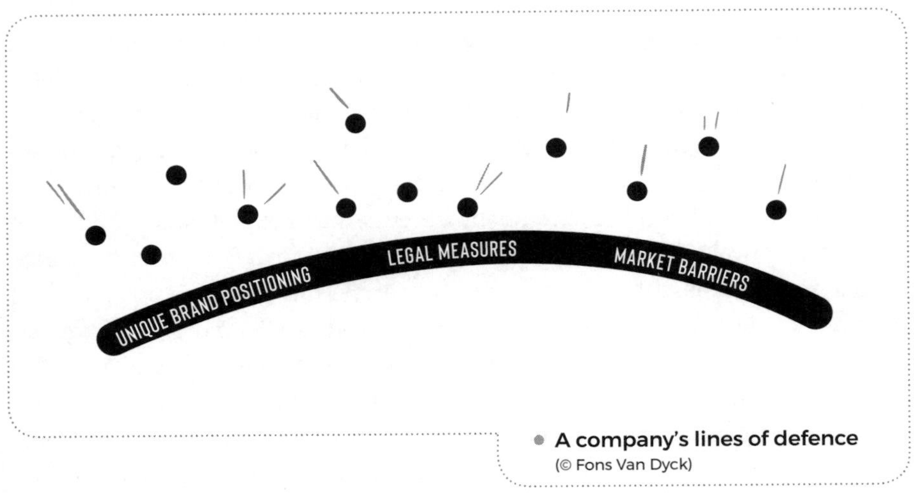

A company's lines of defence
(© Fons Van Dyck)

Unique brand positioning

In the previous chapter, I discussed at some length the importance of having a strong brand positioning and how this can be achieved; for example, through the creation of value propositions. It is inherent in a strong branding that the brand must clearly differentiate itself from the rest of its environment. In other words, it needs to stand out from the crowd, so that it can attract the attention of customers. Marketing specialist Kevin Keller talks about 'points of difference'. The brand must be relevant for its customers, must be fundamentally different from its competitors, and must keep its promises, not just now but also in the future. Brands that succeed in further strengthening these points of difference over time have a good chance of surviving in the long run.[188] That being said, it is not easy for companies to distinguish themselves in terms of content. For many consumers, most brands in a particular product category look much the same. For this reason, it is important for brands to establish an identity based on visual characteristics: name, logo, colours, symbols, design, general look-and-feel, etc. This visual identity is the first 'signpost' of the brand, since it is one that the customer cannot ignore, even if he wants to. As you might expect from Apple, its visual identity (which has changed little over the years) is a unique and highly distinctive weapon that signals its difference from its 'grey' competitors. Research has confirmed that distinctive brand elements of this kind create a more powerful distinguishing capacity in the minds of consumers and stakeholders than strategic positionings, which work brilliantly on an office drawing board, but are not always picked up by the outside world.[189]

Market barriers

If you want to be successful, it is useful to mark off your own territory in the market, a territory in which you alone are king. In other words, where no other players worth mentioning are active. In this way, you create your own new category or sub-category. If you can succeed in doing this, and at the same time can make yourself relevant and attractive to the consumer, you have a good chance of making a good profit. However, you need to set up market barriers to deter 'pirates', who might want to steal your ideas or muscle in on your territory. The art is to make competition too expensive or the likelihood of profits too small for it to be worth your rivals making the effort to become active in your new product category.

As listed below, there are different ways to stake your claim to your territory, some of which are described in the theories of Aaker and Kapferer.[190]

- ∞ Discourage investments by protecting your technology, by offering a superior performance or by developing a closed network of related products (cf. Apple).
- ∞ Emphasise your authenticity, so that other brands are quickly labelled as inferior 'copycats' (cf. Starbucks).
- ∞ Ensure that the customer can identify with your brand, so that he can feel connected to it (cf. Nike and Adidas).
- ∞ Dominate distribution and communication in your market (cf. Coca-Cola).
- ∞ Develop close ties with opinion-makers and decision-takers (cf. Tesla, up to 2018). This applies in particular to business-to-business brands.
- ∞ Keep production costs very low to create a lasting competitive advantage (cf. Dell).
- ∞ Focus on innovation, even if only incrementally, to remain relevant for new generations of consumers (cf. Procter & Gamble, L'Oréal).
- ∞ Create extra margin with more expensive products (cf. Nespresso capsules or Gillette razors).

Manning the barricades, with legal measures if necessary

Companies have good reason to defend their territory with every means at their disposal. Companies threatened by competitors attempting to break into their market risk losing market share and income. Worse still, if you allow someone into your territory, it is very difficult to get them out again. This can have serious consequences for you in the long term.

One way to discourage people from attacks on your territory is to show that you will react strongly to even the mildest of threats. There will be no messing about with you! Companies that have a reputation for being combative and unyielding will be attacked less frequently than weaker companies.

What you certainly must not do is make it easy for or even encourage others to enter your territory. You would be surprised how often this happens. For example, when companies with a unique technology allow others to make use of it on a license basis. Or when they enter into joint agreements whereby they both give each other access to their differentiating business information. These kinds of strategy can perhaps be interesting in the short term, because of the recurring income they can yield, but in time you may find that you have simply helped to create another competitor. Many companies that have set up collaborative projects in China have discovered this to their cost. Patents and intellectual property rights are an efficient way to prevent this from happening.[191]

If you are thinking of making an attack on someone else's territory, you need to be aware that you can expect a hard fight. What's more, in general it is not a successful strategy. Professor Tim Calkins of the Kellogg School of Management compares it with passing someone in the street and punching them in the face. In that case, you can also expect a strong reaction! If you want to attack someone, it is better to opt for a strategy that allows you make your attack from the flank. This involves making your pitch to the consumers who receive less attention from the dominant market player. For example, Apple did this in the 1980s when it focused its Macintosh on the creative and graphic sectors.[192]

Defending your boundaries the Apple way

Apple has always shown itself to be a strong and resilient player in the market. If you look back through the company's history, you can see that the FBI story with which we opened this chapter is by no means an isolated incident. This is something that warrants further examination. Where did Apple set its boundaries? Where did the threats come from? What resources did the company commit to defend itself? Did it sometimes make compromises?

The way in which Apple protected its unique operating system in the 1980s is a classic example of territorial defence. In the process, the company came into conflict several times with Microsoft and IBM. One of the pillars of this defence was Jobs' stubborn refusal to make IBM-compatible products. He explained his reasoning as follows: 'A lot of people thought we were nuts for not being IBM-compatible, for not living under IBM's umbrella. There were two key reasons we chose to bet our company on not doing that: the first was that we thought – and I think as history is unfolding, we're being proved correct – that IBM would fold its umbrella on the companies making compatible computers and absolutely crush them.' His second reason was his belief in the quality of Apple's products: 'If we can just get lots of computers to lots of people, it will make some qualitative difference in the world.'[193]

When IBM introduced its PC in 1981, Apple immediately profiled itself as the unapproachable dominant market player, whose technical supremacy IBM would never be able to equal. Mike Markulla, who was then CEO at Apple, reacted to the IBM threat in cheerful mood: 'We're the guys in the driver's seat... It's IBM who is reacting and responding to Apple... Short of World War III, nothing is going to knock us out of the box.' A few days later, Apple placed a full-page advertisement in *The Wall Street Journal* to welcome IBM to the PC market.[194] Bill Gates, who was on a visit to Apple on the day that IBM launched its computer, later commented on his surprise at what he saw: 'They didn't seem to care. It took them a year to realise what had happened.'[195]

Apple in trouble: selling the family jewels

There were long discussions over many years at Apple Computer about whether or not they should conclude licensing agreements with third parties for their operating system. Jobs had always vetoed this idea and so too did Sculley during his early years. But by the 1990s the computer landscape had changed dramatically. The so-called Wintel coalition between software developer Microsoft and micro-processor manufacturer Intel had taken over the lead from hardware producers like IBM and Apple. Apple was also having great difficulty in reaching its ambitious financial targets. A change of management led to a change of strategy in an attempt to make this possible. This change involved a 180° U-turn: the company decided that from then on it would enter into collaboration agreements with others, including arch-rival IBM.

The aim of this new strategy was to acquire a bigger market share, so that Apple could attract more developers and make more and even better products. Gil Amelio commented: 'Our first aim is to extend our platform. We will be enthusiastic licensors.'[196]

The results of this disastrous decision are well known. Apple continued to lose market share – and money – to its cloning licensees. As a result, the company found itself in a downwards spiral and soon hit rock bottom. Worse still, Apple had sold its soul to the enemy.

What, if anything, could the company do to escape from the hole it had dug for itself? For those who genuinely cared about Apple, one question was more important than all the rest: what was going to happen with the Mac OS? There were three options: start from scratch and develop a new OS; use an existing OS under license; or buy a new OS. The company decided to go for the third option and their choice fell on the NeXT Step operating system, owned by... Steve Jobs. Apple bought the system for 430 million dollars,[197] at the same time opening the door for founder Jobs return to the company where he had been sacked 10 years previously.

The Trojan horse

With Jobs back in the saddle, everyone in the company was confident that Apple would no longer be willing to make compromise deals for the use of its unique operating system. And indeed, one of Jobs' first decisions was to end collaboration with the cloners and to re-invest in Apple's own technology as a way to differentiate itself from its competitors. However, this determination was tempered by common sense. Apple and Jobs had learnt that in the 21st century it was sometimes necessary to weigh ideological principles against commercial objectives. As a result, Jobs did not hesitate to cut a deal with former 'enemy' Microsoft, so that Apple could make use of their popular Windows software programs. Microsoft even became an Apple shareholder. The announcement and the appearance of Bill Gates himself at the launch event was greeted with scepticism and even booing by the die-hard Apple fans, but Jobs knew it was the only way to throw his company a lifeline.

And it was much the same with the 2003 decision to make the iTunes Music Store available to Windows PC users. Jobs had originally adopted an 'over-my-dead-body' approach to the idea that Windows users should be give access to the iTunes Store, although he left the door slightly ajar for a possible change of heart: 'Until you can prove that it will make business sense, I'm not going to do it.' However, his team was eventually able to prove it to him, primarily with the argument that by opening up iTunes in this way, millions of Windows users would be able to sample the Apple experience. iTunes would therefore become a kind of Trojan horse, which would make it possible for Apple to win further share in the PC market. This made, to use Jobs' own words, perfect 'business sense'. He declared publically: 'iTunes for Windows is probably the best Windows app ever written.' In response to which, Bill Gates sent an e-mail to his Microsoft colleagues with the simple message: 'We're smoked.'[198]

Legal cases against Google and Samsung

Apple is much less amenable when others try to penetrate into the heart of its territory. Apple always regards this as a slap in the face and will spare no effort to defend what it believes is rightly theirs – as Google, for example, found to its cost. For many years, both tech giants had lived comfortably enough alongside each other, each operating in their own domain. Google was master in the search engine market, Apple dominated with its outstanding technological devices and applications. Between August 2006 and August 2009, Google's CEO Eric Schmidt even was a member of the Apple board. The problems started when both companies began to hunt in the same territory: for control over digital content, the related software and the tools to gain access to it. At the end of 2007, shortly after the launch of the iPhone, Google effectively declared war on Apple when it launched Android, its own operating system for smartphones. The tension between the two companies – now clearly rivals – exploded into open conflict in January 2010 when Google rolled out its Nexus One, its first telephone, developed in collaboration with HTC. As with Apple phones, it was possible to operate the screen by using your fingers to swipe, zoom, wipe and double-click. Jobs was convinced that these were all things that had been invented by Apple. The Google team countered with the argument that Apple could never prove this legally, because there was enough evidence to show that other companies had been developing comparable technology at the same time. Undeterred, Apple initiated legal action against both Google and HTC. Jobs was furious: 'I am going to destroy Android,' he said, 'because it's a stolen product. I am willing to go to thermonuclear war on this.'[199]

The court battle against Google clearly demonstrates the boundaries that Apple will allow no-one to cross unpunished. 'We did not enter the search business. They entered the phone business,' Jobs told his Apple employees. 'Make no mistake: Google wants to kill the iPhone. We won't let them.'[200] In May 2014, Apple and Google mutually agreed to drop all legal proceedings against each other. No further explanation was given.[201]

The legal run-ins with Samsung also demonstrate the lengths to which Apple is prepared to go to defend its boundaries. In 2010, the Korean company had brought a smartphone to market that looked identical to the iPhone 3GS, with a large screen and a metal frame. The user interface was also almost identical, as was the design of the agenda, clock and note-making function. With the marginal difference of just four icons, the main screen was a copy of the Apple model. Jobs and Cook were not prepared to take this lying down. They invited the chairman of Samsung, Lee Jae Yong, to Apple headquarters in Cupertino to issue him with a very clear warning: Samsung must stop copying Apple products – or else! Unfortunately, Yong failed to get the message. In February 2011, Samsung launched the Galaxy Tab 10.1, which looked even more like the iPad. It was now clear that Samsung would continue to make Apple replicas until it was forced to stop. And the only way to do that was in the courts. It was now open warfare between the two tech giants.[202]

Apple instigated a number of legal actions against Samsung, claiming billions in compensation, and even demanded that the sale of Samsung smartphones should be forbidden in the US. Apple won its cases in several American courts, but this hardly made up for the commercial losses it had suffered. As a result, the two companies continued their worldwide battle until 2014. They then agreed to a global ceasefire and to a settlement for their American dispute: Samsung agreed to pay Apple 548 million dollars in damages. This was exactly the amount that the US courts had suggested, but was less than the 1 billion dollars that Apple had originally claimed and much less than the 2.75 billion in losses that Apple believed it had incurred.[203]

A seventh myth: 'open'

It is another popular myth that companies must be 'open' to the outside world in order to succeed and survive in the long term. Perhaps. But that is only part of the story. The 'A' function of the AGIL paradigm certainly prescribes that companies need to carefully monitor external evolutions and, if possible, shape them to their own advantage. But at the same time, it is also vital to long-term survival that companies should set and manage their own clear boundaries. Throughout its history, Apple has always done this at crucial moments. If necessary, with legal action, like against Google and Samsung. Or even against the government, as in the case of the FBI. The company sees this as its duty: both Jobs and Cook have defended the company's defensive tactics as 'a matter of values'.

In reality, the question of whether a company should be 'open' or 'closed' is an irrelevant debate. The important thing is how you deal with your boundaries. In the case of Apple, for example, it is necessary to make a distinction between its fanatical defence of its 'crown jewels' (the unique technology of its operating system) and its more pragmatic approach to collaborative projects when this was compatible with commercial or financial interests and respect for its own borders. This was the case, for instance, with iTunes for Windows, when Apple was willing to temporarily open its borders to a dominant player like Microsoft. If Apple had failed to do this, it would eventually have found itself isolated. But because the company did decide to do it, it had the opportunity to make new customers and could continue to grow (the Trojan horse strategy).

The concept of 'border protection' illustrates that a company will only collaborate with another company if there is no other alternative or when the collaboration brings it the biggest share of the benefits. Business is not about altruism. In the first instance, it is about serving your own interests. That is the real strength of Apple, a strength that it owes not least to Steve Jobs.

THE DO'S-AND-DON'TS

- ∞ Carefully define and mark your territory.
- ∞ Define your 'points of difference': what makes your company unique and allows you to stand out from the crowd?
- ∞ Communicate your differentiating brand identity, but never lose sight of the basics: your name, logo, colours, symbols, design, general look-and-feel, etc.
- ∞ Make use of powerful internal drivers that allow you to distinguish yourself from and defend yourself against (hostile) external forces.
- ∞ The idea of 'the enemy without' has a motivating effect on both employees and loyal customers.
- ∞ If you want to be successful, it is useful to mark off your own territory in the market, a niche in which you alone are king.

- ∞ Set up market barriers, so that potential pirates and invaders are discouraged from entering your territory.
- ∞ If outsiders do attempt to enter your territory, react strongly, even to the mildest of threats. Companies that have a reputation for being combative and unyielding will be attacked less frequently than weaker companies.
- ∞ Do not be afraid to take legal action, if necessary.
- ∞ Do not make it easy for competitors to enter your territory by giving them access to what makes you unique.
- ∞ If you want to enter someone else's territory, you can best do this from the flank.
- ∞ When it serves your interests, use a Trojan horse: open your borders to another player, so that in time you can attract new customers and continue to grow. Only use this strategy when there is something in it for you.

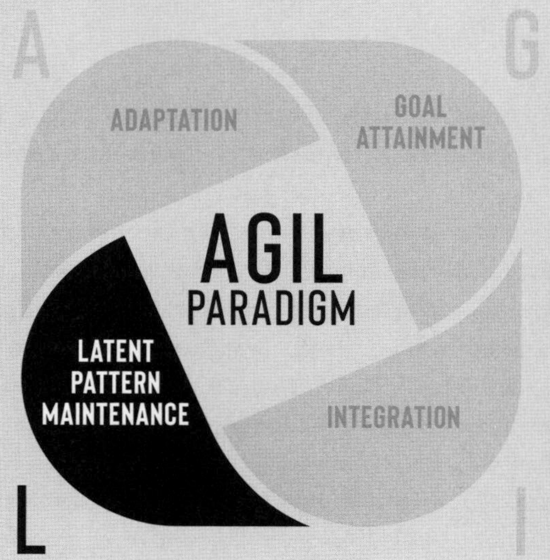

A

G

ADAPTATION

GOAL
ATTAINMENT

AGIL
PARADIGM

LATENT
PATTERN
MAINTENANCE

INTEGRATION

L

I

AG

L

LATENT PATTERN MAINTENANCE

L

LATENT PATTERN MAINTENANCE (LONG-TERM STABILITY)

In a disruptive environment, it is important to be able to adapt, but it is also necessary to keep hold of certain key elements that make your company what it is. You certainly need to mark out your boundaries and defend them, but the ultimate binding agent that will keep your company together and the ultimate compass that will guide you to safer waters are anchored in your identity and culture. Immortal companies have a unique identity and are deeply rooted in their internal culture. This identity and culture provide continuity and consistency over the long term and are the main constituents of the 'L' function of the AGIL-paradigm. This is the most important function of the paradigm, since it touches the very core of the company and is interwoven into its latent patterns, which must be cherished and preserved at all costs. As we shall see, this is most definitely not a 'soft' function and is much more than a 'nice to have'.

In chapter 7, I will look more deeply at the different dimensions of a company's identity, including its brand organisation. We will also see how in immortal companies this identity scarcely changes over time. It functions as a guiding star for the taking of all important decisions. In chapter 8, I will explain what we mean by the term 'company culture': not just the slogans and images projected at the outside world, but what really lives and breathes at the heart of the company. This will take us beyond formal structures and organograms, to reveal the informal and often difficult to discern relationships and circuits that can make all the difference. It is only by fully understanding the 'L' function, by appreciating and cherishing its value, by cultivating it internally and by passing it on from generation to generation that a company will ultimately be able to survive.

7 THE DNA OF THE COMPANY

An immortal company builds, cultivates and defends a unique identity that remains consistent over time.

When Steve Jobs returned to Apple in 1997, he saw an important glimmer of hope among the wreckage he inherited: 'The great thing is that Apple's DNA hasn't changed.'[204] Even so, he knew that a lot of repair work still needed to be done. The choices made by his predecessors as CEO – Sculley, Spindler and Amelio– had driven the company further and further away from its core identity. Jobs understood that he needed to get the company back on the right track as quickly as possible, but also realised that he would need to do this step by step. Gradually, this process became visible to the outside world. In 1998, *Fortune Magazine* wrote: 'Apple is becoming itself again.'[205] The use of the word 'itself' is significant: it meant that there was still an awareness among the public and the press of the things for which Apple stands. The DNA of an organisation is deeply rooted and in many cases outlives founders, owners, board chairmen and managing directors.

In this chapter, I will go in search of that identity. In the many books so far published about Apple and Steve Jobs, this is a subject that has received surprisingly little attention. The biographers and Apple experts have examined the history of the company and the actions and personality of Steve Jobs in great detail, but have seldom delved under the surface to see what really made Apple tick. Its deepest core remained largely unexamined. And that is precisely what I now intend to put right. What makes Apple so unique and so different from the rest? Where are its roots? How have these evolved over the years? What is the higher ideological goal and purpose of Apple, in addition to selling and developing computers? How has the company succeeded in maintaining its identity over the past 40 years? But also: what happens to a company when it strays away from its core?

The leading function

The search for the identity of Apple brings us back again to the AGIL paradigm of Talcott Parsons. In fact, we have arrived at one of its most crucial aspects. In the previous chapters, I have already explored the 'A' function (adaptation) and the 'G' function (goal attainment). Both these functions are focused on the outside world and are often found in one form or another in popular management books and training courses. It is the 'I' (integration) and 'L' functions (latent pattern maintenance or long-term consistency) that make the Parson's paradigm so interesting, because he takes things a stage further than the traditional literature. Both these latter functions are internally focused. While the ' A' and 'G' functions facilitate change and keep moving the company forwards, the 'I' and 'L' functions are the guardians of the company's identity. They make sure that things do not change too dramatically or too quickly, so that the company can remain in contact with its roots.

Within the AGIL paradigm, the 'L' function serves as a compass for the guidance and continued existence of the company. At moments when important decisions need to be taken, a successful management team will always test the decision against the company's DNA, to see if the company is moving in a direction that is compatible with its fundamental essence. It is this essence or identity that guarantees the company's consistency and continuity over the long term. In this sense, the 'L' function is also the most important and most defining function of the AGIL paradigm. This, then, leads us to the first principle of that 'L' function: 'An immortal company builds, cultivates and defends a unique identity that remains consistent over time.'

The three dimensions of identity

The essence of a company is best translated in its identity as an organisation brand. There are two different ways you can look at a brand. There is a minimalistic way, which focuses on the most basic elements: name, logo, colours, graphic design, etc. In this respect, Apple is once again a classic example. But there is also a more holistic way that takes account of a wider range of factors and therefore looks beyond the straightforward packaging and marketing of the brand, regarding it instead as a total 'gestalt'. A brand embodies the DNA of the company: its roots, its culture and its values – or that, at least, is what it should do. In this way, an organisation brand is the total sum of all the tangible experiences with a company and its activities (from technology through products to customer service), allowing the brand to create relevant value for its customers in the four dimensions of the ISP model. However, an organisation brand is also intangible, in the sense that it gives expression to all the unfulfilled wishes, dreams and aspirations of its employees, stakeholders and customers. The brand is therefore a relationship-builder. In my analysis of the survival chances of a company, I consciously adopt this holistic and integrated interpretation of the brand concept.

Following in the footsteps of and inspired by reputed academics like Theodore Levitt and Kevin Lane Keller, we can distinguish three dimensions of the identity of an organisation as a brand:[206]

The core identity

The core identity defines the reason for the company's existence. It describes its DNA, which has its origins in the founding of the company and is often summarised in the vision or mission statement. It reflects the company's view on societal themes, on the way people live, and on the future. In the case of Apple, this means the company's desire to 'change the world through technology'. For Volvo, it is 'safety'. For Coca-Cola, it is 'happiness in a bottle'. For Nike, it is 'everyone can be an athlete' (whatever your age, gender, religion, or ethnicity).

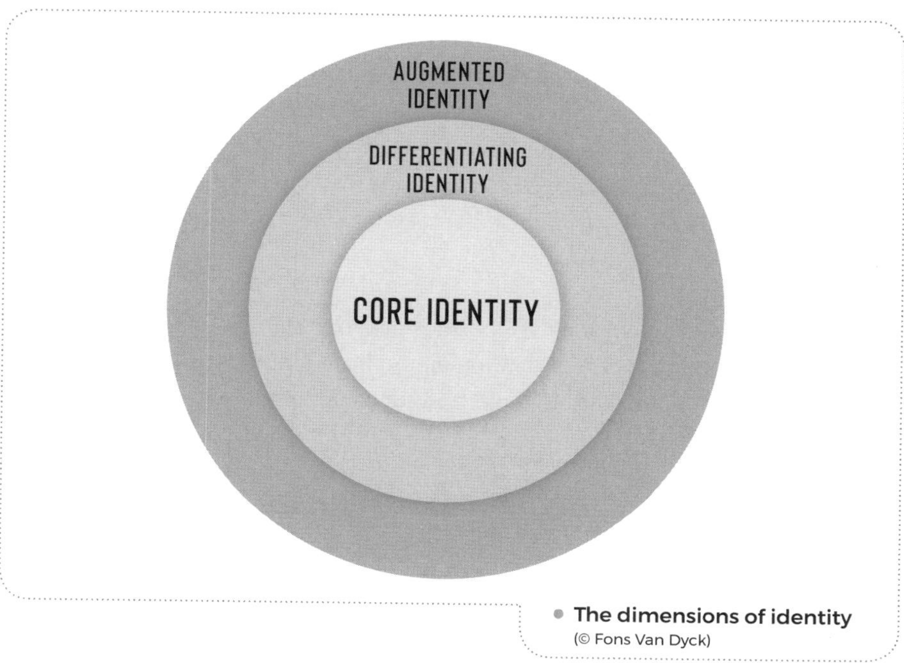

The dimensions of identity
(© Fons Van Dyck)

The differentiating identity
The differentiating identity determines what makes a company different from other comparable companies or brands. What are they better at than everyone else? What makes the brand unique? For a perfume, it might be a particular blend of fragrances. For Harley Davidson, it is the sound of the engine. For Apple, it is its unique and closed operating system that sets it apart from other computer companies. The App Store only contains applications approved by Apple and specially developed for its hardware. In this way, Apple forces consumers to make a choice. And if you choose for Apple, you have to go 'all the way'. It is their way or the highway. Love them or hate them. There is nothing in between.

The augmented identity
The augmented identity reflects all the elements that allow a company to truly shine for its customers. It defines the 'extras' that the brand offers to consumers over and above the generic product or service and is therefore additional to what is strictly necessary to satisfy those consumers' basic needs. It is these extras that make the customer feel happy, surprised or pleasantly challenged – and it is these sensations that tie customers to the brand for life. In the case of Apple, these extras are its simplicity and user-friendliness.

If you map out these three dimensions for a brand, you will have a good idea about its 'total' identity. This, in turn, will give you a good insight into its 'immortality' or sustainability. What makes it possible for a company to deal with change, without betraying its fundamental nature? This total identity acts as a compass for managers and shareholders across the generations. It is the key driver of the internal culture and the key determinant of the external image held by customers and stakeholders.

What do these three dimensions of identity mean for Apple in concrete terms? And how has the company succeeded in remaining itself (with just a few brief exceptions) throughout the trials, tribulations and successes of the past 40 years?

Apple's core identity: making the world a better place

The young Steve Jobs was a drop-out: he left university after his first year of studies, liked taking LSD and walked around on his bare feet. Together with Steve Wozniak, he was a child of the countermovement in Silicon Valley, where hippies and tech-nerds began to make their appearance in the late 1960s and early 1970s, with their dreams of changing the world and improving people's lives through technology. This is fundamentally where the deepest roots of Apple are to be found.

In his biography, Steve Wozniak wrote: 'We were talking about a world – a possible world – where computers could be owned by anybody, used by anybody, no matter who you were or how much money you had.' The two Steves saw the computer as an instrument to achieve social justice. Cheap computers would make it possible for people to realise ambitions that they had only been able to dream about in the past. 'Low-cost computers would empower people to do things they never could before... There was a lot of talk about being part of a revolution. How people lived and communicated was going to be changed by us, changed forever, changed more than anyone could predict exactly... In this, we were revolutionaries.'[207] During those early years, Jobs and Wozniak both often referred consciously and publically to these rebellious and revolutionary ideals. The same language also found its way into Apple's marketing campaigns. During the presentation for the launch of the Macintosh in 1984, Jobs quoted directly from his favourite Bob Dylan song: 'For the loser now/Will be later to win/For the times they are a-changing.' His biographer Isaacson commented that in this way the multi-millionaire linked these verses not only with the company's 'resurrection' but also with his own rebellious self-image.[208] Lee Clow, creative director at Chiat/Day, the advertising agency that made the '1984' commercial for the Mac, remembers: 'It explained Apple's philosophy and purpose – that people, not just governments and big corporations, should run technology.'[209] Or as another commentator put it: 'It was to be the establishment versus the counterculture'.[210] Sculley, who came to Apple from Pepsi-Cola, later wrote in his biography that during his initial recruitment interview Jobs had asked him: 'Do you want to spend the rest of your life selling sugared water or do you want a chance to change the world?' And he added: 'Apple grew from a desire not to make money but to make a difference in the world.'[211]

This same sub-text is also clearly evident in the 'Think Different' campaign, which ran between 1997 and 2002, in which Apple's image was again linked directly to revolutionary thinkers like Martin Luther King Jr., Mahatma Ghandi and John Lennon.

Tim Cook continued with this alternative, almost militant approach, but in a different manner. Jobs projected his message to the world via spectacular commercials and public appearances. Cook prefers to give his highly personal opinions on societal themes in newspaper interviews and opinion pieces. In his office he has photographs of Martin Luther King Jr. and Bobby Kennedy, two of the leading campaigners for equal civil rights in the US in the 1960s. Even today, he still regards them as his great heroes and examples. He once explained: 'Everyone deserves a basic level of human rights, regardless of their colour, regardless of their religion, regardless of their sexual orientation, regardless of their gender.'[212] In contrast to many other CEOs, he does not shirk from taking a clear standpoint, even if he knows it is not likely to be popular. On occasions, Cook has even expressed criticism of the American president, Donald Trump. In particular, he took strong exception to the proposal of the president's policy-makers to withdraw the protected status of the so-called Dreamers and put them out of the country. It is also known that he personally phoned the president to urge him not to withdraw from the Paris climate agreement.[213] As he commented in *The Washington Post*:: 'I think every generation has the responsibility to enlarge the meaning of human rights. I take the view that a CEO of Apple today should participate in the national discussion on these types of issues.'[214] Cook also has a special connection with the LGBT community. In 2013, he wrote an opinion piece for *The Wall Street Journal* in which he supported proposed legislation that would offer better protection to homosexual, lesbian, bisexual and transgender employees. A year later, he made his own homosexuality public in another opinion piece, this time published in *Business Week*: 'While I have never denied my sexuality, I haven't publicly acknowledged it either, until now. So let me be clear: I'm proud to be gay, and I consider being gay among the greatest gifts God has given me.'[215] Each year, thousands of Apple employees, including Cook, take part in the annual San Francisco Gay Pride Parade.

Wanting to change the world is a noble ambition, but there is one other important question that needs to be asked: how does this square with the importance of the company's financial results? In 2012, Apple was briefly the most valuable company in the world and was closely followed by analysts and investors. Even so, in a 2014 interview with PBS Cook left no doubt about where Apple's priorities lie: 'Values come before value.' He continued: 'Too many companies focus on trying to get the largest market cap. And that doesn't drive people… but changing the world – these are the things that people work for.'[216] At a shareholders' meeting, an Apple investor once insisted that the company should only invest in sustainability initiatives if they promised a good ROI. Cook immediately told him: 'We do things because they are the right thing to do, and protecting the environment is a critical example.' When the investor continued to press his point, Cook is reported to have answered: 'If you can't accept our position, you shouldn't own Apple stock.'[217]

An eighth myth debunked: ideological campaigns

It is often said that the strong ideological leaning of Apple (the 'why') and the rebellious nature of Steve Jobs have been the key factors in the company's success. In particular, the '1984' and 'Think Different' campaigns are cited as examples to support this claim. It is no doubt true that campaigns of this kind helped to keep the most loyal Apple fans on board at the most critical times in the company's history. But if you look at the figures – the actual return on investment – there is only one possible conclusion: notwithstanding the massive marketing budgets for these ideological campaigns, they did not result in the hoped-for commercial success. In the case of '1984', income from sales lagged a long way behind the expenditure on PR and advertising, which was one of the reasons why Jobs was forced to leave. And the 'Think Different' campaign was primarily intended to encourage Apple's own staff and retain the confidence of the company's most dedicated customers. But for average computer users at the end of the 1990s, revolution and the counterculture were nothing more than a distant echo, far removed from the more pressing concerns of their everyday lives. They felt no connection whatsoever with Apple's tribal group of radical free thinkers.

Ideology is certainly important for an immortal company, as an internal compass and as a binding agent. But ideology alone will not help you to make it in the tough outside world of business. This is the lesson of the ISP model that we discussed in chapter 2. Again, the history of Apple confirms this: it was not enough for the company simply to keep on reminding people time after time about the counterculture of the 1970s. It needed a more relevant and more meaningful positioning – which it finally achieved with the 'i' series – if it wanted to attract new generations of customers and secure enough income to break into new markets worldwide, particularly in the emerging Chinese economy.

Apple's differentiating identity: proprietary technology

From its earliest years, Apple has differentiated itself from other companies by putting its unique technology at the heart of its activities. Technology, Apple has always believed, can save the world. But only if that technology is the very best in the world. And that means Apple technology.

When Steve Jobs and Steve Wozniak first founded Apple Computer, they envisaged that everything would be geared around the engineers, the actual 'computer builders'. These engineers had to be given the time, space and resources they needed to develop the best PCs on the planet. They were the organisation's core and they practiced 'one of the most worthwhile professions in the world'.[218] Jobs and Wozniak took as their example Hewlett-Packard, a company which also had an extremely strong engineering culture. Wozniak, who was more or less the living embodiment of superior technology-nerd, wrote in his autobiography: 'We wanted Apple to have the amazing employee moral we thought HP had got from treating its engineers like upper-class citizens.'[219]

And the Apple engineers did indeed develop the company's own unique and highly individual operating system with a technology that was very different from the MS-DOS standard system that was bring used by IBM. For Jobs and Wozniak, innovation was their greatest asset and neither man wanted to lower himself and their company by building a computer that was compatible with other computers. This would mean limiting themselves to technology that (in their eyes) was already by definition outdated. This they could never do, because they believed passionately that they and their engineers were better than that; better, in fact, than all the rest. And (if the stories are true) they behaved accordingly. Engineers and designers were treated like royalty at Apple, much more so than the managers. This attitude was sometimes described in Silicon Valley circles as the 'NIH culture', standing for 'Not Invented Here'. In other words, if Apple didn't make it, it must be no good.[220] Be that as it may, there is no disputing that Apple's unique and superior operating system was the jewel in the company's crown. As John Sculley once put it: 'What made Apple different and continues to make it different from any other of our competitors is that we own the crown jewels, our own systems software technology. Nobody else does. And nobody can clone the Macintosh like they can clone IBM PCs.'[221]

As we have already seen, there were other periods during Apple's history when engineers were not treated with quite the same reverence. Following the failure of the Newton, the R&D budget was drastically cut and there was a disastrous U-turn in company policy that made it possible for third parties to clone the Mac. Although this almost resulted in bankruptcy, Apple managed to survive and Steve Jobs was called back just in time to save the day, by giving back to the company's own technology the prominent position he felt it deserved. He had a very good reason for doing so. As he explained: 'That way, we can set our own priorities and look at things in a more holistic way from the point of view of the customer.'[222]

From the turn of the century onwards, Apple devoted increasing attention to the interfaces in its devices. Thanks to the symbiosis between its own software and hardware applications, Apple was able to offer its customers superior ease of use, while the rise of the internet enhanced the customer experience even further. At that time, Microsoft was doing precisely the opposite to Apple: it offered PC manufactures licences to use their Windows operating system. Some critics encouraged Jobs to do the same, but he refused point blank. And he was right, because it was this stubborn refusal that later made possible the remarkable success of the iPhone and the iPad. Even after Jobs died, Apple continued to set its focus on technological superiority. Tim Cook expressed this commitment to excellence in the following terms: 'We want to make the world's best products that really enrich people's lives. That hasn't changed. And we do that through owning the primary technologies. So from my point of view, the most important thing is the same...the core is the same. The value, the value system is the same.'[223]

Apple's augmented identity: simplicity

'Simplicity is the ultimate sophistication.' This saying, thought to have been made originally by Leonardo da Vinci, had pride of place on the brochure for the launch of the Apple II in 1977. It also formed the basis for what Jobs would try to apply throughout the rest of his career: simplicity and user-friendliness as the most important criteria. Making products simpler and better was the mission of everyone working at Apple, but always combined with refined design. That is still the way the company operates today and explains why customers often become 'fans' of the Apple brand.

Jobs and his team were strongly influenced by the prototype computer they had seen during a visit to the Xerox PARC in 1979. It was the first machine to have an interface with icons, which could be operated by the device that later became known as a 'mouse'. Jobs' biography recalls how he experienced that seminal moment: 'I could see what the future of computing was destined to be.'[224]

Jobs was equally impressed by the functional design of the German Bauhaus movement from the 1920s. This group of artists, craftsmen and architects believed that art should be simple but expressive, making use of pure lines and forms to symbolise rationality and functionality. The movement's founder, Walter Gropius, summarised its philosophy in two brief sentences: 'God is in the details' and 'Less is more'. The designs of the German consumer electronics manufacturer Braun also appealed to Jobs' love of simplicity. He made this crystal-clear at a design conference in 1983, when he commented: 'What we are going to do is make the products high-tech, and we're going to package them cleanly, so that you know they're high-tech. We will fit them in a small package, and then we can make them beautiful and white, just like Braun does with electronics.'[225] This was a message Jobs continued to emphasise: 'We will make them bright and pure and honest about being high-tech, rather than having a heavy industrial look of black, black, black, like Sony. That's our approach. Very simple, and we're really shooting for Museum of Modern Art quality. The way we're running this company, the product design, the advertising, it all comes down to this: let's make it simple. Really simple.'[226] The Macintosh was the first Apple product to be designed exactly the way Jobs wanted it: 'We need it to have a classic look that won't go out of style, like the Volkswagen Beetle.'[227]

Later, at the end of the 1990s, Jobs found a design 'soul mate' in Jonathan Ive. Ive had started working for Apple in 1996 and, like Jobs, he was a big fan of the German industrial designer Dieter Rams, who worked for Braun. Ive continued to play the simplicity card but took it to the next level, commenting: 'You have to deeply understand the essence of a product in order to be able to get rid of the parts that are not essential.'[228] Ive's ultimate objective was to make design so simple that it almost 'disappeared'. The best example of this aspiration is undoubtedly the iPod. This was designed as a single enclosed whole, without an on-off button or a battery door. In fact, the device was so simple you could almost forget it had been designed at all.[229] Much the same is true of the iPhone, where Apple succeeded in making a highly complex piece of technology both elegant and, above all, user-friendly. 'I was really designing interfaces that my father could use,' recalled one of the Apple design team. 'We were trying to create systems that people could use intuitively, that they could trust.'[230]

Even today, quality design and ease of use remain the twin mantras for Apple employees worldwide. These are the characteristics automatically associated with the Apple identity in the minds of customers and suppliers alike. It is also this same simple, elegant and functional design that transform loyal customers into brand ambassadors, who often promote Apple products with a fanaticism that other brands can only dream of.

Apple in trouble: no soul, no heart

The three layers in the identity of Apple have perhaps changed and evolved through time, but they have always remained latently present, right from the company's founding, up to the present day. And as we have already done throughout the book, we can learn from Apple's mistakes in this respect. Because the periods when things went badly for Apple coincided with moments when the company forgot to respect its own identity in its rush to try and adapt to a rapidly changing world. This not only resulted in a public loss of face, but was also a betrayal of everything the company stands for.

Consider, for example, the 1980s. Although Apple had already been able to reap the rewards of its unique and differentiating nature, it was having major problems to establish itself in the fast-growing market for personal computers. Ideology alone was unable to set the company on the right track. It was clear that the period of the early followers was now over, but it was less clear where Apple was going to find its new customers. Should it target the private or the professional market? The Apple III and the Lisa had both missed the boat and Jobs knew that he needed to do something quickly to put things right. That was why he recruited Sculley, with his marketing knowledge and experience at Pepsi-Cola. Unfortunately (although perhaps with the best of intentions), Apple now opted for a radical change of course. Instead of concentrating on 'great products' as its first priority, it decided to shift its focus to commercial and financial objectives. In effect, Apple stopped being a computer engineering company and became a marketing company. The days of proudly launching groundbreaking products onto the market, of surprising its customers with new applications and graceful design, of letting its engineers 'do their own thing': all this was now swept away. Instead, Apple went hunting for more and more customers and didn't really care how or where it found them. As a result, it no longer made the effort to try and attract them with top-class innovation, which had always been the secret of the company's success in the past.

Wozniak – who designed the Apple II from scratch – readily admitted how difficult it was for him as an engineer to accept that the marketing department now ruled the roost: 'This is going to be a marketing company. The product is going to be driven, in other words, by demands that the marketing department finds in customers. This is the very opposite of a place where engineers just build whatever they love, and marketing comes up with ways to market them. I knew that it was going to be a challenge for me.'[231] Some years later, Wozniak quietly left the company he had co-founded.

But things weren't all that easy for change manager Sculley either. When he arrived at Apple he found a deep-rooted experimental culture that he soon discovered was not all that easy to alter. Internal opposition to his new strategy quickly grew. In his autobiography, he wrote of this period: 'Now I knew what one wag at Apple's advertising agency meant when he joked: "What's the difference between Apple and the Boy Scouts of America? The Boy Scouts have adult supervision."'[232]

Inevitably, it soon came to a clash between Jobs and Sculley. The cause of their disagreement was the price of the Macintosh. Jobs was furious at Sculley's plans to increase margins: 'It will destroy everything we stand for. I want to make this a revolution, not an effort to squeeze out profits.'[233] In the end, Sculley got his way but the results were disastrous. Twenty-five years later Jobs was still angry when he thought about it: 'It is the main reason Macintosh sales slowed and Microsoft got to dominate the market.' Apple had landed in its first mega-crisis and its own identity was at stake.

After the departure of Wozniak and Jobs, Sculley wanted to make Apple 'a more disciplined, grown-up company'.[234] And that is precisely what he did. For many years, Apple was just an 'ordinary' company that made and sold computers, where the staff did their work diligently and all the rules and regulations – neatly set down on paper – were respected. The company followed the wishes of its customers, made sure its people were kept happy, and provided added value to its shareholders. But the drive and passion of the early years were gone. One member of staff commented anonymously: 'They've cut the heart out of Apple and substituted an artificial one.'[235] Apple had turned its back on its own identity. Unique design was replaced by mainstream design. Premium products were no longer a priority. Instead, other companies were now licensed to clone Apple's technology. In short, Apple had lost its way. Worse still, it had lost its soul.

The value of the brand

When Jobs arrived back at Apple towards the end of the 1990s, he found that there was not much left to build on, except for one thing: the Apple brand. That Jobs appreciated the value of this brand should surprise no-one: for him, the brand had always been the core of the company. All that was necessary was to breathe new life into it. In a 1998 interview with *Time* he commented: 'What are the great brands? Levi's, Coke, Disney, Nike. Most people would put Apple in the same category. You could spend billions of dollars on marketing to create a brand, but you still couldn't rival Apple. But for now, Apple is doing nothing with that big advantage. What does Apple actually stand for? Apple stands for people who follow the paths that others don't follow, for people who use computers to change the world, to create things that can make a difference and not for people who only want to use a computer for work.'[236]

Although Apple's image had been seriously damaged, Jobs was determined to keep the same name and logo, whereas many companies in similar circumstances would have changed both name and logo, in an attempt to turn the tide. The only thing Jobs changed was to replace the rainbow colours with a monochrome colour. 'Water' and 'glass' themes would follow later.

Jobs had every reason to be grateful that 'his' brand had survived the company's recent troubles. Battered and bruised, but still more or less intact. This was a strong trump card and Jobs knew that it would have been madness to throw it away. Academic research has demonstrated the many advantages that this kind of strong brand can confer:[237]

∞ an improved perception of the performance of the product;
∞ greater customer loyalty;
∞ reduced vulnerability to competition and market crises;
∞ bigger margins;
∞ easier customer reaction in response to product price rises or decreases;
∞ wide support from and collaboration with partners;
∞ more effective marketing actions;
∞ increased opportunities for brand extensions and licensing agreements.

Of course, it is also crucial to know if your brand is just as important for each product and in each country. This, too, has been the subject of much research, which has confirmed that there are indeed product and country variations. These variations can be explained by factors such as age, gender, how much information per product is needed, etc. For example, a comparison of twenty products in five countries has revealed that brands are most important for medium-sized cars and cigarettes, and have least value for paper handkerchiefs and drug store products. The mobile phone category made it into the top five in countries such as France, Spain and the UK, and showed a high level of stability over a longer period (2006-2008).[238]

In 2002, professors Thomas J. Madden and Susan M. Fournier, together with financial expert Frank Fehle, investigated the influence of investments in marketing on the creation of added value for shareholders.[239] They monitored the financial results of the strongest brands (based on a list compiled by Interbrand) between 1994 and 2001, and compared these with the results of companies that had invested less in their brand(s). Their conclusion was that the strong brands do significantly better on the stock market. Investing in brand identity generates extra income, not only for brands that still need to prove themselves, but also for established brands.

A Swedish study has also shown that companies with a strong brand generally generate twice as much profit as companies that do not invest in their brand.[240] In fact, it is widely accepted that brands determine a large part of a company's market value; up to 30 %, according to a report by Milward Brown Optimor. For some brands this figure is even higher; the 'Nike' brand, for example, is estimated to represent 84 % of the value of the controlling company.[241]

In 2017, 20 years after Jobs' return to the company, Apple was assessed by marketing consultant Interbrand as having a brand value of 184 154 million dollars, a 3 % increase on the previous year and a figure that far outstripped brands like Google and Microsoft.[242] There can be no doubt: the strength of Apple is first and foremost the strength of the brand, in its most holistic sense.

Consistency wins in the long run

It is not enough simply to build up a strong brand for your company; you need to maintain that brand and its identity over a long period in the face of all the challenges and changes that you will inevitably meet along the way. That is the most important conclusion from the book *Built to Last* by Jim Collins and Jerry Porras. Their research has revealed that sustainable companies almost without exception are visionary companies with a strong ideological component, clear values and a higher goal. Their entire operations are geared to these differentiating characteristics, also in the long term. This conclusion runs contrary to what has often been assumed in popular management literature, where disruption and adapting to change are usually put forward as the best survival strategies.[243]

Collins later examined the difficulties experienced by Apple in the 1990s. He concluded that Apple got into trouble not because its recipe for success no longer worked, but because it lacked the discipline to remain true to this original recipe.[244] When Jobs returned in 1997, he immediately took the company back to its successful roots and was able in this way to avoid further damage. Collins concluded that no company operating at the highest level can survive without finding a balance between continuity and change. Failure to do this leaves you open to the potentially destructive power of external forces.[245]

Being consistent in terms of your identity also helps to reduce costs. We have already seen earlier in the book how it is important for a company to be ever-present and to continue attracting new customers. For the group of incidental customers in particular, this means being almost constantly and identifiably in the picture. If a brand transforms too radically, it may confuse this large and important group of its customers. They no longer recognise the brand they thought they once knew. As a result, all the credit and confidence that has been so carefully built up over the years can be irretrievably lost, almost overnight. Companies in transformation must always be aware of this risk and must seek to find the right balance between past and future for their image, house style and identity.[246] Above all, it is important to resist the temptation to surf on the latest trends and hypes. All too often, these are here today and gone tomorrow. Companies must certainly continue to have an eye for changes in their environment and must adjust accordingly, but without compromising their true nature.

Triangulation

Although continuity is a decisive factor in brand identity, it is also necessary for a company to evolve in a credible manner. Markets become more fragmented and products fall in and out of fashion. Brands need to adjust to the new needs of customers. In this respect, it is important that every new product embodies the core values of the company producing it. To make this possible, the company needs to search for higher and common points of reference that can bind people to the product. This is a process known as 'triangulation'. It is best to keep these reference values as simple and as limited as possible. At the same time, they must be a source of inspiration that can be grafted onto every product and can be experienced by the customers. The more a company deviates from its original 'recipe', the stronger its 'intangible' identity must be.[247]

Triangulation also has an impact on the naming of products. When Apple Computer introduced the new Macintosh in 1998, it added the prefix 'i' to the product name: iMac. During the launch event, Steve Jobs spent a full 30 minutes explaining what this 'i' stood for: initially for 'internet', but also for a number of other aspects related to computers, such as 'individual', 'instruction', 'information' and 'inspiration'. Of these, the first – the importance of the individual – was probably the most relevant in the company's eyes. Apple later continued with this pattern of naming, resulting in iTunes, iMovie, iPhoto, iBook, iPod, iPhone, iPad, iCloud and iOS.

In 2007, when the iPhone was launched, Apple decided to drop the word 'Computer' from its name. From then on, Apple was just plain Apple. In this way, the company wanted to make clear that it had entered into the consumer electronics market. It was a smart move. Apple's non-computer products would very quickly account for more than half its income.

In 2014, Apple decided that the time had come to drop the 'i' prefix from its new products; hence Apple Watch and Apple Pay. There was no official communication from the company about this change, but it was rumoured to be a patents issue: in Europe, the iWatch name was already registered by Probendi Ltd.[248]

Of course, new names can also be an indication that Apple continues to work on new products and technologies: self-driving cars, payment systems, smart watches, etc. But the powerful brand name 'Apple' always makes clear that these new products come from the same impressive and reliable stable. This is significant. As the market continues to expect increasingly more, financial analysts have a clear preference for strong corporate brands like Apple above individual product brands. The wishes of the Chinese and Asian market (now Apple's second largest market), where they attach huge significance to strongly integrated brands, are also a factor that needs to be taken into account.

Subtle changes of name of this kind indicate that the brand is evolving with equal subtlety. This is necessary in a market that is constantly in movement. But the uniqueness and identity of the brand always remains intact.

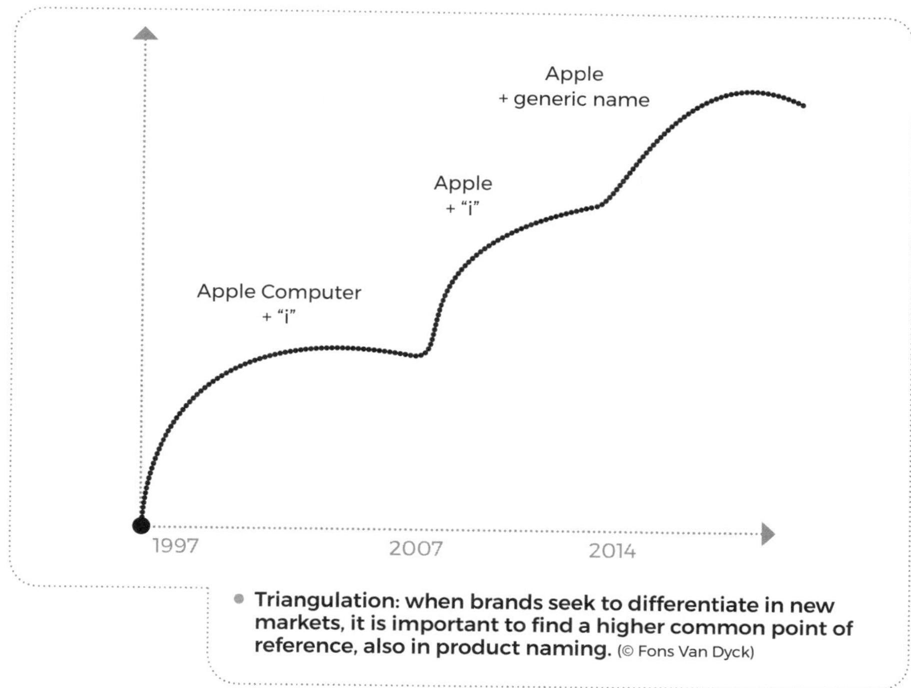

Triangulation: when brands seek to differentiate in new markets, it is important to find a higher common point of reference, also in product naming. (© Fons Van Dyck)

Finally...

Stock-listed companies often use the excuse that it is impossible for them to cultivate a long-term identity and set long-term objectives because of their need to meet short-term financial targets each quarter. This, however, is a fallacy, and has been proven as such by various reliable studies. McKinsey, for example, concluded that companies like Unilever, AT&T and Amazon, which do not allow themselves to be pressurised by quarterly deadlines, perform better in almost every area than comparable companies with a more short-term focus. The figures leave no room for doubt: the average turnover growth and profit, measured between 2001 and 2014, were up to 47 % higher for the companies with a more long-range perspective. What's more, society benefits as well: this strong group of companies created 12 000 more jobs during the review period than their counterparts.[249]

Working for the long term is therefore beneficial, although you sometimes need plenty of patience and perseverance. Look at Apple: it took Jobs 7 years (1997-2004) before he could get the company back on the right track and see this effectively translated into higher sales figures and a higher share price. But in the end his persistence paid off. He who dares, wins.

L

THE DO'S-AND-DON'TS

- ∞ Be true to your identity, also in the long term. Make this identity explicit: map it out carefully and give attention to all its different dimensions: core identity, differentiating identity and augmented identity.
- ∞ Adapt to market change, but without betraying your roots. Search for the right balance between necessary adjustment and maintaining your identity.
- ∞ Avoid change for change's sake or disruption for disruption's sake.
- ∞ Always keep your higher ideological goal firmly in view. Maintain your focus and drive. Never switch to 'automatic pilot'.

L

- ∞ Be disciplined enough to stick to your original recipe for success. Resist the temptation to opt for the easiest solution in the short term.

- ∞ Remember that continuity and a consistent identity can also reduce costs.

- ∞ Never use the excuse that a long-term approach is impossible because of your need to satisfy shareholders with good results each quarter.

- ∞ For a brand to survive, it takes time, courage and money. Be patient and persistent. It will pay off in the end.

- ∞ The identity of a company can never be encapsulated in KPIs, dashboards or due diligence.

L

8 THE HIDDEN FORCE OF CULTURE

An immortal company is based on a deeply anchored culture that is difficult to change.

'Steve's greatest contribution and gift is the company and its culture. He cared deeply about that.' So said Tim Cook in an interview during which he reflected on Jobs' legacy.[250] 'Culture' is a crucial key concept for the immortality of a company. In chapter 7, I discussed the importance of a company's identity as an essential element within the 'L' function of the AGIL paradigm. In this chapter, I am going to take things a stage further and look at the influence of culture on a company's performance and its continued existence. This leads us to the following principle: 'An immortal company is based on a deeply anchored culture that is difficult to change'. A company's culture is the foundation on which its identity and values are built. It is the basis of how everything works within the company: how it deals with its staff and its customers, how it organises and agrees its procedures, how it assesses and judges people and events, etc. For each of these aspects (and many more besides), it always takes the same shared identity and values as its starting point. Sometimes this culture is formally present; often it is slumbering informally, just beneath the surface. In this latter respect, Parsons refers to 'latency'. Whichever form it takes, the company's culture is translated every day through its identity and values into actual practice. Professor Edgar H. Schein (Sloan School of Management at MIT), who has devoted his entire career to the study of company culture, defines culture as 'a pattern of shared basic assumptions learned by a group as it solved its problems of external adaptation and internal integration'.[251]

It's the culture, stupid

'Corporate culture' is a popular subject nowadays in management literature; in particular, how it applies to young start-ups that feel a powerful need to differentiate themselves from everyone else. To do this, they often make use of a stimulating and 'hip' culture as a way to attract promising new talent. That being said, company culture continues to be a concept that is difficult to pin down and even harder to change. It is more than just posters on office walls and teambuilding activities. But what exactly?

There are probably as many definitions of culture as there are academics and consultants writing about it. Through a synthesis of the seminal work by Schein, Shalom Schwartz, Geert Hofstede and other leading scholars, Harvard Business School academics and Spencer Stuart Consultants have recently identified four generally accepted attributes:

Shared. *Culture is a group phenomenon. It cannot exist solely within a single person, nor is it simply the average of individual characteristics. It resides in shared behaviours, values and assumptions, and is most commonly experienced through the norms and expectations of a group; in other words, its unwritten rules.*

Pervasive. *Culture permeates multiple levels and applies very broadly within an organisation. Sometimes it is even equated with the organisation itself. It is manifest in collective behaviours, physical environments, group rituals, visible symbols, stories and legends. Other aspects of culture are unseen, such as mindsets, motivations, unspoken assumptions and 'action logics' (mental models of how to interpret and respond to the world around you).*

Enduring. *Culture can direct the thoughts and actions of group members over the long term. It develops through critical events in the collective life and learning of a group. People are drawn to organisations with characteristics similar to their own. Conversely, organisations are more likely to select individuals who seem to 'fit in', while over* *time those who do not fit in tend to leave. In this way, culture becomes a self-reinforcing social pattern that grows increasingly resistant to change and outside influences.*

Implicit. *An important and often over-looked aspect of culture is that despite its subliminal nature, people are effectively 'programmed' to recognise and respond to it instinctively. It acts as a kind of silent language.*[252]

In his original description of culture, Schein makes a direct link with the leadership in a company. According to the professor, culture and leadership are two sides of the same coin. You cannot have one without the other and you cannot understand one without understanding the other. Leadership within the company must ensure that certain essentials patterns, which form the company's core, are preserved, also in the long term. Once again, this involves the challenge of finding the right balance between long-term patterns of behaviour and identity on the one hand and adjusting sufficiently to a changing environment on the other hand. For leaders in today's volatile markets this is no easy task.

Schein argues that if a leader is an entrepreneur who founds a new company (cf. Jobs), he can install the culture he wants by repeatedly attempting to persuade his people to accept the importance of certain convictions, values and opinions. If he succeeds, this is the start of a shared culture. The concept of 'leadership' within a company therefore represents everything that the (founding) leader believes. Over time, all these different elements will coalesce to create what people within the company will come to regard as 'appropriate leadership'.[253] It is also important to note that a culture can outlive its leader, continuing to shape the company's way of doing things long after the leader has gone. This has twice been the case at Apple; first after Jobs' dismissal in the 1980s and again after his death in 2011. The Apple culture has survived the demise of the Apple leader.

Collective dream, individual struggle

Although Apple has been the subject of much attention in the literature, there are very few public sources that can accurately chart the nature and progress of the company's culture during its 40-year history. One of the rare exceptions is a study made by Professor Schein in 1991. He was called in as an external consultant by CEO Sculley to investigate how the culture within Apple might best be used to influence growth and also what people would be needed to achieve this growth.

Schein's study was part of a long-term project focusing on HR issues and his report was not made public until almost a decade later (in 2000). It represents a reliable assessment of the assumptions and opinions that were commonplace during the Sculley era at the end of the 1980s and the first half of the 1990s. Schein concluded that the personnel felt they not only had to work to achieve commercial success, but also to serve a higher ideological goal: 'To change society and the world, create something lasting, solve important problems, and have fun.'[254] There was also a strong belief in the power of the individual: the individual had the right and the duty to be a total person. This translated itself into comments like: 'individuals are powerful, can be self-sufficient, and can create their own destiny; a group of individuals motivated by a shared dream can create great things; people have an inherent desire to be their best and will go for it.'[255]

These opinions also had a downside. Schein discovered that at Apple the realisation of a task or project was regarded as being much more important than the method of working or manner of collaboration. When you failed at Apple, you failed alone and were cast adrift. Seniority, loyalty and experience all counted for nothing. You were only as good as your last performance. Relationships that were initiated at work seldom lasted, since they were regarded as something temporary that simply served a particular project. In this sense, Schein concluded, Apple could be seen as a club or a community, but not as a tight-knit family.[256]

Or to express it in slightly different terms, the Apple culture is a unique mix of the collective dream to make the world a better place through technology, combined with a continual desire to achieve the best possible levels of individual performance and fulfilment. Sculley summarised this neatly in the late 1980s with a new Apple motto: 'The power to be your best'. He also converted all the opinions revealed by Schein into strict guidelines. The professor, who visited the company on several further occasions in later years, confirmed that these opinions continued to hold sway in the late 1990s and early 2000s, and certainly after the return of Jobs in 1997.

Professor Schein's conclusions have been corroborated to some extent by a limited number of usually anonymous testimonies from (ex-) Apple employees in media publications. For example, these remarks in *Business Insider*: 'On the one hand, you have "Think Different" propaganda posters all over the wall (you have all seen these ad campaigns and you know what they are about). On the other hand, Apple has the strictest rules of any place I have worked. Apple cares about its brand image above all else.'[257] This type of comment and the fact that there is so little published material about the internal culture at Apple has led many observers to wonder about the current state of play within the company. The available evidence suggests that its original culture is still present (in a largely latent form), is deeply rooted, and is transferred from generation to generation.

The Californian ideology

Where did this cultural identity at Apple – collective dream, extreme individualism and a strong performance orientation – originate? Whoever wants to investigate the roots of a company and its culture usually needs to start with the life and personality of its founder. In the case of Apple, it is clear that Steve Jobs was a hugely influential factor (I will be returning to this later in the chapter). But to understand the influence of the founder, you also need to understand the spirit of the times that shaped his or her thinking. Where and when did they grow up? What were the prevailing social mores? Viewed in these terms, the roots of Apple are to be found in mid-1970s California and, more particularly, in the Homebrew Computer Club, which brought together enthusiasts from the many cultural clans of the digital Bay Area. By sharing information and exchanging tips, the members of the club hoped to develop a 'do-it-yourself pack' for the building of a personal computer. In this way, they hoped to make computer technology more widely available to the general public. This was in keeping with the counterculture and the hippie movement of the 1960s, in which free spirits tried to live their lives as independently as possible, liberated from the shackles of institutions, authorities and rules. This was epitomised by the Whole Earth Catalog, compiled by Steward Brand to inform people about the best ways to acquire (or even make) a wide range of products, including technological ones. It is in this context that the Homebrew Computer Club, where Jobs and Wozniak were amongst the keenest members, needs to be placed. This is something of which Wozniak in particular was especially proud. In later years, he wrote more than once that the club was much more than just a bunch of computer nerds, but was driven by a desire to democratise the access to technology. 'In this, we were revolutionaries,' commented Wozniak in his autobiography. 'That had been my goal, too, for years and years before that. So I felt right at home there.'[258] In other words, as the 1970s progressed there was an important shift in people's approach to technology. What had first been seen as an instrument of bureaucratic control now came to be regarded as a symbol of individual self-expression and liberation. California was the crucible of this change and Jobs and Wozniak were its heirs.

According to media experts Richard Barbrook and Andy Cameron: 'Apple's culture is a clear demonstration of the so-called California ideology in the daily practice of a Silicon Valley company.'[259] This mental attitude, they claim, was a combination of the freewheeling spirit of the hippies from the 1960s with the entrepreneurial drive of the yuppies from the 1980s. It turned out to be a unique and highly explosive cocktail.

The cult of the individual

As Schein identified, the Apple culture is about much more than collective dreams and altruism. Visitors to Apple speak of a company were internal discussions are conducted in terms of 'me' and 'my products', rather than 'we' and 'our products'.[260] This cult of the individual was derived in part from the mentality that dominated at Stanford University, the intellectual breeding ground for many Silicon Valley companies. It is a university that certainly embraces democratic values, but links this to the encouragement of a continual and intensive process of self-development.[261]

During the early 1980s, this cult of the individual and the 'duty' of self-realisation became institutionalised at Apple. The company formally enshrined its values in a document that reads more like a creed than an official statement: 'Each person is important; each has the opportunity and the obligation to make a difference. (...) We recognize that each member of Apple is important, that each can contribute to customer satisfaction. Our results come through the creativity, craftsmanship, initiative, and good work of each person as a part of a team.'[262]

In other words, Apple stimulated the intensive self-development of its employees. The Apple University offered a variety of training programmes, invited inspirational speakers and organised excursions to the Pacific, where mountain-climbing instructors encouraged Apple managers to explore the limits of their abilities. The purpose of all these initiatives was to create a network of super-motivated individuals who all shared the same vision. What's more, most of these Apple recruits were in their twenties, which meant that they could work hard for twelve hours a day and still have energy to spare. With this in mind, the company allowed them to finish work early on Friday afternoons, so that they could get together for a relaxing beer and a chat, all at the company's expense.[263]

Of course, the HR managers at Apple were not stupid. They knew that the promotion of individual entrepreneurship would not always be compatible with collective team spirit, and that friction would sometimes arise. As a result, they set up a work group to chart and clarify conflicting values within the company. Their conclusions and guidelines were issued in a series of internal memos, spread throughout the company at all levels. One of these memos emphasised: 'Apple is more than just a company... It is an attitude, a process, a point of view and a way of doing things.' The values that the company sought to project also reflected this fundamental duality within the Apple culture: empathy for customers and users on the one hand, combined with far-reaching self-fulfilment on the other hand. If this led to a degree of healthy conflict and aggression, so be it: 'We set aggressive goals and drive hard to achieve them. We recognize that this is a unique time, when our products will change the way people work and live. It's an adventure, and we're all in it together.'[264]

A ninth myth debunkes: the garage

One of the most persistent myths about tech-entrepreneurs is that they nearly all began in a small garage, a myth that started with the garage of the founders of Hewlett-Packard in Palo Alto in the 1940s. In this myth, the garage stands as a symbol for the American Dream and a meritocratic society, in which the enterprising and creative individual can achieve great things.

In keeping with the traditions of this myth, it is now often claimed that not only was Apple originally founded in a garage at 2066 Crist Drive in Los Altos, California (Steve Jobs' home), but also that the first personal computers were developed and built there. Steve Wozniak has denied that this was the case. 'The garage didn't serve much purpose, except it was something for us to feel was our home. We had no money. You have to work out of your home when you have no money.'[265]

Two researchers from the Haas School of Business in Berkeley, Pino Audia and Chris Rider, have also nuanced the garage myth. They argue that the myth serves to conjure up the image of the lone maverick, who develops super-products by relying exclusively on his (or her) own exceptional effort and talent. However, their research shows that this is simply not true. Most of the famous technology developers were the product of other tech-organisations. This applies both for Wozniak, who was working for Hewlett-Packard when he developed the Apple I, and for Jobs, who was employed at Atari. Similarly, a study of tech-companies financed by venture capital revealed that 91 % of these companies were engaged in activities that bore some relation to the previous job of their founder. This demonstrates that the success of entrepreneurs does not usually result from the iconoclastic work of a single individual, but can more commonly be attributed to the impact of their wider social environment. Would Wozniak and Jobs ever have achieved what they did if they had never been members of the Homebrew Computer Club?[266]

Yet even though academic research has proved it to be false, even today the garage myth continues to symbolise a creative class of young start-ups, from which the next Apple, Google or Facebook is destined to emerge. In the case of Apple, the myth helped to create an aura of innovation, creativity and entrepreneurship around the company. As such, it serves as a powerful metaphor for Apple's (desired) culture, even though it stands in sharp contrast to the reality of their daily practice.

The drop-out culture

During the 1980s, there was a huge gap between Apple's values and principles as set down on paper and actual daily practice in the company. It was a place where counterculture – some might even say a touch of anarchy – ruled. In many companies, for example, people wear badges to show who they are. At Apple, one employee went around for years with a photo on his badge of him wearing an eye-patch. The photo was taken on his first day back at work after he had turned up at a Halloween party dressed as one of Steve Jobs' 'pirates'...[267]

This was typical of the 'alternative' culture at Apple. Similarly, functional titles meant very little. They were usually intended more as a kind of joke, such as 'Software Wizard' or 'Corporate Mouthpiece'. Respect and reputation were acquired through your ability and intellect or, occasionally, because you were prepared to bang your fist on the table. The only titles that meant anything, Sculley later confirmed, were those of 'founder' and 'biggest shareholder'.[268]

One of the most striking results of this unconventional way of running a business was that Apple quickly developed a strong consensus culture. Before a project was started or continued following an evaluation, everyone had to be in agreement. All the managers had the power to call a project to a halt, even if they were not the most senior in the hierarchy. Jobs tolerated this form of disagreement within the company, and was also more than capable of some fist banging himself, if he felt it was called for. In fact, it was the kind of behaviour he encouraged. His basic philosophy was that an idea was only good enough to succeed if it was first able to overcome all internal disagreement. According to Sculley, this was a good example of the Apple DNA, one of the elements that was originally derived from Jobs and continued long after his departure.

In his autobiography, Sculley called Apple a 'third wave company', which typically relies more on consensus management than on the top-down hierarchy applied in second wave companies like Pepsi, where Sculley had previously worked. In third wave companies, knowledge is more important than rank. If the doorman has a fantastic idea, it is taken seriously. Another typical characteristic is the absence of both a dress code and fixed working hours: as long as the work gets done, people are free to come and go as they like. Such matters are left entirely to the discretion of the individual employees.[269]

Apple in trouble: wild horses

Steve Jobs was forced out of the company in the mid-1980s, following a series of failed product launches that he had been unable to put right. Was this a consequence of the culture that Jobs himself had installed? This question was certainly asked at the time, and it is a fact that during the next 10 years various CEOs brought in from outside the company (Sculley, Spindler, Amelio) all attempted to get a grip on that same culture and turn the company's results around – and they all failed. Because throughout the book we have tried to learn from Apple's mistakes, in this chapter I want to look in more detail at this less than glorious period in the company's history, with a focus on the cultural perspective.

It is probably fair to say that when Jobs left Apple it was more a cult organisation than a real company. This implied that within the company, just as in more bureaucratically organised companies, small baronies had developed and that occasionally a knife was stuck into the back of an unfortunate colleague. As time passed, this situation worsened.[270] The culture remained essentially the same but its 'dark side' – the side which said 'do whatever you want and to hell with everyone else' – increasingly gained the upper hand. The outcome was inevitable: half decisions (or no decisions at all), chaos and a sinking ship.

By the mid-1990s, this was also the analysis of the press. Based on dozens of interviews with serving and former managers at the company, *Business Week* came to the conclusion that a pattern of mismanagement had developed at Apple, as a result of which strategic decisions failed to have the desired effect, resulting in turn in a confusing zig-zag course between different strategies. The seeds of this problem, according to the analysts, had already been sown in Apple's earliest years. The fact that Jobs and Wozniak had consistently stimulated a 'drop-out culture' was cited as one of main causes: 'Create your own thing, defy the naysayers, and ignore the Establishment – one person can change the world.' When things were going well, this non-conformist attitude could lead to spectacular successes; for example, to the Mac, a groundbreaking computer whose fans saw it not simply as a utilitarian machine but as a versatile tool that they came to love. But there was also a reverse side to this coin: 'The culture has incredibly powerful elements – Jobs' perfectionism, for one,' commented a former Apple manager. 'But the other side of that is unharnessed and uncontrolled.'[271]

When Gil Amelio arrived as CEO, he quickly came to the same conclusion: the company did not have a single coherent strategy, but went off in several directions at once. All the managers did more or less whatever they pleased. There was no culture of collaboration and no-one seemed to know how to work together in teams. Amelio described Apple as the most 'Balkanised' company he had ever seen: 'It's divided into principalities, each ruled over by a top executive who, like the prince of a city-state, could do damn well what they wanted without anyone else's by-your-leave.'[272] Consensus decision-making might be a noble ideal, but in practice it led to inertia and indecisiveness. When it was not possible to reach a consensus – which was most of the time – everyone just 'did their own thing', which was often inconsistent with what their colleagues were doing! As a result, the collective long-term interests of the company were sacrificed on the altar of self-interest and short-term gain.

Although Sculley, Spindler and Amelio all saw the problem, none of them succeeded in fundamentally changing the values and culture that had been ingrained in the company from its very beginning. Projects such as the possible cloning of the Mac OS and the development of the new Copland operating system are good examples of the kind of inertia that gripped Apple. Because no consensus could be found, the discussion of these crucial projects dragged on endlessly, so that by the time a decision was eventually taken – and a half-hearted decision at that – it was too little too late. In consequence, the company stumbled from one fiasco to the next. A former marketing manager, Michael Mace, said of this period: 'It was a hard place to manage in those days. It was like ten thousand wild horses, none of which had been broken to the saddle.' Another employee who had worked for Apple for years commented that it almost seemed as if the evil spirit of Steve Jobs was still haunting the company, infecting it with all his bad qualities, but none of his good ones.[273] As fate would have it, it was left to that same Steve Jobs to return to the company he had founded to tame those wild horses and rein in the culture he had helped to create.

Cultural heritage: options for new leaders

The fact that a succession of new CEOs at Apple found it difficult to transform the existing culture illustrates that culture in general is capable of surviving its creator and can often be highly 'conservative' (i.e., stubborn). To such as extent, in fact, that it can sometimes put the positive forces in the company at risk. And if a new management team seeks to change the existing culture, but without taking account of the original and more balanced concept of that culture as it was initially intended, things can turn out even worse.

Leaders need to be very careful when they first join a new company. In this respect, it is worth recalling Schein's theory, which argues that culture and leadership are two sides of the same coin. In other words, it is the culture in an organisation that determines what kind of leadership will work. Schein offers four different options for dealing with this situation:

1. The first option is the most radical. Destroy the existing culture by getting rid of the key figures who most clearly represent that culture. This will often mean senior people in the company. Once you have done this, seek to install your own convictions, values and assumptions on the remaining personnel by implementing a new code of conduct. The disadvantage of this approach is that you lose a lot of the company's store of knowledge and experience, so that the company's performance may suffer at first. This is also the reason why so many mergers and

takeovers fail: culture is very resistant and will not allow itself to be eradicated without a fight.

2. Fight the existing culture by imposing your convictions, values and assumptions on all personnel, including the senior figures. The risk here is that the organisation only changes superficially and waits until the new leader moves on, before returning to its old ways. In other words, there is a good chance that the old culture will win in the end, unless the new leader is someone with exceptional charisma. This was option tried at Apple by both Spindler and Amelio. They failed. The existing culture was stronger than the 'outsiders' had thought.

3. Surrender completely to the existing culture by giving up your own convictions, values and assumptions. This risk in this case is that all the elements of the old culture will remain intact, even if some of those elements are now outdated and inefficient. This conciliatory option was chosen by Sculley following his appointment at Apple, although he later admitted the situation required more desperate measures.

4. Adjust as well as you can to the existing culture and take the time to discover how you can get things done within the company. Once you have gained this insight, introduce new guidelines and codes of behaviour step by step, based on different convictions, values and assumptions. For many leaders and organisations this is the most efficient way to implement cultural change management.[274] It is a pragmatic approach that focuses on gradual improvement.

Schein also notes that any cultural change creates massive anxiety and resistance. Only a small – but important – group will openly welcome and applaud the change. In many cases, 'change masters' will be met by scepticism ('yes, but'), cynicism ('we will watch them fail from our ivory tower') and even by sabotage and active opposition. The only way to overcome this internal resistance is to build up a coalition of the willing around your 'ambassadors', attempting to rally the sceptics and even the cynics. The process needs to be an active one: if you don't manage cultural change, it will manage you. Always start with the individual and answer the burning question that nearly everyone will have: 'What's in it for me?'. Be transparent and do not leave people with their anxieties: that will only feed the cynics and arm the saboteurs. Remember to make clear not only what the change means for their teams and for the company as a whole, but also how the transformation will improve the lives of their customers and what benefits it can offer to wider society. Even then, you will still find that implementing cultural change is seldom easy.

The history of Apple shows that only CEOs who were appointed from within the company – and were therefore familiar with the culture – have made a success of things. This was the case with Jobs after his return in 1997 (in spite of his wilderness years, he had always remained an Apple 'insider') and with Tim Cook, who was a Jobs' protégé. In contrast, all the 'outsiders' failed, some more disastrously than others. This illustrates how difficult it is for people from outside a company to fully understand its culture. It is not only a question of understanding the 'general culture' – which is usually the most visible – but also the different sub-cultures developed by individual managers, departments, production lines and geographical units. It is crucial for leaders to gain insight into the workings of these sub-cultures, but often this is only possible (or at least much easier) for an insider.

This means that leaders have an additional task: they not only need to know how their company differentiates itself from other companies in general cultural terms, but must also try to get all the companies different sub-cultures to work together in pursuit of the company's collective business objectives.[275] How exactly did Steve Jobs (after his reappointment) and Tim Cook achieve this? Let's find out.

The return of the emperor

When Jobs agreed to return to Apple, he knew beforehand that the situation was dramatic. But when he arrived, he found that things were far worse than even he had thought. He told *Fortune Magazine*. 'The people had been told they were losers for so long that they were on the verge of giving up. The first six months were very bleak, and at times I got close to throwing in the towel, too. I'd never been so tired in my life.'[276]

Jobs realised all too well that to turn things around would require something more than the touch of his charismatic leadership. 'This is not a one-man show,' he informed *Business Week*.[277]

He decided to adopt a more egalitarian course: no more business class flights, no more special privileges for executives, etc. Everyone in the company was to be treated the same (except him, of course!). The changes he implemented were often

minor (no dogs at work, a smoking ban, etc.), but sometimes they were of major importance, such as an absolute prohibition on the release of information relating to production processes or the development of new products.[278]
The impact of Jobs' return was far-reaching. His aim was to create a large and healthy company capable of dealing with large-scale projects, but working with the enthusiasm and entrepreneurial mentality of a start-up. It took him 2 years to achieve it. He scaled down departments, reorganised procedures, recruited new engineers. He cut the number of production lines and replaced cash bonuses for senior managers with share allocations. Talking about this 'new' Apple, he told *Fortune Magazine*: 'A start-up could never do the new iMac. Literally 2 000 people worked on it. A start-up could never do Mac OS X. It's not easy at a big company either, but Apple now has the management and systems in place to get things like that done. I can't emphasize how rare that is. That's what makes Sony and Disney so special.'[279]

With the launching of the iMac, Jobs had reinstalled another element of the original Apple culture: successful innovation. This gave back to the workforce some of the self-esteem they had lost in recent years. Jobs commented: 'What they didn't have before was a good set of coaches, a good plan. A good senior management team. But they have that now. The first thing to invigorate people is winning again.' The people working for Jobs' Apple no longer felt they were losers.[280]

As so often before, there was also a reverse side to the coin. The employees were now self-proclaimed winners, but they were expected to give 100 % to the company – and more. Jobs swept through Apple like an 'enlightened despot', correcting here, criticising there. Many of his people actually came to fear him, even though he was their hero.

All this has been confirmed by various testimonies and studies made of Apple's culture since the year 2000. Leander Kahney, who has devoted several articles and books to the company, tells how Apple's expectations of its personnel were extremely high under the new regime: not only Jobs' expectations of his managers, but also the managers' expectations of their teams. People were constantly anxious, fearful of losing their job for the slightest mistake or lack of effort. At the same time, they were constantly hoping to score that one big hit that would please the big boss and make their career. In spite of all the tension, everyone loved their work and all were utterly loyal both to the company and to Steve Jobs personally.[281]

Sometimes Jobs took things to fairly extreme lengths, but he knew what he was doing and his motives were sound. Or as Stanford management professor Robert Sutton put it in his 2007 bestseller *The No Asshole Rule. Building a Civilized Workspace and Surviving One That Isn't*: 'He made people feel terrible; he made people cry. But he was almost always right, and even when he was wrong, it was so creative it was still amazing.' A Palo Alto venture capitalist expressed it even more succinctly: 'Democracies don't make great products. You need a competent tyrant.'[282]

Even the development of the biggest of Jobs' successes – the iPhone – was only possible after the requisite amount of blood, sweat and tears. In *The One Device* by Brian Merchant, a female employee working on the project commented: 'The Cupertino campus teemed with Apple fanatics, a number of whom made no secret of their Steve Jobs idolatry. "Apple is kind of a weird place," Strickton is quoted as saying. "You've even got people dressing like Steve." (...) The ultimate question was, of course, what would Steve Jobs think? After all, Jobs was the ultimate authority – he could kill the project with a word, if he didn't see the potential.'[283]

The result of this culture was that people were prepared to give a lot, an awful lot, to achieve success for the company – and keep their jobs. One of the most popular euphemisms in Silicon Valley at that time was: 'Work hard, play hard'. This was certainly the case at Apple. The staff had to work long days, but they were handsomely rewarded. 'At Apple, people are so committed that they go home at night and don't leave Apple behind them. What they do at Apple is their true religion,' said one senior engineer interviewed by journalist Adam Lashinsky.[284] It is even said that the marriages of many Apple employees fell apart during the development of the iPhone. If this is true, it would seem that the 'work-life balance' so prized by Generation Y is not much in evidence at Apple.

The Cook doctrine

Tim Cook, a civil engineer who had previously worked as head of sales at PC manufacturer Compaq, was recruited by Steve Jobs in 1998 as senior vice-president worldwide operations. His task was to make Apple function more efficiently, amongst other things by reducing the supply of components to less than a month. This not only meant a significant reduction of costs, but also guaranteed just-in-time delivery for Apple. For his efforts, Cook was known within the company as 'the Attila the Hun of inventory'.

Jobs had always pushed Cook forward as his possible successor. In 2004, Cook replaced Jobs briefly as chairman of the board and then for a longer period in 2009. It seemed logical to make the appointment permanent after Jobs' death in 2011. Cook had always said that continuity would be the basis of his strategy. In 2009, he made this concrete by drawing up a manifesto that became known as 'the Cook doctrine'. This document confirmed Jobs' heritage, but smoothed off some of the rough edges. Amongst other things, he emphasised the principles of innovation and simplicity, as well as underlining the need for Apple to control the technology on which its products were based. 'We believe in saying no to thousands of projects, so that we can really focus on the few that are truly important and meaningful to us. We believe in deep collaboration and cross-pollination of our groups, which allow us to innovate in a way that others cannot. And frankly, we don't settle for anything less than excellence in every group in the company, and we have the self-honesty to admit when we're wrong and the courage to change. And I think regardless of who is in what job those values are so embedded in this company that Apple will do extremely well.'[285]

Tim Cook has never concealed the fact that his policy is a continuation of Jobs'. He confirmed this with an eloquence that was almost worthy of his great predecessor: 'Steve's DNA will always be the base of Apple. It's the case now. I want it to be the case in 50 years, whoever is the CEO. I want it to be the case in 100 years, whoever is the CEO. Because that is what this company is about. (...) It's like the Constitution, which is the guide for the United States. It should not change. We should revere it.'[286] With these comments, Cook illustrates again just how deeply a culture can be embedded in a company, how little room it leaves for change, and how it can survive numerous changes in leadership.

At the same time, this was a conscious choice on Cook's part. He would not want it any other way. The need for continuity was already institutionalised as early as 2008 with the founding of the Apple University, an alternative training school to ensure the perpetuation of Apple's core values once Steve Jobs was no longer around. Jobs was very clear on this point. He said he wanted to create a forum 'that could impart Apple's DNA to future generations of Apple employees'. The opening of the new campus at Cupertino in 2017 is yet a further signal that Apple will continue to follow the same path far into the future.

A culture of change or a change of culture?

Most companies regard an innovative culture as desirable. Most leaders claim to understand what such a culture entails. So why are they so hard to create and sustain? Harvard Business School professor Gary Pisano believes that the vast majority of managers only understand part of the innovation culture equation. They concentrate on the popular aspects, but often forget that this is only one side of the coin. The freedoms generated by an innovation culture need to be offset against a series of responsibilities – and these are often anything but popular. As Pisano puts it: 'A tolerance for failure requires an intolerance for incompetence. A willingness to experiment requires rigorous discipline. Psychological safety requires comfort with brutal candour. Collaboration must be balanced with individual accountability. And flatness requires strong leadership. Innovative cultures are paradoxical. Unless the tensions created by this paradox are carefully managed, attempts to create an innovative culture will fail.'[287]

All change is difficult, but cultural change is especially so. In one sense, organisations are like clubs, with the organisational culture setting out the rules of membership. If a leader wishes to change this culture, he is effectively – and unilaterally – changing those rules. In these circumstances, it is hardly surprising that people will resist, with those benefiting most from the existing rules shouting the loudest. The only way to confront this resistance is by being fully transparent right from the very start, both about the need for change and about harder realities of innovative cultures. If you only do this later on, people will be understandably cynical, when they realise that the rules are being changed halfway through the process. It will then seem as though you have been pulling the wool over their eyes.

Some leaders try to shortcut this process by breaking down the organisation into smaller units, in the belief that this will allow these units to 'imitate' an innovative start-up culture. This seldom works, Pisano confirms. There is no correlation between scale and culture. Just because a business unit becomes smaller, this will not magically imbue it with an entrepreneurial spirit. In the vast majority of cases, they will simply perpetuate the same culture as in their larger 'parent' organisation.

Cultural change always demands strong management measures to shape new norms, values and behaviours. This is doubly so in the case of innovative cultures, since they have a greater tendency to be unstable, so that the field of tension between the perceived positive and negative aspects of the proposed change can easily be thrown off-kilter. 'Leaders need to be vigilant for signs of excess in any area and intervene to restore balance, when necessary.' It is equally important that leaders are aware of any excessive tendencies in themselves. 'If you want your organisation to strike the delicate balance required, then you as a leader must demonstrate the ability to strike that balance yourself.'[288]

In other words: practice what you preach. And practice – leading by example – is more effective than preaching.

The perfect transformation

There is a two-way relationship between a company's culture and its structure, with the latter often reflecting the former. For example, a company that has an overtly collaborative culture might develop incentive systems to reward collective effort and the attainment of shared goals. Conversely, well-established organisational constructions can sometimes help to create a culture over time. It needs to be recognised, however, that this is a much more difficult process to achieve successfully: it is always easier to align structure to culture, rather than the other way around.[289] The events occurring at Apple in the 1990's are an example.

That being said, it can, nevertheless, still be achieved. The 'turn around' of Microsoft under its new CEO, Satya Nadella, is a classic example of this kind of 'cultural renaissance', as he calls it in his book *Hit refresh*.[290] For Nadella, the 'C' in CEO stands for 'culture': 'The CEO is the curator of an organisation's culture.'[291] Nadella admits that when he arrived he found the Microsoft culture to be extremely rigid: 'Each employee had to prove to everyone that he or she knew it all and was the smartest person in the room.'[292] The result of this mentality was what Nadella called 'a confederation of fiefdoms'.[293] He needed to teach his people to rediscover the art of listening to customers rather than to themselves. He wanted the company to become diverse and inclusive rather than monolithic and restrictive. His new motto was: 'We are one company, one Microsoft.' He also had the good sense to realise that this is a mission that will never be completed: 'It's not a program with a start and end date. It's a way of being.'[294] Although everyone now recognises his success, Nadella found out the hard way that cultural change is difficult and can be painful. The fundamental source of resistance to change, he acknowledges, is fear of the unknown. People keep on asking big and important questions, for which there are not always easy and conclusive answers: 'Sometimes it feels like a bird learning to fly.[295]' The situation is further complicated by the fact that its positive results only become evident in the longer term: there are no 'easy fixes' or 'quick wins' when it comes to culture. Even so, Nadella's achievement again underlines the importance of continuity and consistency across actions and over time. This is the only way to build trust, without which the entire change process is doomed to failure.[296]

Insider or outsider?

There is much discussion about whether it is wiser to appoint someone from inside the company or from outside the company as CEO. At Apple, as we have seen, the insiders have usually performed better than the outsiders. Even so, it is a subject worth debating, because a change in CEO can have a huge influence on the running of the company and its results.

It is hard to overestimate the importance of aligning culture and leadership. The character and behaviour of a CEO and of other top executives can have a profound effect on culture. At the same time, a company's culture can also limit or improve a leader's ability to perform effectively. Data produced by Spencer Stuart has revealed that lack of a proper cultural fit is responsible for up to 68 % of recruitment failures at the senior leadership level.[297] As a factor for success, cultural fit is as important as a leader's capabilities and experience.

What further light can Apple's past shed on this? Sculley and Amelio came from outside the company. Spindler was an old Apple retainer. In general, shareholders tend to look to external candidates when things are not going well (cf. Jobs in 1997) and are happier to see an insider come through the ranks when the company's performance is positive (cf. Cook in 2011).

A change of CEO can affect the reputation of a company in different ways. Research at 241 of the Fortune 500 companies has shown that a change of CEO not only has an impact on the internal culture, but in general also enhances the company's reputation – except in the case of companies that already have an excellent reputation, where some temporary fall-off is experienced. In other words, a change at the top can sometimes have a dislocating effect and may put a good reputation at risk, if allowed to go too far. This applies mainly to very large companies, which receive more media attention and are therefore watched more closely. A company with a poor reputation may see that reputation boosted by a new CEO from outside, who brings with him/her the promise of change. In general, however, the research suggests that companies with an internal promotee as CEO perform better and book better results than companies that appoint an external candidate. An internal successor is seen as being more likely to maintain the status quo. This avoids uncertainty about possible disruption and the future direction of the company. In this respect, Jobs' decision to groom Cook as his successor – a man who after 10 years in the company was an insider through and through – has brought Apple nothing but good fortune. In fact, it was probably the most visionary of all Jobs' decisions.[298 299]

Equally interesting in this context is the study conducted by Collins and Porras. They concluded that visionary companies are more likely than other comparable companies to prepare, select and promote internal management talent. They do this consciously to protect their core business and values. It is not so much the quality of leadership per se that distinguishes visionary companies from the rest, but rather the continuity of that quality of leadership. This was the case in fifteen of the eighteen companies they investigated.[300]

Apple has already been thinking about a possible successor for Tim Cook. At the end of 2017, it was rumoured that Cook had not only recruited Angela Ahrendts to reorganise Apple's retail and online stores, but also saw her as his eventual replacement. The company denied this but the rumours persisted. If Ahrendts had been able to align herself with the internal Apple culture, this might not have been a bad idea. However, in February 2019 it was announced that Ahrendts would be leaving the company that April. As a result, at the time of going to press Apple is still looking for a new candidate to become the future face of the organisation.

L

THE DO'S-AND-DON'TS

- ∞ Leadership and culture are two sides of the same coin. Leadership ensures that culture can be preserved, also in the long term. Culture determines the form that leadership can take within the company.

- ∞ The challenge for leaders is to find the right balance between long-term patterns of behaviour and identity on the one hand and adjusting sufficiently to a changing environment on the other hand.

- ∞ Create structures that transmit the culture: training, information, transparency, good coaches, good management.

- ∞ Do this consistently and ensure that all levels of the company, from top to bottom, are suffused with the same philosophy.

- ∞ Culture is more than just posters on office walls and team-building activities.

- ∞ Be aware that an existing culture can often be highly 'conservative' (i.e., stubborn), to such as extent that it can sometimes put the positive forces in the company at risk.

- ∞ Remember, as a new leader, that if you want to change an existing culture, but fail to take account of the original and more balanced concept of that culture as it was initially intended, things can turn out even worse.

L

- ∞ Adjust as well as you can to the existing culture and take the time to discover how you can get things done within the company. Once you have gained this insight, introduce new guidelines and codes of behaviour step by step, based on different convictions, values and assumptions. Take into account that this will not be an easy task.

- ∞ Sometimes you need to be an insider to know what lives on the inside of a company.

- ∞ Leaders not only need to know how their company differentiates itself from other companies in general cultural terms, but must also try to get all the companies different sub-cultures to work together in pursuit of the company's collective business objectives.

- ∞ Successful companies with an internal promotee as CEO perform better and book better results than companies that appoint an external candidate. An internal successor is seen as being more likely to provide continuity and certainty.

- ∞ Innovative cultures only succeed with plenty of discipline.

- ∞ A company with a less good reputation may see that reputation improve by appointing an external CEO, provided he/she is seen by the outside world as someone who can bring change.

- ∞ It is not so much the quality of leadership per se that distinguishes visionary companies from the rest, but rather the continuity of that quality of leadership.

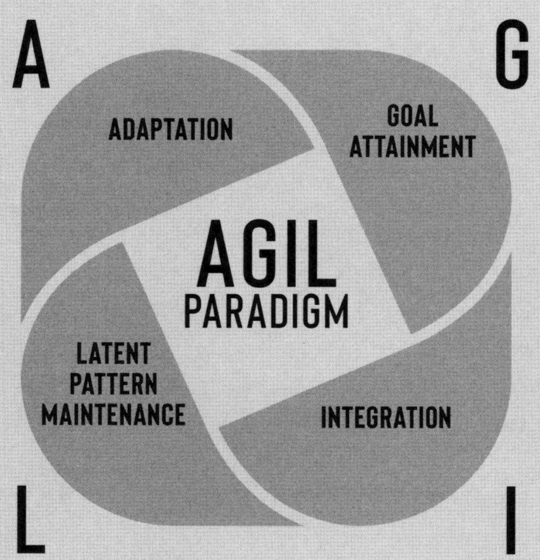
A
G
ADAPTATION
GOAL
ATTAINMENT
AGIL
PARADIGM
LATENT
PATTERN
MAINTENANCE
INTEGRATION
L
I

A MOVING EQUILIBRIUM BETWEEN CHANGE AND STABILITY

An immortal company must continuously pursuit a moving equilibrium between the need for change and the need for stability.

When reporters asked Tim Cook in 2015 if he planned to distance himself in any way from the legacy of Steve Jobs, he answered simply: 'The values in the core remain the same as they were in '98, as they were in '05, as they were in '10. I don't think the values should change. But everything else can change.'[301]

This comment perfectly summarises the survival strategy that a company like Apple – or any other company, for that matter – always needs. Companies must be able to deal with what Talcott Parsons described as 'a very fundamental dilemma': on the one hand, remaining faithful to your core values, your deepest DNA; on the other hand, adapting to change and making compromises, even if, at first sight, this seems to go against those values. If companies fail to respond in an effective manner to this seeming paradox, conflicts can easily arise, both internally and with the outside world. And when this happens, your stability is in danger.[302]

In essence, this means that it is necessary for companies to find a balance between the four AGIL functions, where the 'A' and 'G' functions facilitate change and the 'I' and 'L' functions facilitate stability, continuity and coherence. All four functions are crucial to a company's survival, but they do not operate autonomously. They are in constant interaction with each other. In this context, Parsons speaks of 'interchanges'. If the balance between the functions is correct, this will generate a fly-wheel effect, in which the sum of the whole produces a greater effect than the four functions can make individually. But if the functions are not in balance – if, for example, one of the four dominates the other three – this can have a paralysing or even a destructive effect. This makes the likelihood of conflict situations much greater.

In their well-known *Built to Last,* Jim Collins and Jerry Porras compare a company's core identity and its progress with the yin and yang of Chinese philosophy. Each element activates, completes and strengthens the other. Collins and Porras argue that visionary companies not only search for a balance between core identity and progress, but at the same time also seek to give expression to both elements in a pronounced way, by combining a deeply embedded and strong identity with a highly progressive mindset. Identity provides a strong basis on which a company can evolve, experiment and change. The desire for change will strengthen the identity, because without continuous change the company will move backwards instead of forwards and will perhaps even cease to exist.[303]

The history of Apple illustrates this point. During its most successful periods, it was able to manage the four dimensions like a symphony orchestra. The synergy within the company strengthened each function individually. During the less successful periods, the opposite happened: the functions got out of balance.

Perhaps it is not so surprising that this sometimes happens. Maintaining the right balance is no easy matter. The rapidly changing environment in the modern business world means that the exercise needs to be repeated time after time. For this reason, Parsons talks of the need for a 'moving equilibrium'. Moving in the sense that the equilibrium becomes disturbed from the very moment it is reached. This implies that the perfect equilibrium– which is both necessary and desirable – can never be achieved. Or more dangerous still: can create complacency, arrogance or inertia.[304]

In the 1980s and the 1990s, the Apple management struggled to find the right moving equilibrium, leading to numerous conflicts as a result. Since the return of Jobs and certainly with Tim Cook in charge, the company has been able to deal with that equilibrium in a productive manner, bearing in mind that the search to achieve it never stops. This is something we will now look at more closely.

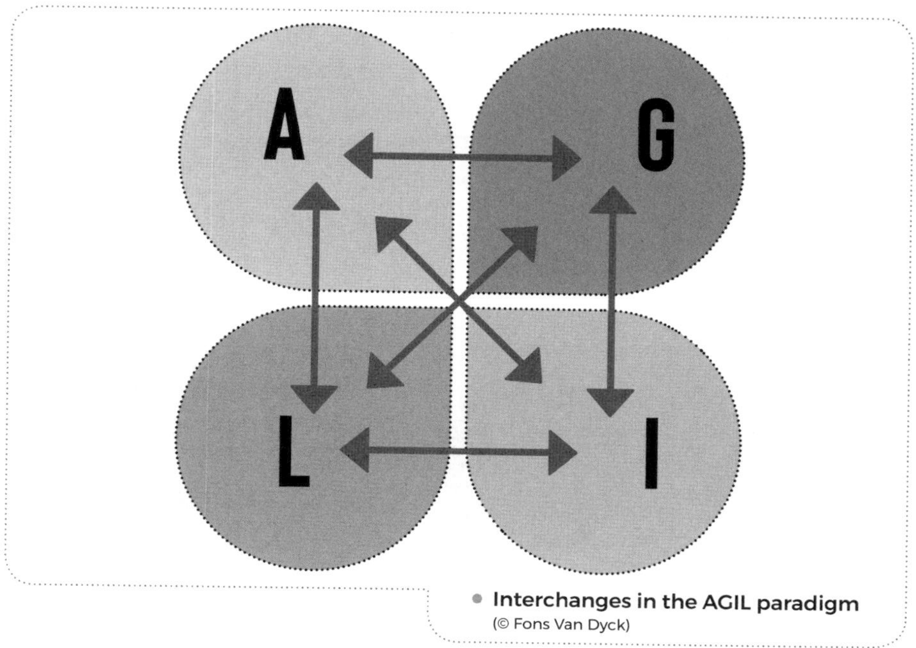

• **Interchanges in the AGIL paradigm**
(© Fons Van Dyck)

The need for change: Apple 3.0

In order to survive as a company, at the end of the 1990s and during the early years of the new century, Apple searched desperately to find ways in which it could adapt to its changing environment. These efforts, which were ultimately successful, transformed the Apple business model completely.

The starting-point for everything was the digital 'hub' strategy, of which the iMac – launched in 1998 – was the first demonstration. This marked Apple's entry into the consumer electronics market, so that it was no longer a company that 'just' made computers. The transformation was not disruptive, but occurred gradually: from the iMac, iPod and iTunes to the iPhone and the iPad. Gradual or not, it was a transformation that appealed to the imagination of many observers: 'It's fascinating that the company is morphing into something else,' wrote one Wall Street analyst. A journalist at *The New York Times* commented that Apple was starting to behave like highly regarded brands, 'such as Nike and Virgin'.[305]

The evolution took quite a long time. It was only in 2003, with the opening of the iTunes Store, that Apple was finally able to halt the downwards spiral in which had been trapped for many years. And it would not be until a full decade after Jobs' return, with the launch of the iPhone in 2007, that the new strategy of the 're-invented' Apple was translated into excellent sales figures.

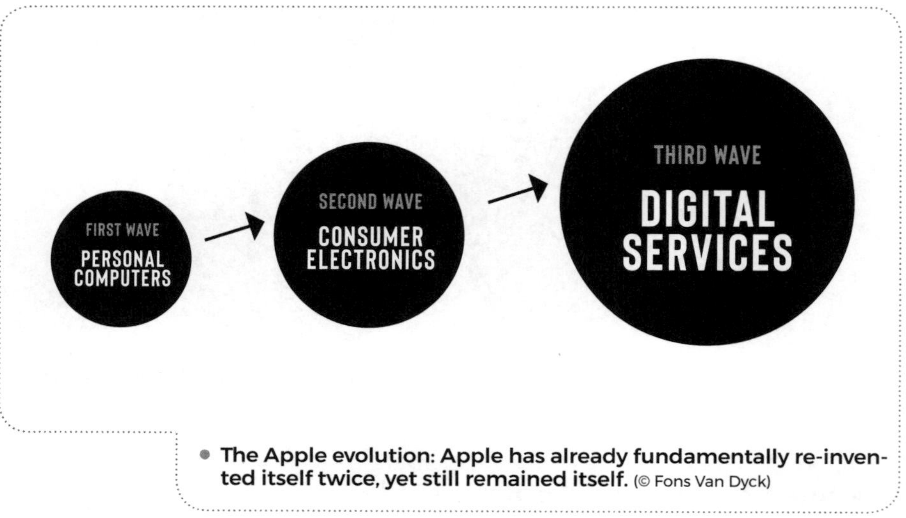

• **The Apple evolution: Apple has already fundamentally re-invented itself twice, yet still remained itself.** (© Fons Van Dyck)

Cook set out to strengthen the existing business model, but also wanted to explore new pathways. In 2016, the company's innovation budget reached a record level of 10.39 billion dollars, almost double what it had been just 3 years previously. Cook declared that in this way he was getting Apple ready to face the future: 'I know people care about quarters, and we care too. But the decisions we make are not for the 90-day clock.'[306]

But the question remains: which direction will Apple take in that future? With the launching of the Apple Watch, the company said it wants to make life 'easier' for people. 'I think it's the beginning of a very long run,' was Cook's comment on the matter.[307] With Apple Care, Cook and Apple have taken a further step along the same road, hoping to surf on the wave of the fast-growing digital health market. In 2016, Apple's digital services, such as iCloud, Apple Care and the App Store, were good for 12 % of income. In 2017, Cook declared that he wanted to double that figure by 2020. This makes clear that Apple is now entering a third wave of transformation: from the PC market via the consumer electronics market to new forms of digital service provision. Analysts have speculated for many years that Apple had plans to break into the entertainment business as a way to increase the attractiveness of the iPhone: from music streaming to online games and TV content. These services all have one thing in common: the use of AI (Artificial Intelligence), whereby Apple uses the data of its customers (with due respect for privacy laws) to provide them with new digital services. Furthermore, they also mark a move away from a traditional acquisition model towards a subscriber model. Cook believes that the opportunities are huge: 'I see a large open field in front of me. And I see no limitations,' he told a meeting of Goldman Sachs investors in 2013.[308]

It is also worth noting that Apple is not a pioneer in this domain, but is again a smart follower (as we saw earlier under the 'A' function). Cook now sees this as a strength: 'We've never been about being first. We've been about being best.'[309] Cook is planning for the long term and that is the message he is selling to potential investors. They will need to be patient until success eventually comes: 'The kinds of investors we seek are long-term, because that's how we make our decisions.' You can't be any clearer than that.[310]

The need for stability: the pole star

Even so, sometimes the question has been asked – both now and in the past – whether or not Apple is in danger of losing its focus. This was, after all, one of the most serious mistakes made by the company in the 1990s. When Jobs returned in 1997, he also demanded a return of focus, lots of focus, even if this is not always easy: 'Focusing is about saying no. You've got to say, no, no, no.'[311] He continued to be very aware of this need for focus and thought carefully about the perimeters within which Apple could operate. As he explained in typical Jobs fashion: 'If Mercedes made a bicycle or a hamburger or a computer, I don't think there'd be much advantage in having its logo on it. I don't think Apple would get much equity putting its name on an automobile, either.'[312]

Jobs' biographer Isaacson believes that it was this ability to focus that finally saved the company. In an interesting study into growth strategies, Chris Zook, a consultant at Bain & Company, has shown that strong companies succeed in growing in a sustainable manner by careful planning brand extensions that border on their core business. In cases where companies deviate too far from their core business, the likelihood of success is less certain. Zook calls this 'the trap of false enthusiasm'. As a result, he advises managers, when contemplating the introduction of something new, to always take account of a number of key economic parameters. Where is the link with our core? Can we acquire a leadership position? How viable and potentially profitable are our plans?[313] Moving too far away from your core also brings with it the danger that your customers will become confused and perhaps even desert you. All the more reason, according to Zook, for maintaining a clear focus – an opinion with which Tim Cook at Apple heartily concurs: 'We'll only do our best work if we stay focused. Frankly, the hardest decisions we made were all about the things not to work on.'[314]

While Apple has undergone successive waves of transformation during the past 20 years, the company has never fallen 'out of equilibrium'. This is because it has always remained faithful to its identity and core principles: simplicity, ease of use, control over their own technology and a desire to change the world. By setting up the Apple University and appointing Tim Cook as Jobs' 'insider' successor, these values were further strengthened and more firmly anchored within the company. The values (though seldom stated explicitly), identity and DNA of Apple have run like a red thread through Cook's public declarations in recent years. Sometimes, he even goes so far as to make comparisons with the American Constitution: 'It should never change. We should revere it.'[315] For Cook and for Apple, this DNA is the company's pole star, giving the company direction and guidance whenever an important choice or decision needs to be made, even if the path ahead is sometimes unclear and unpredictable.

Jobs expressed this in almost philosophical terms: 'The place where Apple has been standing for the last two decades is exactly where computer technology and the consumer electronics markets are converging. So it's not like we're having to cross the river to go somewhere else; the other side of the river is coming to us.'[316] The only difference for Apple under Cook is that the river has increased dramatically in size.

In *Great by Choice*, Jim Collins and Morton Hansen investigated the success formulas of companies whose performance far outstrips that of their rivals. One of their conclusions was that they change these formulas far less frequently than their competitors. Even so, they continued to evolve, but always driven forwards by a coherent, connective concept and a strict methodology. As the authors rightly commented: 'Those who bring about the most significant change in the world, those who have the largest impact on the economy and society, are themselves enormously consistent in their approach.'[317] These findings underline yet again the importance of the 'L' function – which guarantees the identity and continuity of a company –as a lever for future growth and survival.

Apple in trouble: for sale

Apple has not always managed to stay in equilibrium. Although Sculley, following his appointment in the mid-1980s, initially seemed to pay lip service to Apple's core values, he very quickly shifted almost the entire focus to the 'G' function of the AGIL paradigm: at all costs, the company wanted to book commercial and financial success. In concrete terms, Sculley aimed to boost turnover from 1 billion to 10 billion dollars, with a gross margin of at least 50 % and a share price of 50 dollars! Sculley brought the company new marketing expertise, allowing him to rationalise the company's finances and turning Apple (temporarily, at least) into a well-oiled machine. But by committing everything to achieve a set of very ambitious short-term targets, the Apple ship soon found itself hopelessly out of balance. The ends – even the surrender of control over their technology through licensing agreements – seemed to justify the means. But as so often when this happens, the results were catastrophic.

The idea that companies need to have ambitious objectives if they wish to achieve long-term success is one of the biggest misconceptions in management theory. In contrast to current thinking, the mantra of 'big hairy goals' usually has the opposite effect to what was intended. Empirical research in this field has revealed that having an excessively one-dimensional focus to achieve highly ambitious targets at all costs can lead to unethical behaviour (like Apple's channel stuffing in the turbulent 1990s), irresponsible risk-taking (often to achieve target bonuses) and blindness to other challenges and opportunities in a rapidly changing environment (so that yesterday's targets are quickly overtaken by tomorrow's new trends). More importantly, the intrinsic motivation of both management and the workforce is lost from sight completely, since everything is sacrificed to the single objective, which in many cases is nothing more than 'making money'. In this way, the established company culture is hollowed out and forgotten.[318]

This is what happened at Apple in the late 1980s and early 1990s. To achieve the greatest possible commercial and financial success, the company was willing to sell its soul. Jobs saw the approaching danger while he was still working for the company first time around. In a visionary interview with *Rolling Stone* magazine, he commented: 'Something happens to companies when they get to be a few million dollars – their souls go away. And that's the biggest thing I'll be measured on: were we able to grow a 10 billion dollar company that didn't lose its soul?'[319] He learnt the answer to this question a year later, when he was sacked from his own company.

Sculley, his successor, booked some immediate short-term successes, but was unable to keep the Apple ship on a sustainable course. With 'change manager' Spindler at the helm, things simply went from bad to worse, with the company trying a variety of different and sometimes contradictory courses, none of which led anywhere. The company stumbled from one half-measure to the next, rudderless in the water. No matter what Spindler tried, he was unable to adjust the deeply anchored Apple culture in any meaningful way. An insider close to Spindler once said: 'The system converts people; people don't convert the system.'[320] The internal tension between changing and staying the same continued to grow and grow. It was a recipe for disaster.

It eventually reached the point where the board saw no other option but to try and find a buyer for the company. There were discussions with Eastman Kodak, AT&T, Canon, Compaq, Hewlett-Packard, Sony and even rival IBM, but no-one was interested in taking over what seemed like a hopeless case. The only offer came from Sun Microsystems at the start of 1996, but was not really serious: just a third of Apple's then market value. Even so, it was an indication of just how low the company had sunk. Apple was literally and figuratively in 'the middle of nowhere': it had failed to achieve its ambitious objectives, failed to adapt its internal culture and failed to find a buyer. Three successive CEOs had been unable to give the company the new balance it so desperately needed. *Time Magazine* described the problem in the following terms: 'Every time the firm has shifted its focus and its strategy, it has lost ground and also some of its identity. Now it is very difficult to identify what Apple Computer really stands for.'[321] Larry Elison, the top man at Oracle (and a friend of Jobs) expressed the same sentiments more graphically. He compared Apple with 'a prodigal daughter, a former homecoming queen, now strung out on drugs and turning tricks on the mean streets'.[322]

A company out of equilibrium – in which the four functions of the AGIL paradigm no longer work in harmony but compete with each other – is a company flirting with its own destruction. This was the situation at Apple in the 1990s.

Does history repeat itself? In June 2019 Jony Ive departed from Apple after nearly 30 years to open his own design firm. The news did not come as a major surprise to Apple insiders. Ive had been growing more distant from Apple's leadership, said people close to the company. Some media even reported that Ive 'grew frustrated as Apple's board became increasingly populated by directors with backgrounds in finance and operations rather than technology or other areas of the company's core business.' Ive's departure indicates that conflicting interchanges had been at play within Apple between the G- and L-functions. Design, and ultimately user simplicity, for which Ive was responsible, are part of the core identity of Apple since the early days (L-function). At the same time Apple was under growing pressure to meet its financial and commercial goals, turning Apple into a 1 trillion-dollar company (G-function). The departure of Ive is indicative of the potential tensions amongst the four AGIL-functions. If a company does not succeed in managing these tensions they might result in conflicts, and in this case one of the figureheads of Apple leaving the company. The underlying tensions and conflicts remind us of the events Apple faced in the mid-1980's after the failed launch of the Macintosh, which at that time caused the forced departure of co-founder Steve Jobs. And of the events that occurred in the mid-1990's when Apple's management was selling out its core identity to reach very aggressive short-term goals, resulting into chaos and almost going bankrupt. If a company does not succeed in managing these tensions and conflicts amongst the four AGIL-functions, its future is at risk.[323 324 325]

A tenth myth: the charismatic leader

In the media and in management books, the success of Apple is often attributed exclusively to the 'genius' of Steve Jobs. According to this belief, the miraculous resurrection of the company after 1997 was the result of his visionary and charismatic leadership: nothing more and nothing less. For many, he was an idol, and his reputation was further enhanced by his tragic early death. In reality, however, the success of Apple is much more than the success of one man. Jobs himself proved as much, with his failure in the 1980s to sustainably anchor the initial success of the Apple II. Moreover, in practice his leadership style was much less charismatic than is romantically portrayed in the media. His behaviour was often autocratic and he was not afraid to give people the sharp edge of his tongue.

By the time he returned to the company in the mid-1990s, his personality had changed. True, he was still as demanding as ever. He was still as omnipresent as ever. And he still breezed through the company like a latter-day Sun King. The biggest difference was that during his absence he had learnt how to manage the four functions of the AGIL paradigm in combination. As we saw earlier in the book, the leader of a company is only 'instrumental'. The company's immortality is dependent on the AGIL functions: these must be kept in a moving equilibrium by the leader; irrespective of the 'style' he chooses to do it. This explains why the authoritarian approach of the extravert Jobs and the more collaborative approach of the more modest Cook have both been able to lead Apple to success.

Lehman Brothers & Sisters

When once asked about his business model, Steve Jobs compared it to The Beatles, pointing out that together the group was bigger than the sum of the four individuals: John, Paul, George and Ringo. We have learned that a company that wishes to survive must fulfil the four AGIL functions in a synchronised manner. We have also learned how the leaders of a company can make the right choices, by searching for the necessary balance between the need for change and the need for stability and consistency.

But what type of leaders and other personnel does a company need to be able to combine these four functions successfully? In reality, putting together your 'immortal dream team' is rather like putting together a powerful and efficient army.

1. To guarantee that your company will be able to adapt quickly and effectively, it first and foremost needs a group of 'explorers'. These are people with a broad view of the world. They have the ability to look beyond the narrow confines of the company framework and can think 'out of the box'. They see no boundaries between the company and its environment, being part of a new generation that is interested in new cultural trends and keen to search for new technologies. They sense that the world is changing and they want both to change with it and to help shape that change.
2. The development of strategy and the realisation of objectives must be entrusted to a group of 'conquerors'. These conquerors or warriors are highly ambitious and result-oriented. They focus on achieving clear and quantifiable goals. What are the criteria that will allow the company to make a difference? Better quality products? More competitive prices? Improved customer service? Conquerors not only wish to understand the world; they want their company, their brand

to win in that world. They give concrete expression to the ideas of the explorers and transform their vision into a set of practical projects. They are not really thinkers; they are more doers.

3. A company also needs a number of 'integrators', who, as the name implies, must ensure proper integration within the company and manage its eco-system. These integrators or diplomats dislike conflict. Instead, they search for allies both inside and outside the company. They combine this with a long-term vision and an ability to build bridges that will serve the company well in the future. Their task is more important than ever in a world that is becoming increasingly fragmented, where conflicts (both internal and external) are inevitably set to multiply.
4. To be able to survive these conflicts, a company must also have a squad of 'guardians'. These protectors attach huge importance to the company's heritage, values and culture, and cherish its 'roots'. They are aware that the company will need to adapt to survive, but their task is to ensure that this adjustment does not lead to a break with the past. They seek to achieve a good balance between change and the preservation of existing values.[326]

These four profiles are very different, but also complementary. Their differences mean that they will sometimes find it hard to work together, but that is perfectly normal: tensions and conflict are part and parcel of the reality of business life. However, their complementarity will ultimately help to steer your company through the difficult and dangerous waters that lie ahead. Which of the four profiles do you need the most? A Deloitte study has concluded that most top leaders in large companies are either explorers or conquerors (or in their original terminology: pioneers and drivers).[327] Why? Because these are the most vocal styles. And probably the most risk-taking. To rephrase the idea: what would have happened to Lehman Brothers if it had been Lehman *Sisters*? Companies that wish to survive should go for a balanced leadership profile, covering all four styles. They need both Brothers and Sisters to survive, but most of all Sisters.

Explorers, conquerors, integrators and guardians: these are the four profiles that a company needs in every department and in every team, if it wants to be successful. If these four profiles can work together in harmony and unison, you will not fail and your survival will be assured. The whole will be greater than the sum of the parts. This is what Bono means in his song *One*, when he sings: 'We are one, but we are not the same.' It might have been a Beatles tune...

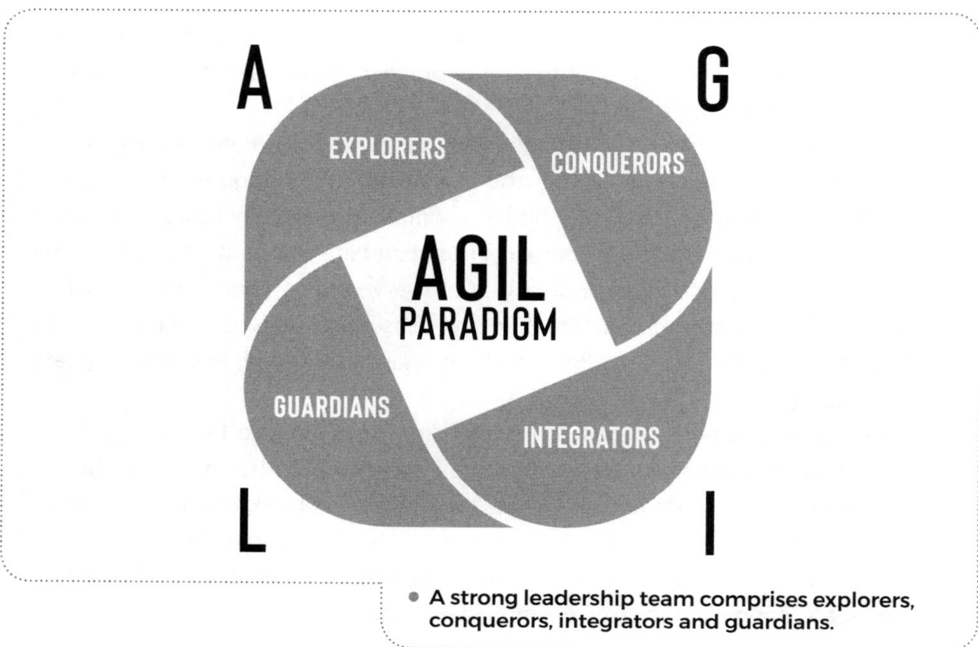

- A strong leadership team comprises explorers, conquerors, integrators and guardians.

The pay-off

In spite of the popular belief about the need for change to be disruptive, it is actually more advisable to adapt to change in your environment progressively and gradually, without straying too far from your identity and core values. Better still, try to change in a manner that strengthens your identity and values. When a brand of long standing changes too drastically, there is a serious risk that it will become weaker or lose influence. The question that needs to be asked, as marketing professor David Aaker has rightly pointed out, is this: 'How can we change while still reinforcing our heritage identity?'[328]

Concepts such as 'culture' and 'identity' have been understood for too long as 'soft' skills: nice if you have them, but no more than that. It is only in recent years that company culture has been treated and managed as a catalyst for innovation and growth. It was Gerard Tellis, a professor at the Marshall School of Business, who first argued that the long-term domination of a market is only possible for companies that carefully cultivate, nourish and maintain a culture of far-reaching innovation. In this context, well-established companies are best placed to innovate and be competitive, because they are usually the companies with the necessary financial resources, experience and expertise.[329]

A study by Booz & Company (now PwC) has further revealed that the companies with a finely tuned culture and a strong innovation strategy generate an additional growth of 30 % in value and 17 % in profits in comparison with other companies. In other words, the closer the link between strategy, culture and innovation, the better a company's financial and commercial performance.[330] This once again disproves the supposed incompatibility of change (innovation) and continuity (culture). Both are necessary to survive in the long term.

And does this 'moving equilibrium' between change and stability pay off, in the end? Rita Gunther McGrath, professor at Columbia Business School, has investigated how many publicly traded companies with a market capitalisation of at least US$1 billion grew by 5 % each year for 10 years, from 2000 till 2009. Only 10 of the 2,347 companies that qualified across that entire period grew their net income by 5 % in all 10 years, and only five grew in terms of both revenues and net income every year. Contrary to conventional wisdom, these findings demonstrate that any growth of the industry they are active in, the type or branch of industry by itself, their size, or even the type of leadership in its management does not make a difference at all. Not even their age does. More than half of the so-called 'outliers' were established in their current form after 1980, but the two most senior companies had been established in 1903 and 1906. Every one of these companies has performed well throughout major shifts in globalization, underlying technology and business practices.

The 'outliers' turned out to share many practices that, although unsurprising in themselves, add up to an intriguing, counterintuitive profile, very familiar to the main findings of my research on the longevity of companies. Although these companies are nimble and adaptive, their leadership, strategy, and values are very stable, McGrath concludes. They pay close attention to values, culture, and alignment (the L and I function in the AGIL-paradigm). They invest significantly in creating an appropriate corporate culture, in employee training, and in executive development. Their stability is what enables these companies to innovate and to maintain steady growth. Coupled with transparent values, it allows employees to feel confident about taking the risks that a spirit of experiment requires. Strong values help maintain ethical standards. Continual small changes keep an organisation from becoming stale. Management continuity permits the building of informal internal networks, which are known to be a factor in successful innovation. The result is a high-performing organisation that delivers consistent results over a reasonably long period in the face of environmental volatility.[331]

Apple forever?

The fact that a desire 'to change the world' has been deeply rooted in the Apple culture right from the very start ensures that even today the company can still continue to slalom effortlessly between these twin poles of change and stability. It has achieved a moving equilibrium that evolves slowly but surely, keeping the company on course but also true to itself. In the second decade of the 21st century, Tim Cook has succeeded in making Apple a bigger success than even Steve Jobs could ever have imagined. The company's future success will continue to be determined by the four functions of the AGIL paradigm, the way its leaders deal with them, and last but not least, its diversified leadership profile. Cook's ambition in this respect, expressed in 2016, is crystal-clear: 'I want Apple to be there, you know, forever.'[332]

FINALLY...

This book does not end here. On the contrary, I hope that it means a new beginning for you and your company; that it will stimulate you to reflect over where your company currently stands today and where tomorrow's opportunities and dangers will emerge.

Together, we have seen what companies need to do in order to survive in the long term. The AGIL paradigm developed by sociologist Talcott Parsons can be applied to every company and, by extension, to every organisation. This makes it possible to map out the conditions for future survival and highlights the possible recipes for both success and failure. Even so, it must be remembered that the AGIL paradigm is not the holy grail. At the end of the day, the owners and leaders of each company must make their own choices and develop their own strategies. In short, they must be responsible for the implementation of their own success or failure.

Our search for the characteristics of the immortal company has taught us the importance of achieving a moving equilibrium between the need for change (the 'A' and 'G' functions) and the need for stability, continuity and consistency ('G' and 'I' functions). At the same time, you must also realise that this is an equilibrium that can never be permanently achieved in a world that is constantly in change – hence the need for movement and progressivity. One thing, however, is certain: a company that remains out of equilibrium over a longer period of time will inevitably go under, no matter how strong its performance might temporarily appear at times. That being said, companies that focus too one-dimensionally on radical change or set targets that are too ambitious are also effectively signing their own death warrant. Survival in the modern business world is more than a matter of Darwinism. For sure, Darwin was right when it comes to the need for adaptation. But adjusting to a changing environment without a clear goal and without the aid of a reliable internal compass is a recipe for disaster in the long term. It risks hollowing out or even destroying the uniqueness of the company, as expressed in its identity and culture. When this happens, the likelihood of internal and/or external fractures and subsequent implosion is very great. The 'L' function, which stands for identity and culture, is therefore the leading function (the pole star of Apple) for every company that wants to survive.

In this book, I have discussed in great detail the paths followed by Apple throughout its existence. At different periods in its 40-year history, it has moved from being on the verge of bankruptcy to become the largest company in the world (measured in terms of market value). By using the four functions of the AGIL paradigm, I hope I have been able to show where and why things went wrong and then went right – and also why Apple under Tim Cook has become even more successful than under the company's founder and spiritual inspiration, Steve Jobs. But remember that this paradigm can also be applied to any company, large or small, public or privately owned.

I have also written this book for the many thousands of young entrepreneurs, who are today in the process of starting up their own business. These pages will have shown how a starting company can succeed in becoming sustainable in the medium term by a balanced rather than a disruptive approach. In many respects, the story of Apple is inspirational, not only because of its successes but also because of its failures at various moments in its history and its ability to climb back out of the hole in which it found itself. Entrepreneurship is often a matter of dusting yourself off and starting again – time after time.

Last but not least, I hope that this book will have made clear to the reader that survival in the long term is more than a matter of indiviual luck, fate or faith. It is, above all, a matter of finding the strength to change, so that you can remain true to your own real nature. This is the only possible way forwards that has any chance of success. You will have to change to stay true to yourself, or even, to become your better self.

IS YOUR COMPANY IMMORTAL?

DO THE AGIL-TEST*

What are the survival chances of your company? Does your company adjust sufficiently to its changing environment? Is your strategy successful in achieving your objectives? Are you managing to keep everything in your company on an even keel? What is the identity of your company in the long term?

After reading this book, would you like to know how your company will fare in the future?

You would? Then why not do the AGIL paradigm self-test on **www.fonsvandyck.com** and see whether your company will still be in business in 5 years' time. Exclusively for readers of *The Survival Paradox*.

And please don't hesitate to contact Fons Van Dyck if you have any questions about what the AGIL paradigm can mean in practice for your company.

Because you don't need to let the future control you; with the right approach, you can control the future!

* © The AGIL methodology for companies, the AGIL self-evaluation survey and the AGIL score are all protected by patent.

ENDNOTES

Introduction

1 *The Economist* (2011). The magician: Steve Jobs and the world he created. 8 October, p. 15.
2 President Barack Obama's speech can be consulted at: https://obamawhitehouse.archives.gov/blog/2011/10/05/president-obama-passing-steve-jobs-he-changed-way-each-us-sees-world.
3 Kane, Y.I. (2014). *Haunted empire: Apple after Steve Jobs.* New York: Harper Collins.
4 Hudson, B. (2014). The prevalence of longevity among leading brands. *Boston Hospitality Review*, Fall.
5 Hill, A. (2011). Nokia: from 'burning platform' to a slimmer management model. *Financial Times*, 25 February.
6 Darrow, B. (2015). Bye-bye HP, it's the end of and era. *Fortune Magazine*, 30 October.
7 Havas Media (2019). Meaningful brands: https://www.meaningful-brands.com/en
8 Van Hamme, K. (2018). Familiebedrijven kloppen de beurs. *De Tijd*, 1 September, p. 35.
9 The most popular biography of Steve Jobs is by Walter Isaacson (ex-CNN and *Time*) and is based on his many conversations with Jobs and his entourage towards the end of his life:
Isaacson, W. (2011). *Steve Jobs: the exclusive biography*. New York: Simon & Schuster.
A more recent biography was written by Brent Schlender and Rick Tetzeli, journalists at *Fortune* and *Fast Company*:
Schlender, B. & Tetzeli, R. (2015). *Becoming Steve Jobs*. New York: Crown Business.
The best documented history of Apple, from the early years to the present day, can be found in the extensive papers of David Yoffie, Professor of International Business Administration at the Harvard Business School. For the brief summary of the history of Apple in this book I used facts and figures extracted from these papers. Also important for its attention to historical details (for the period up to the launching of the iPod) is:
Linzmayer, O.W. (2004-2008). *Apple confidential 2.0. The definitive history of the world's most colorful company.* San Francisco: No Starch Press.
For fascinating insights into Apple's wilderness years, see, amongst others:
Carlton, J. (1997). *Apple: the inside story of intrigue, egomania and business blunders.* New York: Random House.
Malone, M.S. (1990). *Infinite loop*. New York: Currency Doubleday.
Moritz, M. (1984-2010). *Return to the little kingdom: how Apple and Steve Jobs changed the world.* New York: The Overlook Press.
Rose, F. (1989-2009). *West of Eden: the end of innocence at Apple Computer*. New York: Stuyvesant Street Press.
Young, J.S. (1987). *Steve Jobs: the journey is the reward.* New York: Lynx Books.
Finally, there are also a number of biographies and autobiographies of other important 'crown witnesses' from the Apple management, often written from a highly subjective perspective, but nonetheless interesting for offering a different angle of approach. See:
Sculley, J. (1987). *Odyssey: Pepsi to Apple*. New York: Harper Row.
Amelio, G. & Simon, W.L. (1998). *On the firing line*. New York: Harper Business.
Wozniak, S. (2006). *iWoz*. New York: W.W. Norton & Company.
Hertzfeld, A. (2005). *Revolution in the valley*. Sebastopol: O'Reilly Media.
McKenna, R. (1986). *The Regis Touch: new marketing strategies for uncertain times.* Menlo Park: Addison-Wesley.
10 Bradshaw, T. (2017). Apple serves up in-house tech to set it apart. *Financial Times*, 14 September, p. 13.
Bradshaw, T. (2017). Apple reclaims crown amid iPhone X launch. *Financial Times*, 5 November, p. 10.

The AGIL paradigm

11 Booth, C. (1997). Steve's Job: restart Apple. *Time Magazine*, 18 August.
12 Reeves, M., Levin, S. & Ueda, D. (2016). The biology of corporate survival. *Harvard Business Review*, January-February, pp. 47-55.
13 Govindarajan, V. & Srivastava, A. (2016). The scary truth about corporate survival. *Harvard Business Review*, December, pp. 24-25.
14 Innosight (2016). *Corporate longevity: turbulence ahead for large organisations.*
15 Kim, E. (2018). Jeff Bezos to employees: 'One day, Amazon will fail' but our job is to delay it as long as possible.' CNBC, published 15 November 2018, updated 27 November 2018.
16 Davis, I. (2014). Reflections on corporate longevity. *McKinsey Quarterly*, September.
17 Foster, R. & Kaplan, S. (2001). *Creative destruction: from built-to-last to built-to-perform.* London: Prentice Hall.
18 Reeves, M., Levin, S. & Ueda, D. (2016). The biology of corporate survival. *Harvard Business Review*, January-February, pp. 47-55.
19 Schein, E.H. (2003). *DEC is dead, long live DEC* (pp. 243-244). San Francisco: Berrett-Koehler Publishers.
20 Schein, H.E. (2010, 4th ed.). *Organizational culture and leadership* (pp. 11, 20). San Francisco: Jossey Bass.
21 Collins, J. & Porras, J. (2000, 3e ed.). *Built to last* (pp. 54-55). London: Random House.
22 De Geus, A. (1997). *The living company*. Boston: Harvard Business School Press.
23 Tellis, G.J. (2013). *Unrelenting innovation* (pp. 241-244). San Francisco: Jossey-Bass.
Rajesh, C. & Tellis, G.J. (2000). The incumbent's curse? Incumbency, size and radical product innovation. *Journal of Marketing*, 64(3), July, pp. 1-17.
24 Sharp, B., Nenycz-Thiel, M., Martin, J., Anesbury, Z. & McColl, B. (2017). *Are big brands dying?* (paper published online).
25 Parsons, T. & Smelser, N.J. (1956). *Economy and society.* New York: Routledge (Paperback issue, 2010).
26 For whoever wishes to learn more about the theories of Parsons, I can recommend the following works:
Alexander, J.C. (1983). *The modern reconstruction of classical thought: Talcott Parsons*. London: Routledge & Kegan Paul.
Bourricaud, F. (1981). *The sociology of Talcott Parsons.* Chicago: The University of Chicago Press.
Fox, R.C., Lidz, V.M. & Bershady, H.J. (2005). *After Parsons: a theory of social action for the twenty-first century*. New York: Russell Sage

Foundation.
Gerhardt, U. (2002). *Talcott Parsons: an intellectual biography.* Cambridge: Cambridge University Press.
Kerkhoff, A.H.M. (2007). *De samenleving in schema's. Een inleiding in het sociologische denken van Talcott Parsons.* Budel: Damon.
Rocher, G. (1974). *Talcott Parsons and American sociology.* London: Nelson.
Segre, S. (2012). *Talcott Parsons, an introduction.* Lanham: University Press of America.
For those who wish to read Parsons in his own words, his most important publications are:
(1937) *The structure of social action.*
(1951) *The social system.*
(1951) *Toward a general theory of action.*
(1951) *Working papers in the theory of action.*
(1956) *Economy and society.*
(1966) *Societies: evolutionary and comparative perspectives.*
(1969) *Politics and social structure.*
(1971) *The system of modern societies.*
(1973) *The American university.*
(1977) *Social systems and the evolution of the action theory.*
(1977) *The evolution of societies.*
(1978) *Action theory and the human condition.*
(1999) *The Talcott Parsons Reader* (edited by Turner, B.S.).
27 Barton, D., Manyika, J. & Keohane Williamson, S. (2017). Finally, proof that managing for the long term pays off. *Harvard Business Review*, 7 February.

1The smart follower

28 Kranz, M. (1999). Jobs' golden Apple. *Time Magazine*, 2 August.
29 Kranz, M. (1999).
30 Schlender, B. (1998). The three faces of Steve. *Fortune Magazine*, 9 November.
31 Schlender, B. & Tetzeli, R. (2015). *Becoming Steve Jobs* (p. 237). New York: Crown Business.
32 Merchant, B. (2017). *The one device: the secret history of the iPhone* (p. 48). New York: Little, Brown and Company.
33 Morris, B. (2008). What makes Apple golden: an exclusive interview with Steve Jobs. *Fortune Magazine*, 17 March.
34 Stone, B. (2011). Steve Jobs: the return, 1997-2011. *Business Week*, 6 October.
35 Isaacson, W. (2011).
36 Isaacson, W. (2011).
37 Gladwell, M. (2011). The tweaker. *The New Yorker*, 14 November.
38 Manjoo, F. (2015). Invincible Apple: 10 lessons from the coolest company anywhere. *Fast Company Magazine*, July/August.
39 Tellis, G.J. & Golder, P.N. (1996). First to market, first to fail? Real causes of enduring market leadership. *Sloan Management Review*, Winter, pp. 65-75.
Tellis, G.J. & Golder, P.N. (2002). *Will and vision. How latecomers grow to dominate markets.* Los Angeles: Figueroa Press.
40 Thiel, P. & Masters, B. (2014). *Zero to one* (pp. 56-58). London: Virgin Books.
41 Bort, J. (2019). Jeff Bezos says the true secret to business success is to focus on the things that won't change, not the things that will. *Business Insider* (consulted online).
42 Christensen, C.M. (1997). *The innovator's dilemma.* Boston: Harvard Business School Press.
43 McGregor, J. (2007). Clayton Christensen's innovation brain. *Business Week*, 15 June.
44 Kahney, L. (2010). John Sculley and Steve Jobs: the full interview. *Cult of the Mac*, 14 October.
45 Keller, K.L. (2008). *Strategic brand management* (pp. 490-541). New York: M.E. Sharpe.
46 Batra, R., Lenk, P. & Wedel, M. (2010). Brand extension strategy planning: empirical estimation of brand Amsand-category personality fit and atypicality. *Journal of Marketing Research*, XLVII (April), pp. 335-347.
47 X. (2018). Re-evaluating incremental innovation. *Harvard Business Review*, September-October, 22-24 (the study 'Newton versus Lorenz: innovation in consumer goods companies', is by Marcel Corstjens, Gregory Carpenter and Tushmit Hasan, and also appeared in the MIT Sloan Management Review).
48 Murphy, M. (2017). Tim Cook on Donald Trump, the HomePod, and the legacy of Steve Jobs. *Bloomberg Business Week*, 19 June.
49 Stone, B. & Tyrangiel, J. (2014). Tim Cook Q&A: the full interview on iPhone 6 and the Apple Watch. *Bloomberg Business Week*, 19 September.
50 Murphy, M. (2017). Tim Cook on Donald Trump, the HomePod, and the legacy of Steve Jobs. *Bloomberg Business Week*, 19 June.

2 The customer first

51 Florida, R. (2002). *The rise of the creative class.* New York: Basic Books.
52 Schlender, B. & Tetzeli, R. (2015). *Becoming Steve Jobs* (pp. 272, 349). New York: Crown Business.
53 Macworld Staff (2013). This is Tim: Cook at the 2013 Goldman Sachs conference (transcript). *Macworld*, 12 February.
54 Bach, D. & Allen, D.B. (2010). What every CEO needs to know about non-market strategy. *MIT Sloan Management Review*. Spring issue, April.
55 Sculley, J. (1987). *Odyssey: Pepsi to Apple* (p. 215). New York: Harper & Row.
56 Kahneman, D. (2016). *Ons onfeilbare denken.* Amsterdam: Business Contact.
57 Isaacson, W. (2011), p. 332.
58 Pine, J.H. & Gilmore B.J. (1999). *The experience economy.* Boston: Harvard Business Press.

59 Reputation Institute (2016). *Global RepTrack 100: the world's most reputable companies.*
60 Sinek, S. (2012). *Begin met het waarom.* Amsterdam: Business Contact.
61 Almquist, E. (2016). *Elements of value. Measuring what customers really want.* Harvard Business Review Webinar (consulted online).
62 WARC (2011). *Apple Macintosh: Mac vs PC.* Cannes Creative Effectiveness Lions.
63 Isaacson, W. (2011), p. 143.
64 Burlingham, B. & Gendron, G. (1989).The entrepreneur of the decade. An interview with Steve Jobs. *Inc. Magazine*, 1 April.
65 Merchant, B. (2017), p. 347.
66 Wilson, M. (2014). 4 myths about Apple design, from an ex-Apple designer. *Fast Company*, 22 May.
67 Vascellaro, J.E. (2012). Turns out Apple conducts market research after all. *The Wall Street Journal*, 26 July.
68 Robinson, B.T. (2013). *Appletopia* (pp. 17, 100, 101). Waco: Baylor University.

3 Follow the money

69 Bradshaw T. (2018). High-priced iPhone X does the trick for Apple. *Financial Times*, 3 May, 13.
70 Bradshaw, T. (2018). Service arms helps push Apple towards $1 tn. *Financial Times*, 29 May, 13.
71 Kahney, L. (2011). Icon of the valley: a personal appreciation of Steve Jobs. *Fortune Magazine*, 11 October.
72 Hern, A. (2017). *Tim Cook: Apple products aren't just for the rich. The Guardian*, 12 September.
73 Grobart, S. (2013). Apple chiefs discuss strategy, market share and the new iPhones. *Bloomberg Business Week*, 19 September.
74 Treacy, M. & Wiersema, F. (1995). *The discipline of market leaders.* Cambridge, Massachusetts: Perseus Books, pp. 37, 40.
75 Treacy, M. & Wiersema, F. (1995), pp. 33, 34, 36.
76 Stone, B. (2013). *The everything store.* New York: Little, Brown and Company, pp. 89-90.
77 Treacy, M. & Wiersema, F. (1995), p. 40).
78 Treacy, M. & Wiersema, F. (1995), p. 45).
79 Crawford, F., Mathews, R. (2001). *The myth of excellence: why great companies never try to be the best at everything.* New York: Three Rivers Press.
80 Kapferer, J.N. (2012). *The new strategic brand management.* London: Kogan Page.
81 Aaker, D. (1991), p. 18.
82 Kane, Y. (2014), p. 39.
83 Keller, K.L. (2008), pp. 206-208.
84 Taylor, D. (2013). *Grow the core.* Chichester: John Wiley & Sons, p. 58.
85 Dendooven, P. (2019): Carlos Britto: De dagen dat één merk dominant was, zijn voorbij. *De Standaard*, 1 March
86 Burggraeve, C.R. (2019). *Marketing is finance is business. How CMO, CFO and CEO cocreate iconic brands with sustainable pricing power in the New Galactic Age*, p. 129-130.
87 Burggraeve, C.R. (2019), p. 133.
88 Sharp, B. (2010), pp. 41, 50.
89 Pringle, H. & Field, P. (2008). *Brand immortality: how brands can live long and prosper.* London: Kogan Page, p. 168.
90 Sheff, D. (1985). Playboy interview: Steve Jobs. *Playboy Magazine*, February.
91 Malone, M.S. (1999). *Infinite loop.* New York: Currency Doubleday, p. 118.
92 Isaacson, W. (2011), p. 105.
93 Sculley, J. (1987), p. 141.
94 Sculley, J. (1987), p. 377.
95 Carlton, J. (1997), pp. 79-80.
96 Carlton, J. (1997), p. 107.
97 Carlton, J. (1997), pp. 135, 181.
98 Amelio, G. & Simon, W.L. (1998), p. 8.
99 Armstrong, J.S. & Green, K.C. (1996). Competitor orientation: effects of objectives and information on managerial decisions and profitability. *Journal of Business Research*. 33, pp. 188-199.
Armstrong, J.S. & Green, K.C. (2007). Competitor-oriented objectives: the myth of market share. *International Journal of Business*, 12, pp.117-136.
100 X. (2007). The 'myth of market share': can focusing too much on the competition harm profitability? *Knowledge@Wharton*, 24 January.
101 Ovide, S. & Wakabyashi, D. (2015) Apple's share of smartphone industry's profits soar to 92 %. *The Wall Street Journal*, 12 July.
102 Bradshaw, T. (2018). High-priced iPhone X does the trick for Apple. *Financial Times*, 3 May, p. 13.
103 Bloom, P. & Kotler, P. (1975). Strategies for high market-share companies. *Harvard Business Review*, November.
104 O'Donnell, N. (2019). Facing possible anti-trust probe, CEO Tim Cook insists Apple is 'not a monopoly'. CBS News, 4 June (consulted online).
105 Keller, K.L. (2008), p. 209.
Sharp, B. (2010). *How brands grow: what marketers don't know* (pp. 156-157). Oxford: University Press.

4 Omnipresent

106 Moritz, M. (1984-2010). *Return to the little kingdom: how Apple and Steve Jobs changed the world* (p. 181). New York: The Overlook Press.
107 *The Independent* (1992). My biggest mistake: Regis McKenna. 11 October.
108 Moritz, M. (1984), p. 34.

109 Malone, M. (1999). *Infinite loop*. New York: Currency Doubleday, p. 3.
110 McKenna, R. (1985). *The Regis touch: new marketing strategies for uncertain times* (pp. 53, 55). Menlo Park: Addison-Wesley.
111 McKenna, R. (1985), p. 56.
112 McKenna, R. (1985), p. 61.
113 Rose, F. (1989). *West of Eden: the end of innocence at Apple Computer* (pp. 150-151). New York: Stuyvesant Street Press.
114 Sculley, J. (1987), pp. 223-224.
115 Villanueva, J., Yoo, S. & Hanssens, D.M. (2008). The impact of marketing-induced versus word-of-mouth customer acquisition on customer equity growth. *Journal of Marketing Research*, XLV (February), pp. 48-59.
116 WARC (2019). Influencer marketing: beyond the hype, published online, February.
117 Keller, E. & Fay, B. (2012). *The Face-to-Face Book: why real relationships rule in a digital marketplace*. New York: Free Press.
118 WARC (2004). Apple Computer: iPod Silhouettes. *WARC: Effie Worldwide Silver Award; Effie Awards.*
119 Apple Computer Inc. (2003). *Annual Report.*
120 WARC (2011). *IDC Worldwide PC Tracker 2010.*
121 Sethuraman, R., Tellis, G. & Briesch, R. (2011). How well does advertising work? Generalizations from meta-analysis of brand advertising elasticities. *Journal of Marketing Research*, 48(3), June, pp. 457-471.
122 De Vries, L., Gensler, S. & Leeflang, P.S.H. (2017). Effects of traditional advertising and social messages on brand-building metrics and customer acquisition. *Journal of Marketing*, 81 (September), pp. 1-15.
123 Joshi, A. & Hanssens, D. (2010). The direct and indirect effects of advertising spending on firm value. *Journal of Marketing*, 74(1), January, pp. 20-33.
124 Yoffie, D. (2007).
125 Sherman, E. (2015). Apple Watch $3M ad spend a drop in the bucket. *CBS Moneywatch*, 10 April.
O' Reilly, L. (2016). Apple mysteriously stopped disclosing how much it spends on ads. *Business Insider UK*, 24 November.
126 Useem, J. (2007). Apple: America's best retailer. *Fortune Magazine*, 8 March.
127 Adamczyk, A. (2016). Remember when everyone thought Apple stores would fail? *Money*, 19 May.
128 Linzmayer, O.W. (2008), p. 300.
129 Isaacson, W. (2011), pp. 369-370.
130 Isaacson, W. (2011), p. 370.
131 Isaacson, W. (2011), p. 374.
132 Macworld Staff (2013) This is Tim: Cook at the 2013 Goldman Sachs conference (transcript). *Macworld*, 12 February.
133 Allen, G. (2014). Numbers revealed: Apple retail is all about community. *Forbes*, 7 December.
134 Manjoo F. (2010). Invincible Apple: 10 lessons from the coolest company anywhere. *Fast Company Magazine*. July/August.
135 Macworld Staff (2013). This is Tim: Cook at the 2013 Goldman Sachs conference (transcript). *Macworld*, 12 February.
136 Reingold, J. (2015). What the heck is Angela Ahrendts doing at Apple? *Fortune Magazine*, 10 September.
137 Danziger, P.N. (2017). Today at Apple: how Angela Ahrendts imagined a new Apple retail experience. *Forbes*, 20 May.
138 Dormehl, L. (2012), p. 377.
139 Markoff, J. (1996). Apple expects it will lose $700 million. *The New York Times*, 10 June.
140 Amelio, G. & Simon W.L. (1998), p. 115.
141 Amelio, G. & Simon W.L. (1998), p. 115.
142 Amelio, G. & Simon W.L. (1998), p. 117.
143 Sharp, B. (2010), p. 55.

5 The alignment pact

144 Dawar, N. (2018). Marketing in the age of Alexa. *Harvard Business Review*, May-June (consulted online).
145 X. (2011). Steve Jobs. *Time, Special Commemorative issue*, pp. 51-52.
146 Sculley, J. (1987), p. 143.
147 Wozniak, S. (2007), p. 265.
148 Isaacson, W. (2011), p. 262.
149 Hansen, M. (2009). *Collaboration* (pp. 18-19). Boston: Harvard Business Review Press.
150 Colt, S. (2014). Tim Cook gave his most in-depth interview to date (PBS News). *Business Insider*, 21 September.
151 McGregor, J. (2016). Tim Cook, the interview: Running Apple 'is sort of a lonely job'. *The Washington Post*, 13 August.
152 Reingold, J. (2015). What the heck is Angela Ahrendts doing at Apple? *Fortune Magazine*, September.
153 McKenna, R. (1985), p. 165.
154 Carlton, J. (1997), p. 139.
Business Week, 1994, 2 October.
155 Linzmayer, O.W. (2008), p. 290.
156 Schlender, B. & Tetzeli, R. (2015), p. 354.
157 Dormehl, L. (2012), p. 458.
158 Blenkinsop, P. (2019). Spofify files EU antitrust complaint against Apple. Reuters, 13 March (consulted online).
159 Van Thillo, C. (2019). Apple makes a lot of money out of our apps. *Financial Times*, 7 June.
160 Keller, K.L. (2008), pp. 73, 87, 389.
Kapferer, J.N. (2012), p. 131.
161 Kahney, L. (2011), p. 28.
Isaacson, W. (2011), p. 322.
162 Schlender, B. & Tetzeli, R. (2015), p. 349.
Kahney, L. (2011), p. 241.
163 Manjoo, F. (2010). Invincible Apple: 10 lessons from the coolest company anywhere. *Fast Company Magazine*, July/August.

164 Isaacson, W. (2011), p. 516.
165 Schlender, B. & Tetzeli, R. (2015), p. 288.
166 Colt, S. (2014).
167 Tetzeli, R. (2016). Tim Cook on Apple's values, mistakes and seeing around corners. *Fast Company Magazine*, 9 August.
168 Siggelkow, N. & Terwiesch, C. (2019). The age of continuous connection. *9*, May-June, pp. 64-73.
169 Forrester Research (2019). Customer service chatbots fail consumers today. 30 January (consulted online).
170 Burrows, P. (1996). Why fewer buyers are bobbing for Apples. *Business Week*, 5 February.
171 Malone, M. (1999), p. 537.
172 Malone, M. (1999), p. 546.
173 Malone, M. (1999), p. 549.
174 Markoff, J. (1996).
175 Belk, R. & Tumbat, G. (2005). The cult of Macintosh. *Consumption, Markets and Culture,* 8 September, pp. 205-217.
176 Linzmayer, O.W. (2008), p. 541.
177 Malone, S. (1999), p. 479
178 Sharp, B. (2010), pp. 108, 111, 327.
Franzen, G. (2009), p. 327.
179 Reinartz, W. & Kumar, V. (2002). The mismanagement of customer loyalty. *Harvard Business Review*, July.
180 Reputation Institute (2016).
181 Fombrun, C.J., Ponzi, L.J. & Newburry, W. (2015). Stakeholder tracking and analysis: the RepTrak system for measuring corporate reputation. *Corporate Reputation Review*, 18(1), pp. 3-24.
Caspar, R. & Thomsen, S. (2004). The impact of corporate reputation on performance: some Danish evidence. *European Management Journal*, 22(2), pp. 201-210.
182 Porter, M. (2011).
183 Kahney, L. (2019). *Tim Cook: the genius who took Apple to the next level.* Portfolio/Pinguin.
184 Cook, T. (2019). Commencement address by Apple CEO Tim Cook. *Stanford News*, June 16 (consulted online).

6 Us against them

185 Grossman, L. & Gibbs, N. (2016). Apple CEO Tim Cook on his fight with the FBI and why he won't break down. *Time Magazine*, 17 March.
186 McGregor, J. (2016). Tim Cook, the interview: Running Apple 'is sort of a lonely job'. *The Washington Post*, 13 August.
187 Parsons, T. (1961), p. 70.
188 Keller, K.L. (2008), pp. 115, 131.
189 Sharp, B. (2010).
190 Aaker, D. (2011), pp. 295-296.
Kapferer, J-N. (2012), pp. 226-227.
191 Calkins, T. (2012). *Defending your brand* (pp. 90, 225-227, 232-233). New York: Palgrave MacMillan.
192 Calkins, T. (2012). p. 245.
193 Sheff, D. (1985). Playboy interview: Steve Jobs. *Playboy Magazine*, February.
194 Linzmayer, O.W. (2008), pp. 67-68.
195 Linzmayer, O.W. (2008), p. 67.
196 Linzmayer, O.W. (2008), p. 254.
197 Carlton, J. (1997), p. 411.
198 Isaacson, W. (2011), pp. 405-406.
Schlender, B. & Tetzeli, R. (2015), p. 291.
199 Isaacson, W. (2011), p. 512.
200 Stone, B. & Helft, M. (2010). Apple's spat with Google is getting personal. *The New York Times*, 13 March.
201 Kane, Y.I. (2014), p. 16.
202 Kane, Y.I. (2014), p.161.
203 Reisinger, D. (2015). Samsung will pay Apple for damages – but wants the cash back. *Fortune Magazine*, 15 June.

7 The DNA of the company

204 Kahney, L. (2008). *Inside Steve's brain* (p. 267). London: Atlantic Book.
205 Kirkpatrick, D. (1998). The second coming of Apple. *Fortune Magazine*, 9 November.
206 Levitt, T. (1986). *The marketing imagination* (pp. 72-93). New York: The Free Press.
Keller, K.L. (2008), pp. 3-5.
207 Wozniak, S. (2007), p. 151.
208 Isaacson, W. (2011), p. 168.
209 Linzmayer, O.W. (2008), p. 109.
210 Malone, M.S. (1999), p. 232.
211 Sculley, J. (1987), pp. 90, 142.
212 Colt, S. (2014). Tim Cook gave his most in-depth interview to date. *PBS News. Business Insider*, 21 September.
213 Griffin, A. (2017). Apple's Tim Cook on iPhones, augmented reality, and how he plans to change the world. *The Independent*, 10 October.
214 McGregor, J. (2016). Tim Cook, the interview: running Apple 'is sort of a lonely job'. *The Washington Post*, 13 August.
215 Cook, T. (2013). Workplace equality is good for business. *The Wall Street Journal*, 3 November.
Cook, T. (2014). Tim Cook speaks up. *Bloomberg BusinessWeek*, 30 October.

216 Colt, S. (2014).
217 Cook, T. (2017). *MIT's Commencement Speech,* 9 June.
218 Carlton, J. (1997), p. 93.
219 Wozniak, S. (2007), p. 232.
220 Carlton, J. (1997) pp. 48, 51, 93.
221 Sculley, J. (1987), pp. 273-274.
222 Morris, B. (2008). What makes Apple golden: an exclusive interview with Steve Jobs. *Fortune Magazine*, 17 March.
223 Tetzeli, R. (2016). It's Tim Cook's Apple now: what WWDC 2016 teaches us about his vision for the company. *Fast Company Magazine*, 14 June.
224 Isaacson, W. (2011), pp. 80, 97.
225 Isaacson, W. (2011), p. 126.
226 Isaacson, W. (2011), pp. 126, 128.
227 Isaacson, W. (2011), p. 128.
228 Isaacson, W. (2011), p. 243.
229 Kahney, L. (2013). *Jony Ive: the genius behind Apple's greatest products* (pp. 268, 269). London: Penguin Books.
230 Merchant, B. (2017), p. 332.
231 Wozniak, S. (2007), p. 233.
232 Sculley, J. (1987), p. 130.
233 Isaacson, W. (2011), pp. 157, 158.
234 Malone, M.S. (1999), p. 396.
235 Rose, F. (2009), p. 328.
Schlender, B. & Tetzeli, R. (2015), p. 90.
236 Kahney, L. (2011), pp. 27-28.
237 Hoeffler, S. & Keller, K.L. (2003). The marketing advantages of strong brands. *Journal of Brand Management*, 10(6), pp. 421-445.
238 Fischer, M., Völckner, F. & Sattler, H. (2010). How important are brands? A cross-category, cross-country study. *Journal of Marketing Research*, 10, pp. 831- 834.
239 Madden, T.J., Fehle, F., Fournier, S.M. (2002). Brands matter: an empirical investigation of brand-building activities and the creation of shareholder value (working paper).
240 Gromark, J. & Melin, F. (2011). The underlying dimensions of brand orientation and its impact on financial performance. *Journal of Brand Management*. 18(6), pp. 394-410.
241 Gerzema, J. & Lebar, E. (2008), *The brand bubble* (p. 12). San Francisco: Jossey-Bass.
242 Interbrand (2017). *Best global brands 2017 rankings.*
243 Collins, J. & Porras, J. (2000), p. 54.
244 Collins, J. & Hansen, M. (2011). *Great by choice* (p. 136). New York: Harper Business.
245 Collins, J. & Hansen, M. (2011). p. 145.
246 Aaker, D.A. (1996). *Building strong brands* (pp. 216, 223). New York: the Free Press.
Aaker, D.A. (1991). *Managing brand equity: capitalizing on the value of a brand name* (pp. 15-16). New York: Macmillan.
247 Kapferer (2012), pp. 245, 292.
248 Bunton, 2015.
249 Barton, D., Manyika, J. & Keohane Williamson, S. (2017). Finally, evidence that managing for the long term pays off. *Harvard Business Review* (online). 7 February.

8 The hidden force of culture

250 Tetzeli, R. & Schlender, B. (2015). Tim Cook on Apple's future. *Fast Company Magazine*, April.
251 Schein, E.H. (2010, 4th ed.). *Organizational culture and leadership* (p. 32). San Francisco: Jossey Bass.
252 Groysberg, B., Lee, J., Price, J. & Cheng, J. (2018). The leader's guide to corporate culture. *Harvard Business Review*, January-February, pp. 44-57.
253 Schein, E.H. (2009), *The corporate culture survival guide* (p. 4). San Francisco: Jossey Bass.
254 Schein, E.H. (2010), p. 336.
255 Schein, E.H. (2010), p. 337.
256 Schein, E.H. (2010), p. 337.
257 England, L. (2015). What Apple employees really think about the company's internal culture. *Business Insider*, 18 July.
258 Wozniak, S. (2007), p. 150.
259 Barbrook, R. & Cameron, A. (1996). The California ideology. *Science as culture*, 6(1), 44-72.
260 Rose, F. (2009). pp. 40-41.
261 Rose, F. (2009), p. 39.
262 Carlton, J. (1997), p. 29.
263 Carlton, J. (1997), p. 29.
264 Rose, F. (2009), pp. 265, 266.
265 Brandon, L. (2014). Apple: Steve Wozniak on the early days with Steve Jobs. *Business Week*, 4 December.
266 Heath, D. & Heath, C. (2007). The myth about creating myths. *Fast Company*, 1 March.
267 Carlton, J. (1997), p. 29.
268 Carlton, J. (1997), p. 32.
269 Carlton, J. (1997), p. 35.
270 Carlton, J. (1997), p. 36.
271 Rebello, K., Burrows, P. & Sager, R. (1996), 5 February.

272 Amelio, G. & Simon, W.L. (1998), pp. 25, 119.
273 Dormehl, L. (2012). *The Apple revolution* (p. 375). London: Virgin Books.
274 Schein, E.H. (2009), p. 5.
275 Schein, E.H. (2009), p. 6.
276 Schlender, B. (1998). The three faces of Steve. *Fortune Magazine*, 9 November.
277 Reinhardt, A. (1998). Steve Jobs: 'There's sanity returning'. *Business Week*, 25 May.
278 Young, J.S. & Simon, W.L. (2005). *Steve Jobs: iCon* (p. 235). Hoboken: John Wiley & Sons.
279 Morris, B. (2000). Apple's one-dollar-a-year man. *Fortune Magazine*, 24 January.
280 Reinhardt, A. (1998). Steve Jobs on Apple's resurgence: 'not a one-man-show'. *Business Week*, 12 May.
281 Kahney, L. (2011). *Jony Ive: the genius behind Apple's greatest products* (pp. 155-156). London: Portfolio Pinguin.
282 Elkind, P. (2008). The trouble with Steve. *Fortune Magazine*, 4 March.
283 Merchant, B. (2017), pp. 17-18, 27.
284 Lashinsky, A. (2012). *Inside Apple* (p. 45). New York: Business Plus.
285 Fiegerman, S. (2014). Tim Cook's philosophy at Apple, in his own words. *Mashable*, 17 September.
286 Murphy, M. (2017). Tim Cook on Donald Trump, the HomePod, and the legacy of Steve Jobs. *Business Week*, 19 June.
287 Pisano, G.P. (2019). The hard truth about innovative cultures. *Harvard Business Review*, January-February, pp. 62-71.
288 Pisano, G.P. (2019). The hard truth about innovative cultures. *Harvard Business Review*, January-February, pp. 62-71.
289 Groysberg, B., Lee, J., Price, J. & Cheng, J. (2018). The leader's guide to corporate culture. *Harvard Business Review*, January-February, pp. 44-57.
290 Nadella, S. (2017). *Hit refresh*. London: William Collins, p. 97.
291 Nadella, S. (2017), p. 100.
292 Nadella, S. (2017), p.100.
293 Nadella, S. (2017), p.102.
294 Nadella, S. (2017), p. 105.
295 Nadella, S. (2017), p. 111.
296 Nadella, S. (2017), p. 135.
297 Spencer Stuart (2017). *The role of culture in search and succession: busting three common cultural myths*, p. 1 (consulted online).
298 Flatt, S., Harris-Boundry, J. & Wagner, S. (2013). CEO succession: a help or hindrance to corporate reputation? *Corporate Reputation Review*, 16(3), pp. 206-219.
299 Rhim, J.C., Peluchette, J.V. & Song, I. (2006). Stock market reactions and firm performance surrounding CEO succession: antedecent of succession and successor origin. *American Journal of Business*, 221(1), pp. 159-171.
300 Collins, J. & Porras, J. (2000), p. 184.

A moving equilibrium

301 Tetzeli, R. & Schlender, B. (2015). Tim Cook on Apple's future. *Fast Company*, April.
302 Parsons, T. (1951). *Toward a general theory of action* (p. 179). Cambridge (MA): Harvard University Press.
303 Collins, J. & Porras, J. (2000), pp. 84, 85, 88.
304 Loubser, J.J., Baum, R.C., Effrat, A. & Lidz, V. (1976). *Explorations in general theory in social science* (p. 7). New York: The Free Press.Rocher, G. (1974). *Talcott Parsons and American sociology* (p. 48).London: Nelson.
305 Markoff, J. (2004). Oh, yeah, he also sells computers. *The New York Times*, 25 April.
306 Elmer-DeWitt, P. (2013). Apple Inc. CEO Tim Cook speaks at Goldman Sachs. *Fortune Magazine*, 12 February.
307 Stone, B. & Satariano, A (2014). Tim Cook interview: the iPhone 6, the Apple Watch, and remaking a company's culture. *Business Week*, 17 September.
308 Macworld Staff (2013). This is Tim: Cook at the 2013 Goldman Sachs conference (transcript). *Macworld,* 12 February.
309 Lashinsky, A. (2015). Apple's Tim Cook leads different. *Fortune Magazine*, 24 May.
310 Lashinsky, A. (2015).
311 Isaacson, W. (2011), p. 336.
312 Schlender, B. (1998). The three faces of Steve. *Fortune Magazine*, 9 November.
313 Zook, C. (2004). *Beyond the core* (p. 139). Boston: Harvard Business School Press.
314 Colt, S. (2014). Tim Cook gave his most in-depth interview to date (PBS News). *Business Insider*, 21 September.
315 Murphy, (2017). Tim Cook on Donald Trump, the HomePod, and the legacy of Steve Jobs. *Business Week*, 19 June.
316 Tetzeli, R. (2016).
317 Collins, J. & Hansen, M. (2011), p. 148.
318 Ordonez, L., Schweitzer, M., Galinsky, A. & Bazerman, M. (2009). Goals gone wild: the systematic side effects of over-prescribing goal setting. *Harvard Business School* (working paper), 09-083, 28.
319 Levy, S. (1984). The birth of the Mac. *Rolling Stone*, 1 March.
320 Rebello, K, Burrows, P. & Sager, I. (1996). The fall of an American icon. *Business Week*, February.
321 Alsop, S. (1996). Exit the King. *Time Magazine* (reprinted: 2011, p. 61).
322 Levy, S. (1994-2000). *Insanely great* (pp. 313-314). New York: Penguin Group.
323 Bradshaw, T. (2019). Jony Ive, iPhone designer, announces Apple departure. *Financial Times*, June 28 (consulted online).
324 Gurman, M. (2019). Inside Apple's long goodbye to design chief Jony Ive. *Bloomberg*, June 28 (consulted online).
325 Mickle, T. (2019). Jony Ive is leaving Apple, but his departure started long ago. *The Wall Street Journal*, June 30 (consulted online).
326 Johnson Vickberg, S.M. & Christfort, K. (2017). Pioneers, drivers, integrators and guardians. *Harvard Business Review*, March-April, pp. 50-59.
327 Johnson Vickberg, S.M. & Christfort, K. (2017), pp. 50-59.
328 Aaker, D. (1991), pp. 230-236.
329 Tellis, G.J. (2013) *Unrelenting innovation*. San Francisco: Jossey-Bass.
330 Jaruzelski, B., Loehr, J. & Holman, R. (2011). Why culture is key. *Strategy+Business*, 65, 16.
331 McGrath, R.G. (2012). How the growth outliers do it. *Harvard Business Review*, January-February (consulted online).
332 Tetzeli, R. (2016). Playing the long game inside Tim Cook's Apple. *Fast Company*, 8 August.

PRAISE FOR *THE SURVIVAL PARADOX*

'When we started Apple, Steve and I assumed that every successful company was immortal. Lasting, rather than selling out, is about wanting to bring good change to the world, more than the money it brings. This book brilliantly captures what Apple has always been about.'

STEVE WOZNIAK | co-founder of Apple Computer

'Optimally balancing continuity and change is critical for the enduring success of any company, but incredibly hard to do. In his thoughtful and highly practical book, The Survival Paradox, *Fons Van Dyck brings the Apple story to life in a powerfully vivid way through his clever application of the AGIL framework. Timely and engaging, the book is full of invaluable lessons for companies young and old.'*

PROFESSOR KEVIN LANE KELLER | Tuck School of Business at Dartmouth College, co-author (together with Philip Kotler) of *Marketing Management*

'The solid argumentation of an expert, the clear pen of a didactitian, the feeling for a smart non-fiction book of a gifted author. World class.'

MARC BUELENS | professor emeritus Vlerick Business School, columnist for *Trends*